INVISIBLE Woman

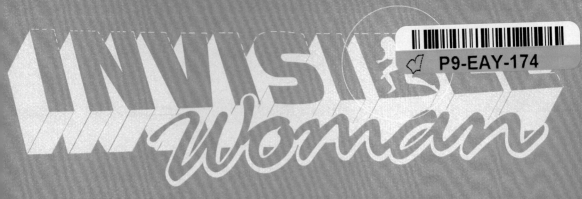

PARTNERS IN CRIME

Mark Waid
WRITER

Mattia De Iulis
ARTIST

VC's Joe Caramagna
LETTERER

Adam Hughes
COVER ART

Shannon Andrews Ballesteros
ASSISTANT EDITOR

Alanna Smith
ASSOCIATE EDITOR

Tom Brevoort
EDITOR

INVISIBLE WOMAN CREATED BY **STAN LEE** & **JACK KIRBY**

COLLECTION EDITOR **JENNIFER GRÜNWALD**
ASSISTANT EDITOR **CAITLIN O'CONNELL**
ASSOCIATE MANAGING EDITOR **KATERI WOODY**
EDITOR, SPECIAL PROJECTS **MARK D. BEAZLEY**
VP PRODUCTION & SPECIAL PROJECTS **JEFF YOUNGQUIST**
BOOK DESIGNER **ADAM DEL RE**

SVP PRINT, SALES & MARKETING **DAVID GABRIEL**
DIRECTOR, LICENSED PUBLISHING **SVEN LARSEN**
EDITOR IN CHIEF **C.B. CEBULSKI**
CHIEF CREATIVE OFFICER **JOE QUESADA**
PRESIDENT **DAN BUCKLEY**
EXECUTIVE PRODUCER **ALAN FINE**

INVISIBLE WOMAN: PARTNERS IN CRIME. Contains material originally published in magazine form as INVISIBLE WOMAN (2019) #1-5. First printing 2019. ISBN 978-1-302-91697-8. Published by MARVEL WORLDWIDE, INC., a subsidiary of MARVEL ENTERTAINMENT, LLC. OFFICE OF PUBLICATION: 135 West 50th Street, New York, NY 10020. © 2019 MARVEL No similarity between any of the names, characters, persons, and/or institutions in this magazine with those of any living or dead person or institution is intended, and any such similarity which may exist is purely coincidental. **Printed in Canada.** DAN BUCKLEY, President, Marvel Entertainment; JOHN NEE, Publisher; JOE QUESADA, Chief Creative Officer; TOM BREVOORT, SVP of Publishing; DAVID BOGART, Associate Publisher & SVP of Talent Affairs; DAVID GABRIEL, VP of Print & Digital Publishing; JEFF YOUNGQUIST, VP of Production & Special Projects; DAN CARR, Executive Director of Publishing Technology; ALEX MORALES, Director of Publishing Operations; DAN EDINGTON, Managing Editor; SUSAN CRESPI, Production Manager; STAN LEE, Chairman Emeritus. For information regarding advertising in Marvel Comics or on Marvel.com, please contact Vit DeBellis, Custom Solutions & Integrated Advertising Manager, at vdebellis@marvel.com. For Marvel subscription inquiries, please call 888-511-5480. **Manufactured between 11/29/2019 and 12/31/2019 by SOLISCO PRINTERS, SCOTT, QC, CANADA.**

10 9 8 7 6 5 4 3 2 1

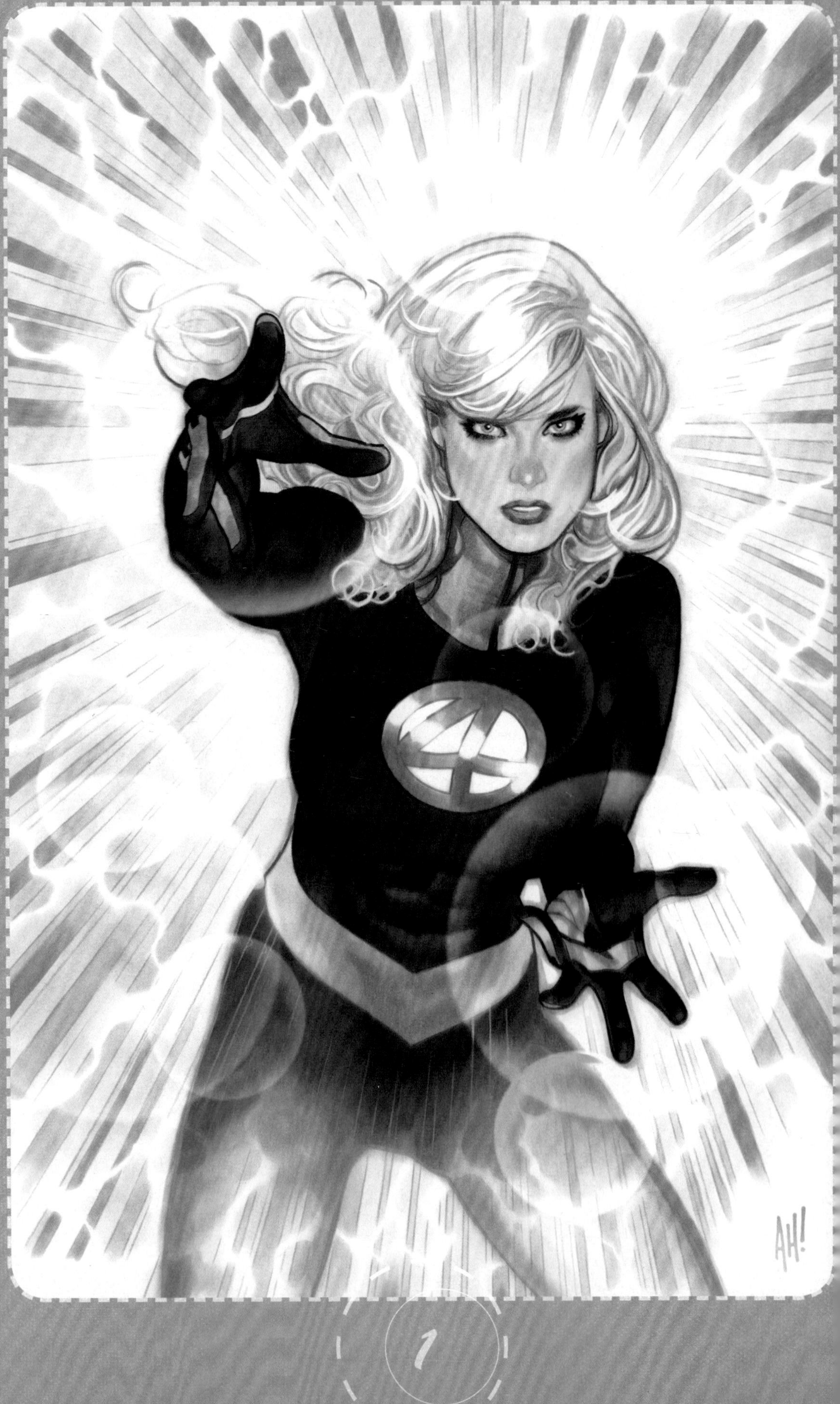
1

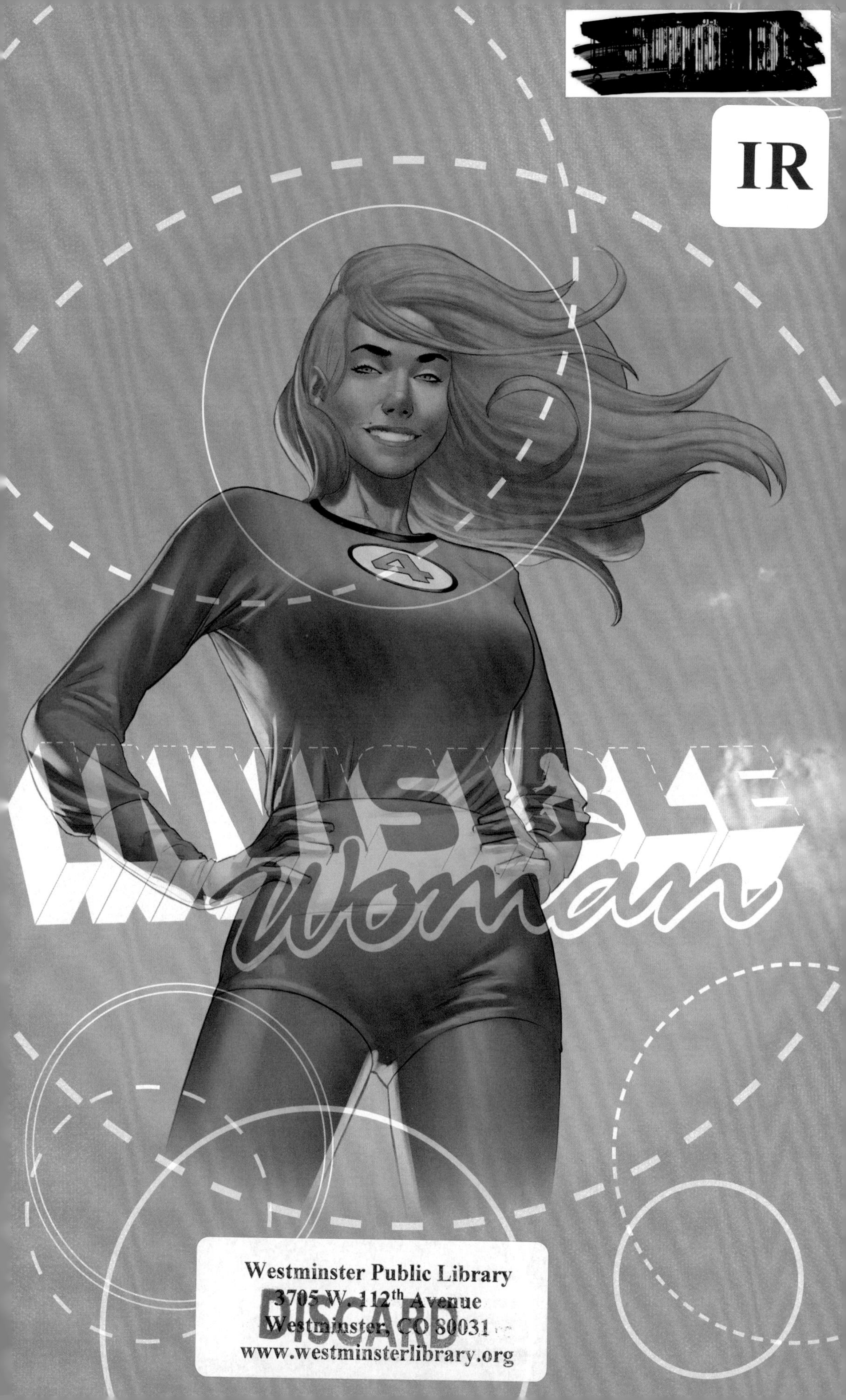
INVISIBLE
Woman

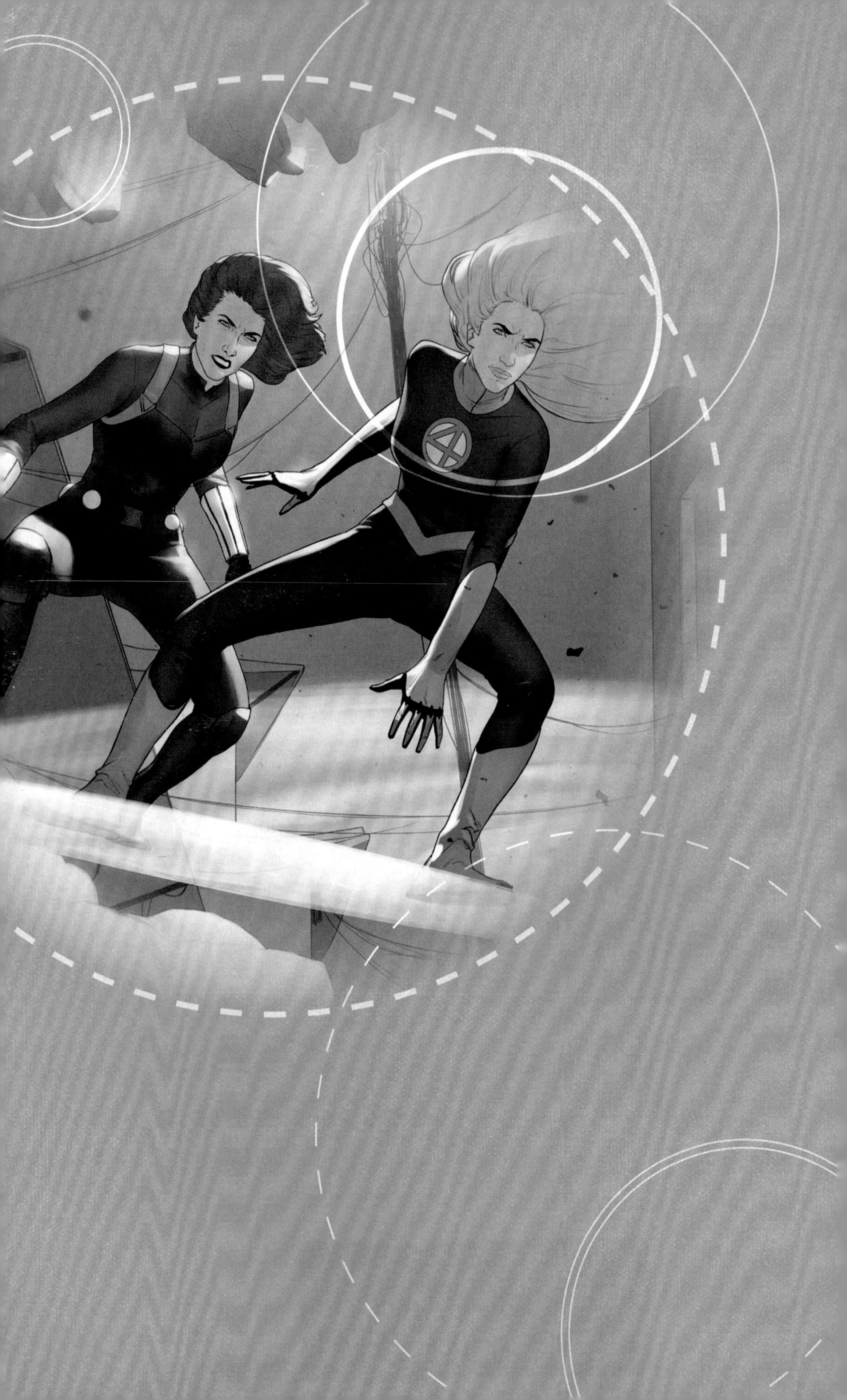

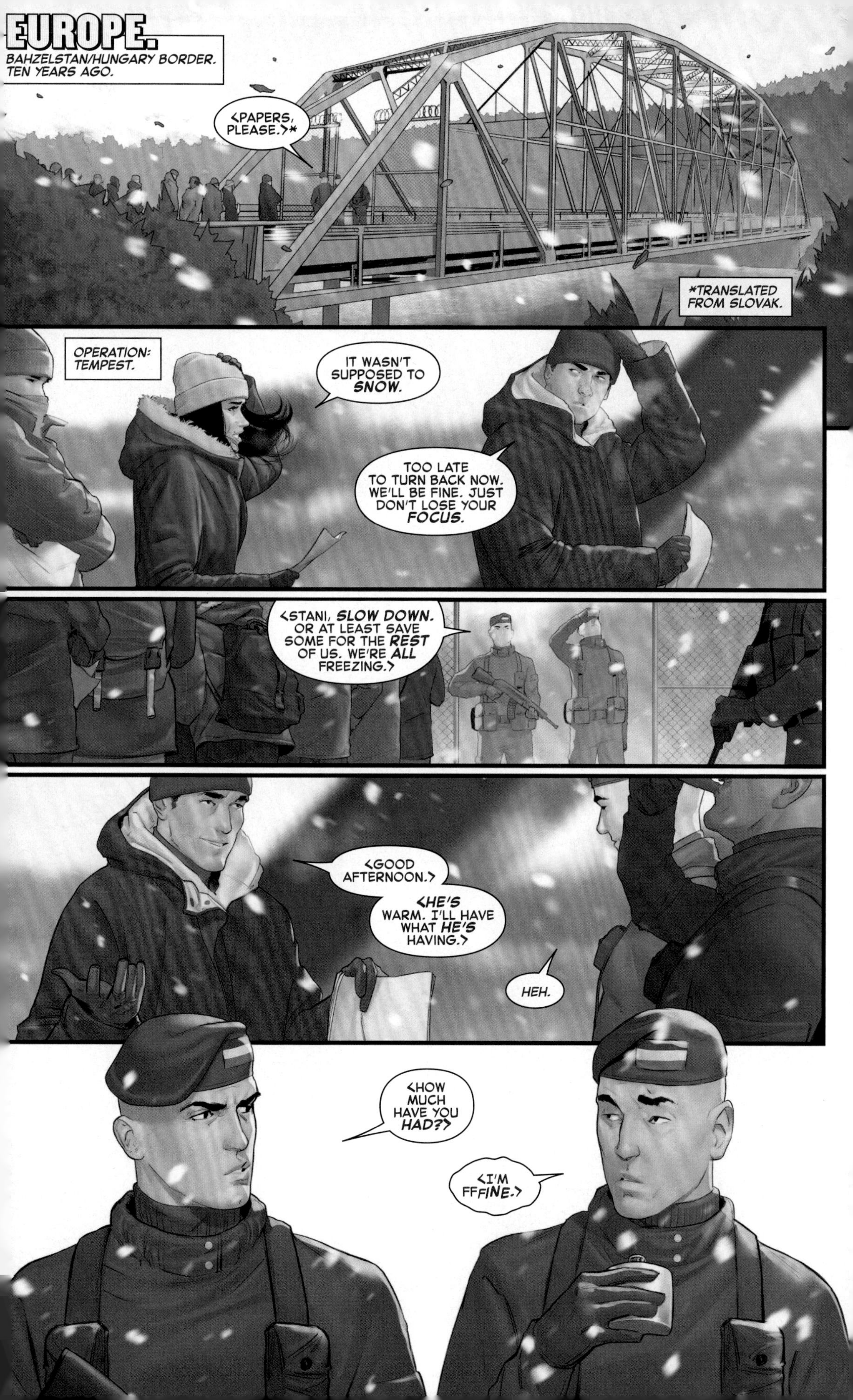
EUROPE.
BAHZELSTAN/HUNGARY BORDER. TEN YEARS AGO.
<PAPERS, PLEASE.>*
*TRANSLATED FROM SLOVAK.
OPERATION: TEMPEST.
IT WASN'T SUPPOSED TO SNOW.
TOO LATE TO TURN BACK NOW. WE'LL BE FINE. JUST DON'T LOSE YOUR FOCUS.
<STANI, SLOW DOWN. OR AT LEAST SAVE SOME FOR THE REST OF US. WE'RE ALL FREEZING.>
<GOOD AFTERNOON.>
<HE'S WARM. I'LL HAVE WHAT HE'S HAVING.>
HEH.
<HOW MUCH HAVE YOU HAD?>
<I'M FFFINE.>

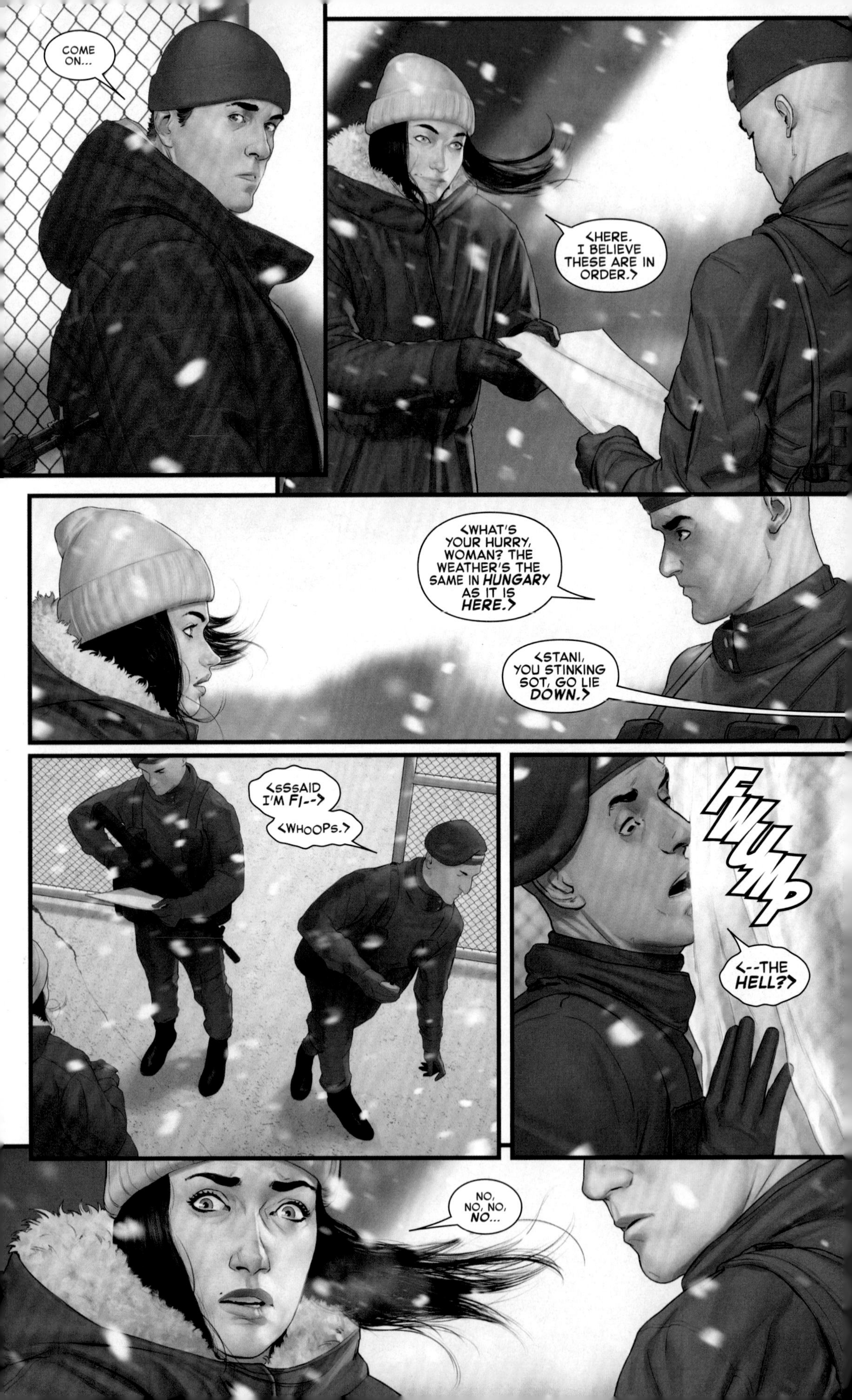
COME ON...
<HERE. I BELIEVE THESE ARE IN ORDER.>
<WHAT'S YOUR HURRY, WOMAN? THE WEATHER'S THE SAME IN HUNGARY AS IT IS HERE.>
<STANI, YOU STINKING SOT, GO LIE DOWN.>
<SSSAID I'M FI-->
<WHOOPS.>
FWUMP
<--THE HELL?>
NO, NO, NO, NO...

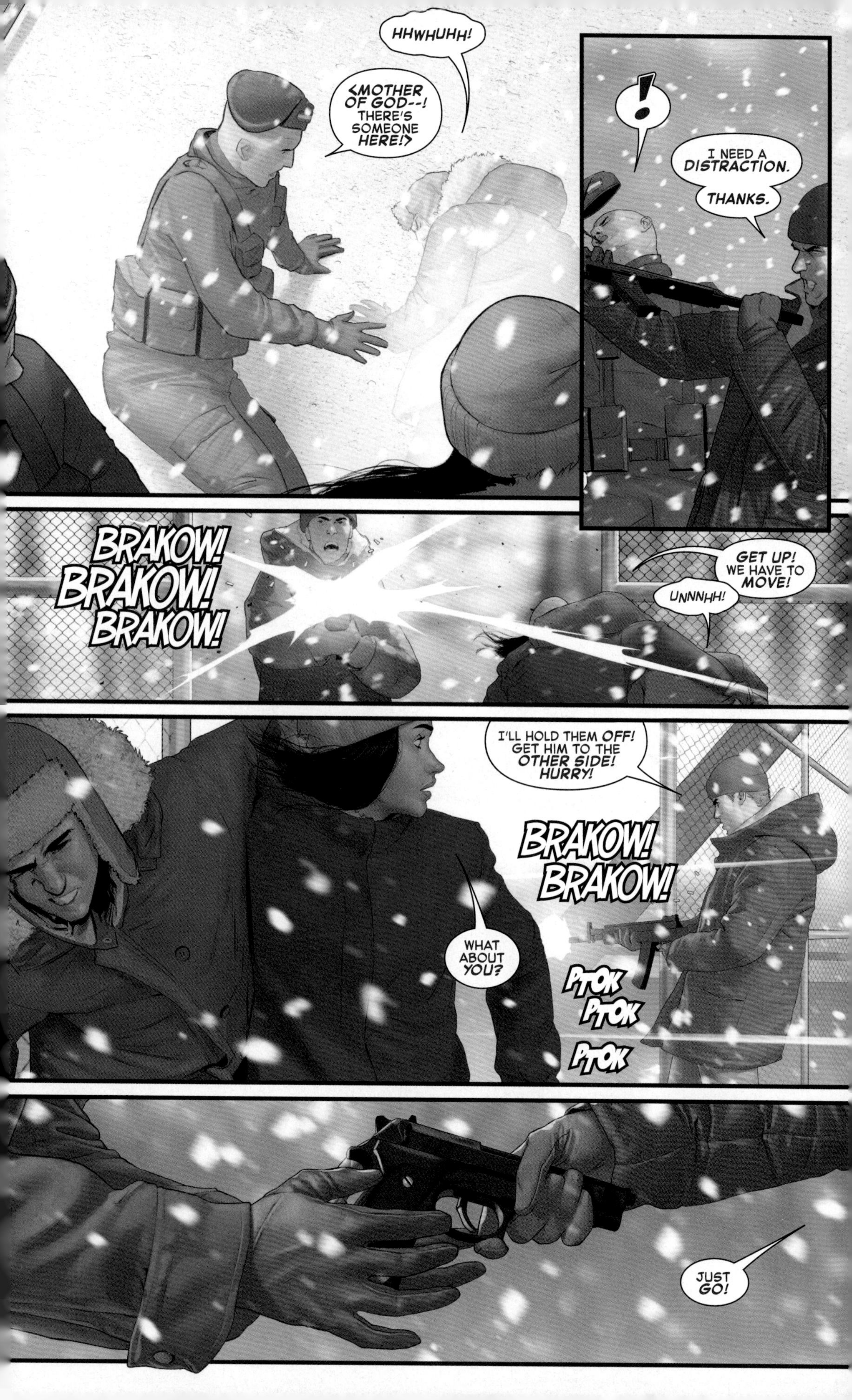

HHWHUHH!
<MOTHER OF GOD--! THERE'S SOMEONE HERE!>
!
I NEED A DISTRACTION.
THANKS.
BRAKOW! BRAKOW! BRAKOW!
GET UP! WE HAVE TO MOVE!
UNNNHH!
I'LL HOLD THEM OFF! GET HIM TO THE OTHER SIDE! HURRY!
BRAKOW! BRAKOW!
WHAT ABOUT YOU?
PTOK PTOK PTOK
JUST GO!

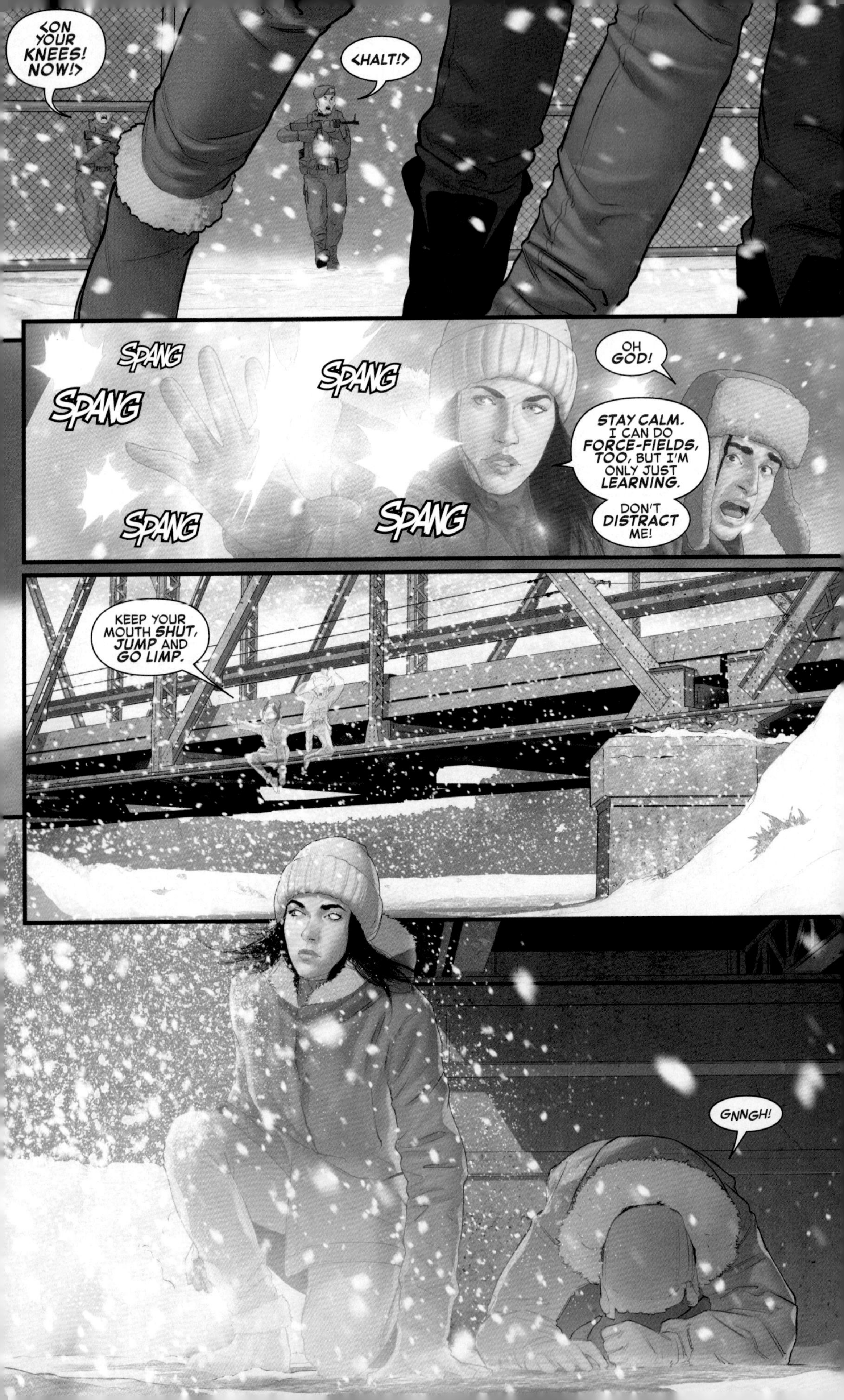
<ON YOUR KNEES! NOW!>
<HALT!>
SPANG
SPANG
SPANG
SPANG
SPANG
OH GOD!
STAY CALM. I CAN DO FORCE-FIELDS, TOO, BUT I'M ONLY JUST LEARNING.
DON'T DISTRACT ME!
KEEP YOUR MOUTH SHUT, JUMP AND GO LIMP.
GNNGH!

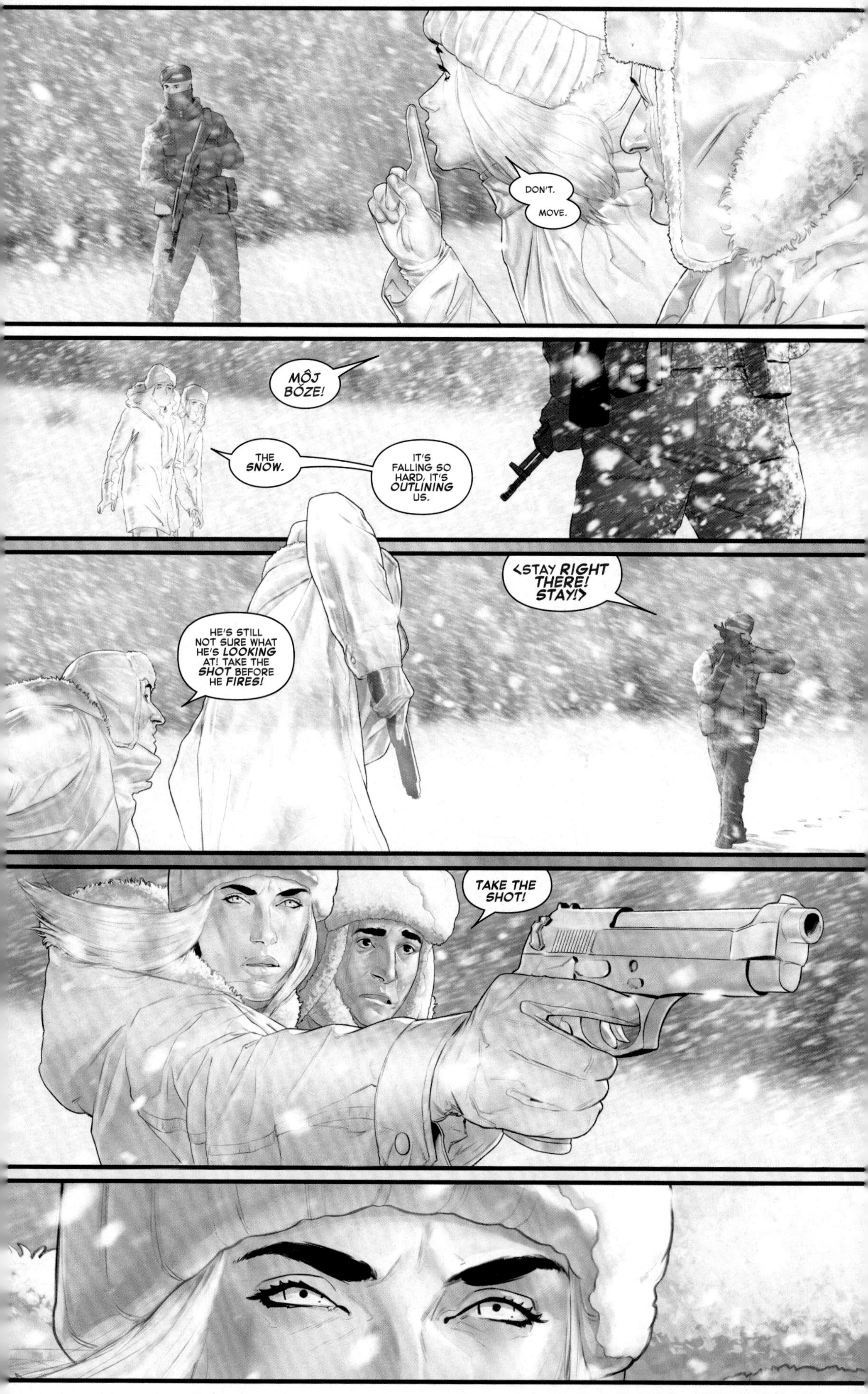
DON'T.
MOVE.
MÔJ BǑZE!
THE SNOW.
IT'S FALLING SO HARD, IT'S OUTLINING US.
<STAY RIGHT THERE! STAY!>
HE'S STILL NOT SURE WHAT HE'S LOOKING AT! TAKE THE SHOT BEFORE HE FIRES!
TAKE THE SHOT!

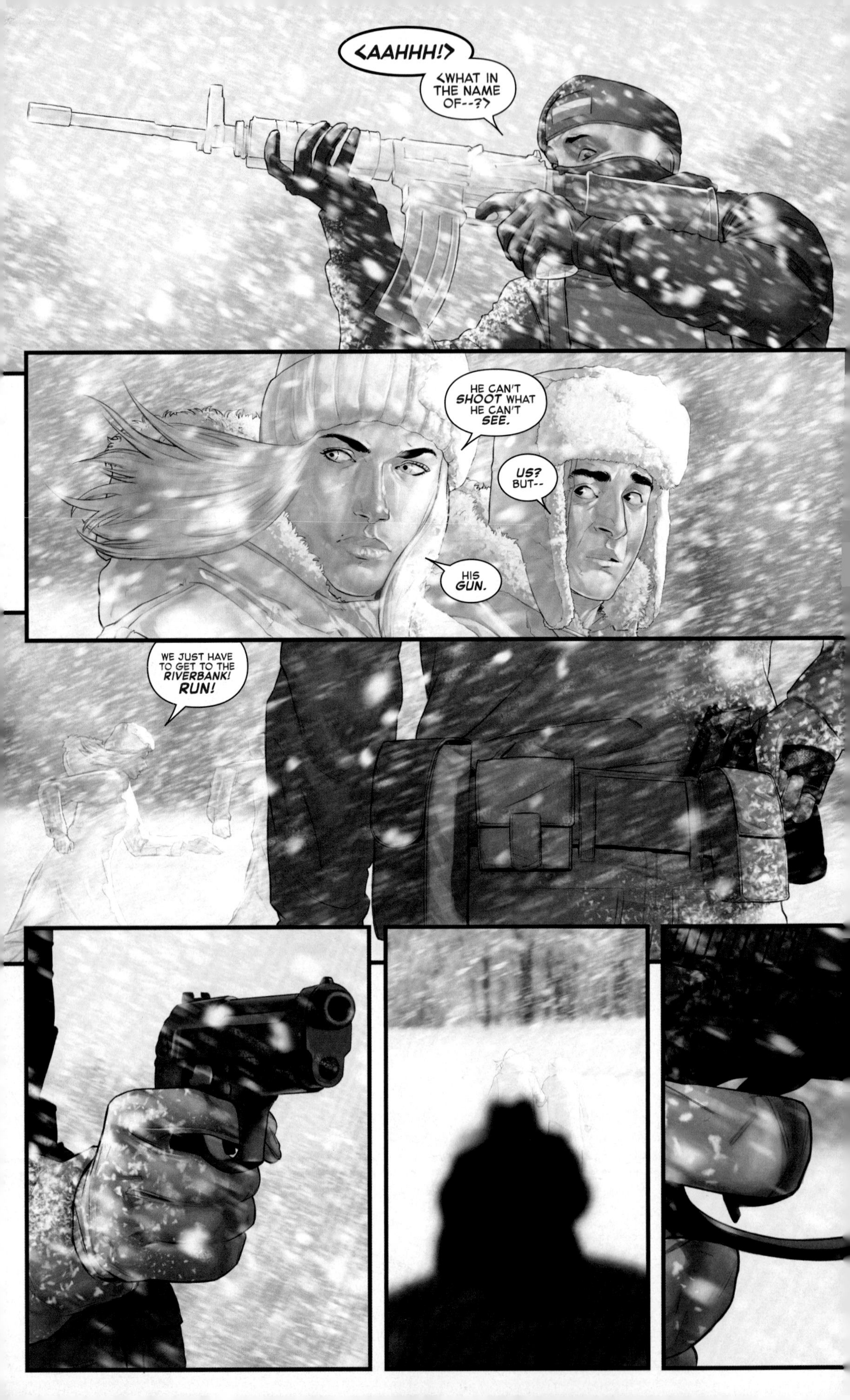
<AAHHH!>
<WHAT IN THE NAME OF--?>
HE CAN'T SHOOT WHAT HE CAN'T SEE.
US? BUT--
HIS GUN.
WE JUST HAVE TO GET TO THE RIVERBANK! RUN!

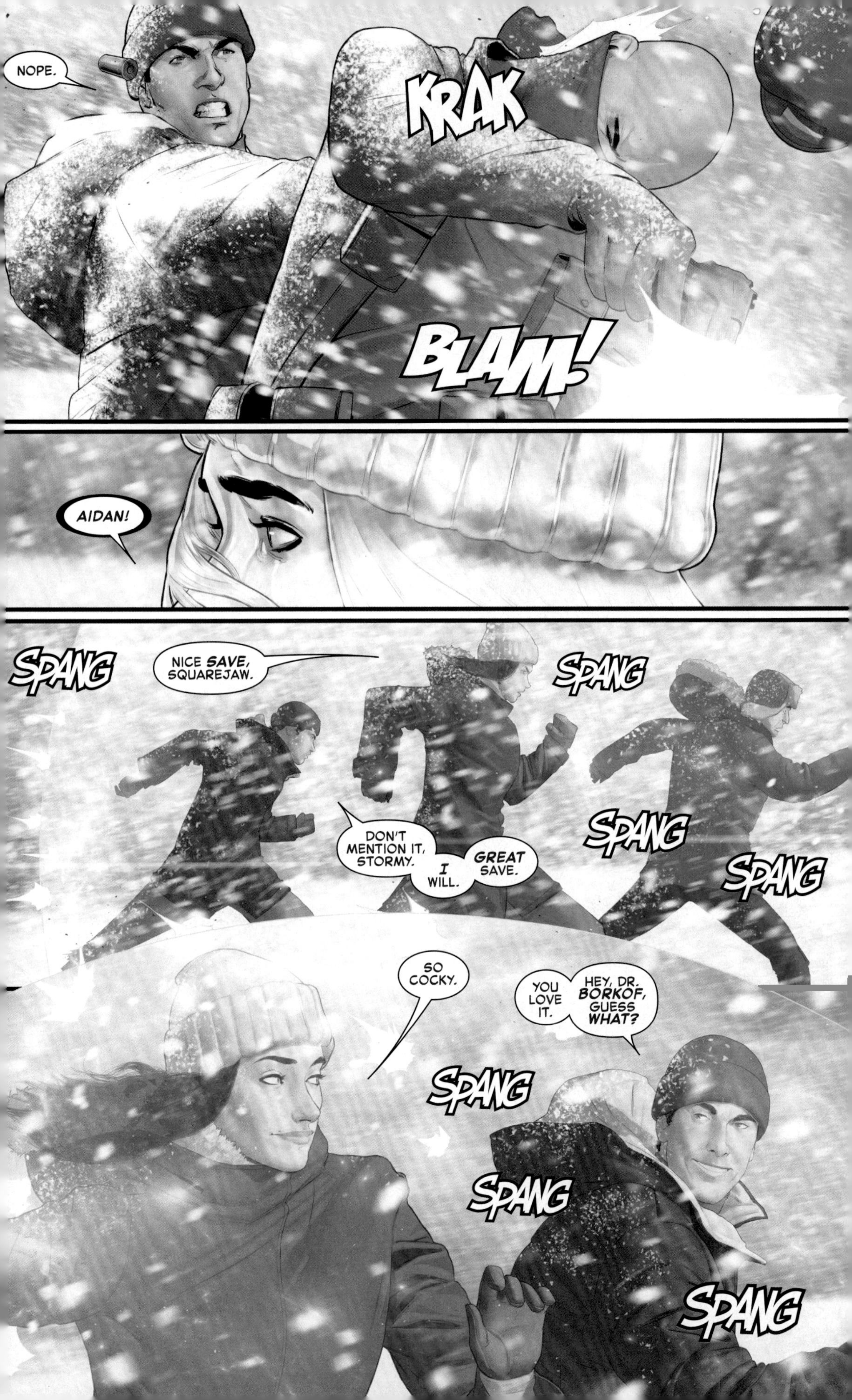
NOPE.
KRAK
BLAM!
AIDAN!
SPANG
NICE SAVE, SQUAREJAW.
SPANG
DON'T MENTION IT, STORMY.
I WILL.
GREAT SAVE.
SPANG
SPANG
SO COCKY.
YOU LOVE IT.
HEY, DR. BORKOF, GUESS WHAT?
SPANG
SPANG
SPANG

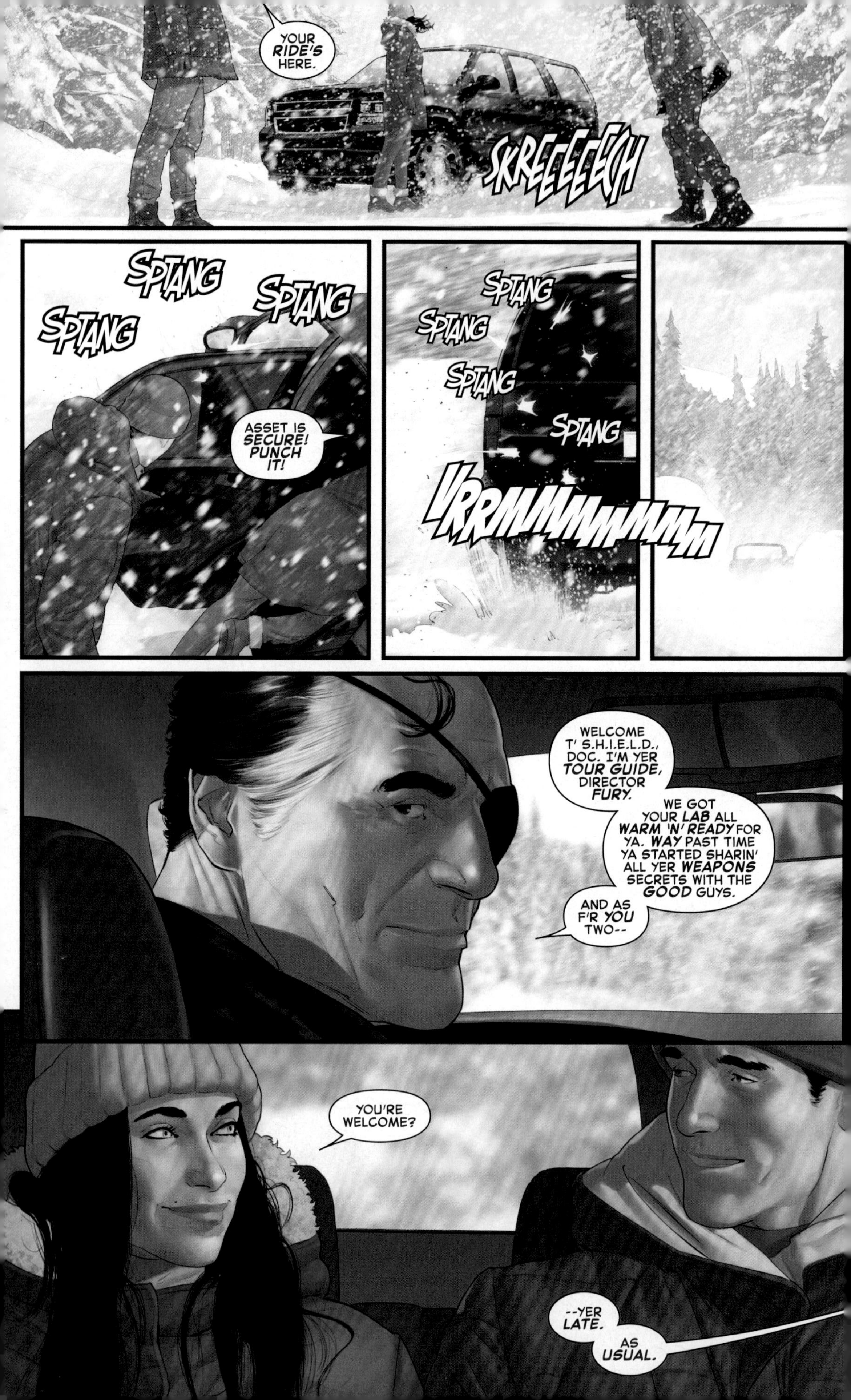
YOUR RIDE'S HERE.
SKREEEEECH
SPTANG
SPTANG
SPTANG
ASSET IS SECURE! PUNCH IT!
SPTANG
SPTANG
SPTANG
SPTANG
VRRMMMMMMMMMM
WELCOME T' S.H.I.E.L.D., DOC. I'M YER TOUR GUIDE, DIRECTOR FURY.
WE GOT YOUR LAB ALL WARM 'N' READY FOR YA. WAY PAST TIME YA STARTED SHARIN' ALL YER WEAPONS SECRETS WITH THE GOOD GUYS.
AND AS F'R YOU TWO--
YOU'RE WELCOME?
--YER LATE.
AS USUAL.

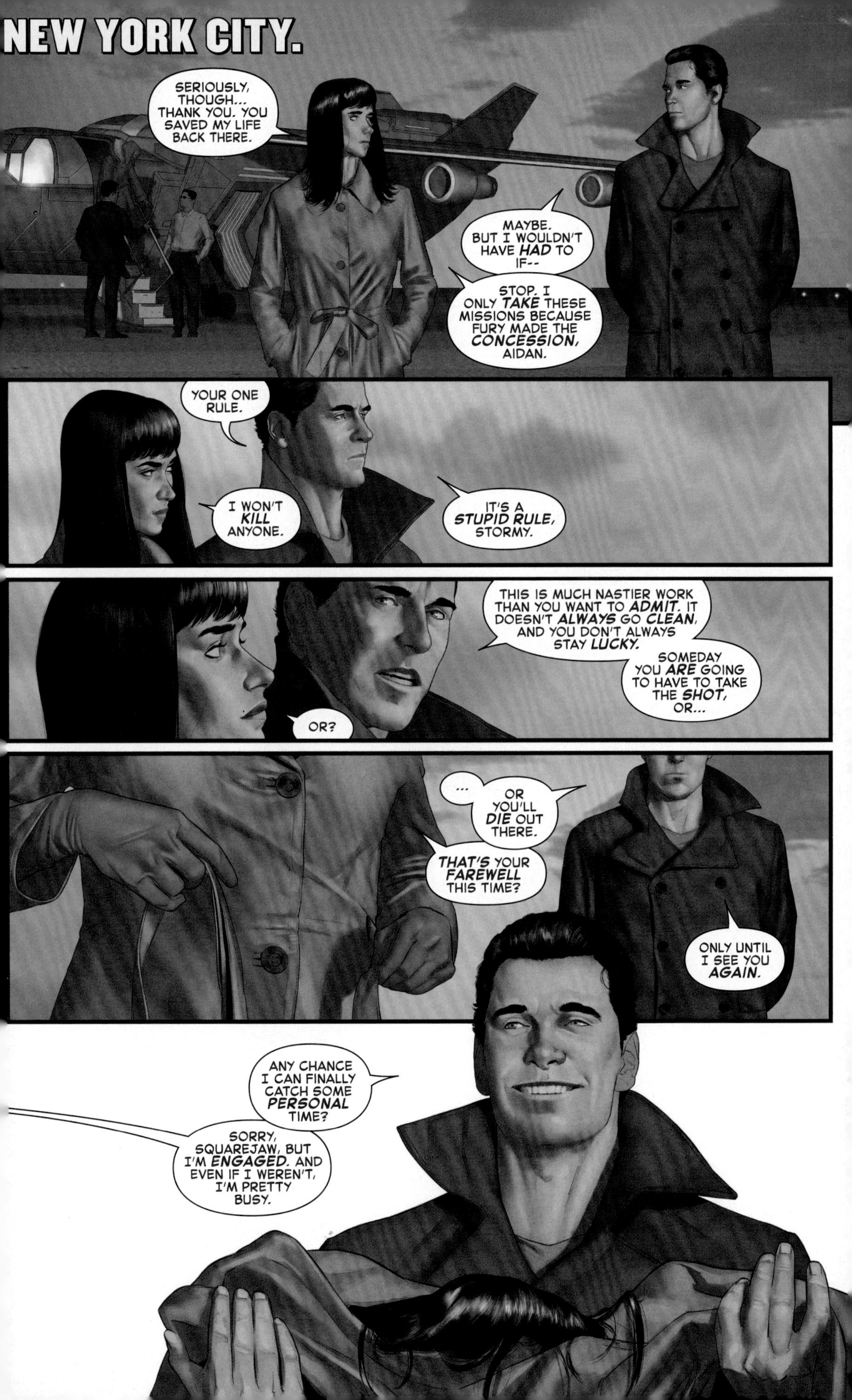
NEW YORK CITY.
SERIOUSLY, THOUGH... THANK YOU. YOU SAVED MY LIFE BACK THERE.
MAYBE. BUT I WOULDN'T HAVE HAD TO IF--
STOP. I ONLY TAKE THESE MISSIONS BECAUSE FURY MADE THE CONCESSION, AIDAN.
YOUR ONE RULE.
I WON'T KILL ANYONE.
IT'S A STUPID RULE, STORMY.
THIS IS MUCH NASTIER WORK THAN YOU WANT TO ADMIT. IT DOESN'T ALWAYS GO CLEAN, AND YOU DON'T ALWAYS STAY LUCKY.
SOMEDAY YOU ARE GOING TO HAVE TO TAKE THE SHOT, OR...
OR?
...
OR YOU'LL DIE OUT THERE.
THAT'S YOUR FAREWELL THIS TIME?
ONLY UNTIL I SEE YOU AGAIN.
ANY CHANCE I CAN FINALLY CATCH SOME PERSONAL TIME?
SORRY, SQUAREJAW, BUT I'M ENGAGED. AND EVEN IF I WEREN'T, I'M PRETTY BUSY.

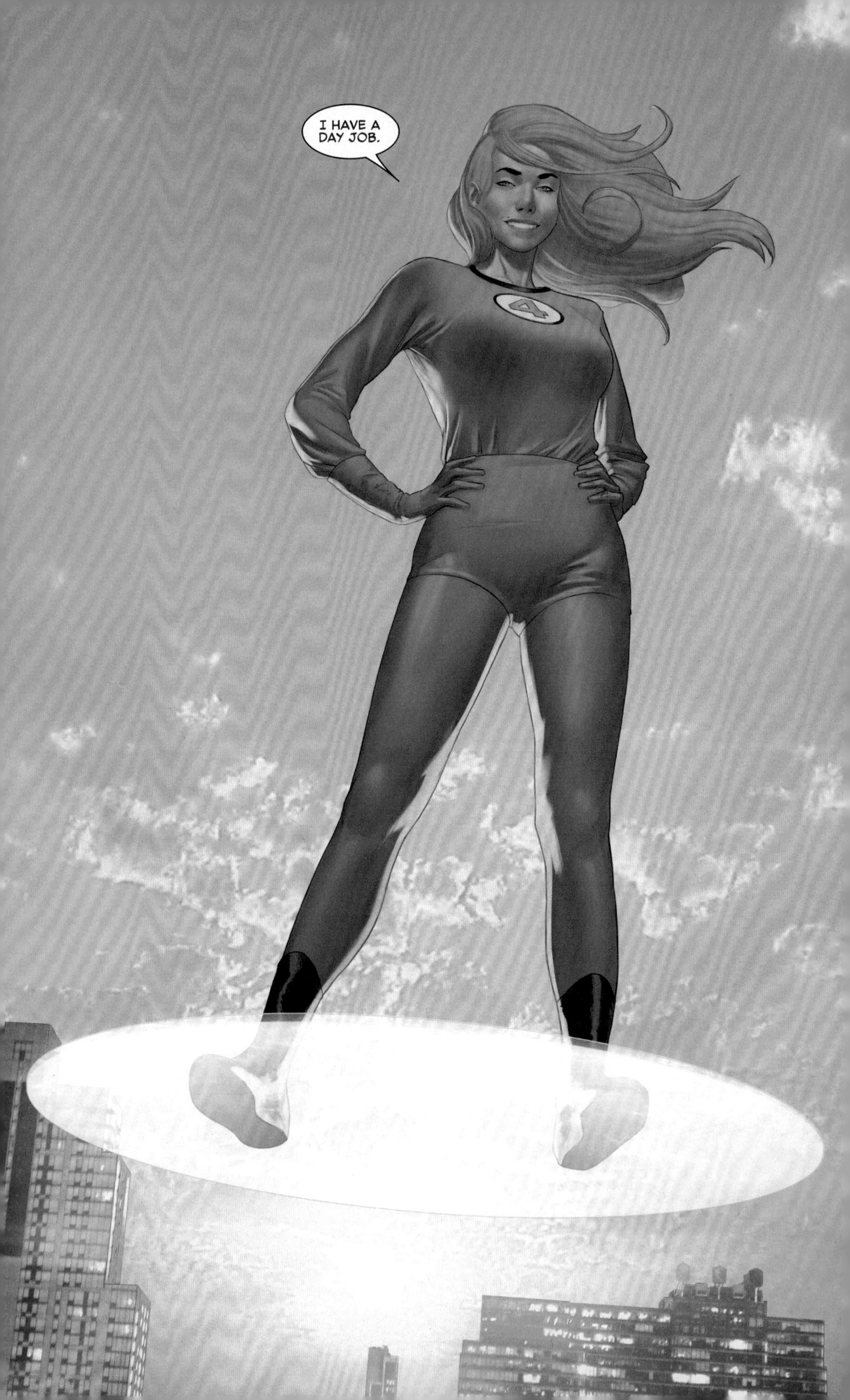
I HAVE A DAY JOB.

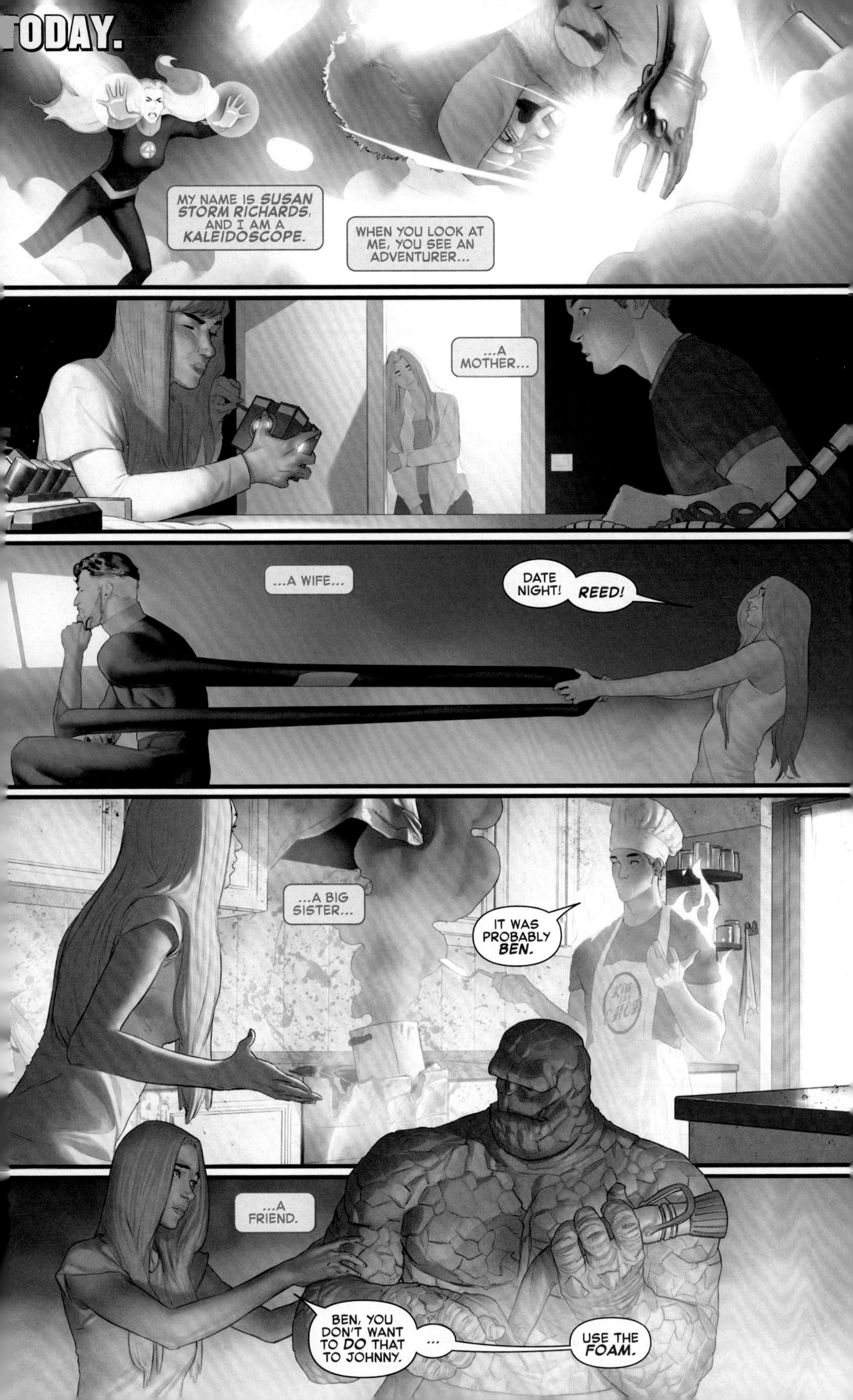
TODAY.
MY NAME IS SUSAN STORM RICHARDS, AND I AM A KALEIDOSCOPE.
WHEN YOU LOOK AT ME, YOU SEE AN ADVENTURER...
...A MOTHER...
...A WIFE...
DATE NIGHT!
REED!
...A BIG SISTER...
IT WAS PROBABLY BEN.
...A FRIEND.
BEN, YOU DON'T WANT TO DO THAT TO JOHNNY.
...
USE THE FOAM.

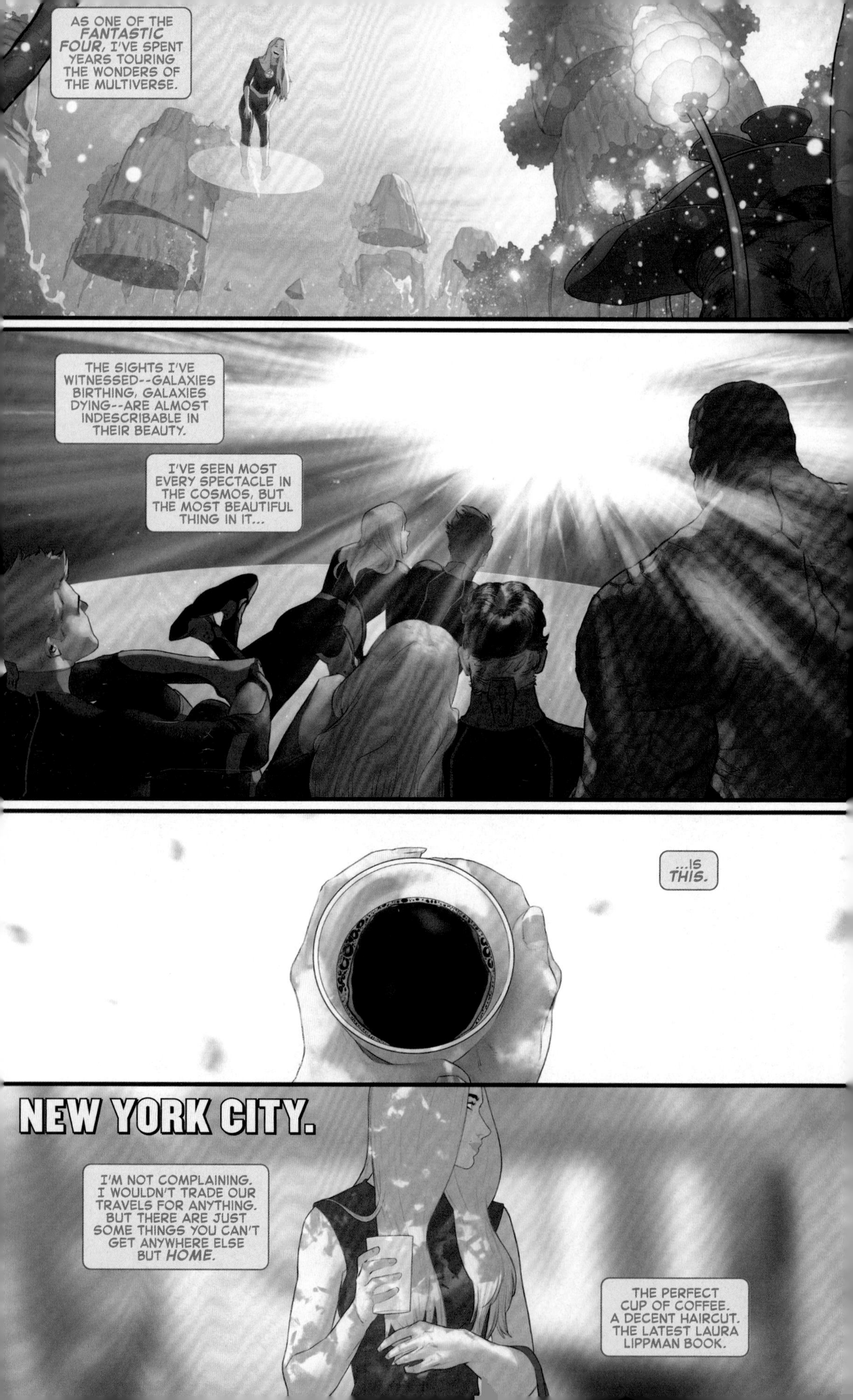
AS ONE OF THE FANTASTIC FOUR, I'VE SPENT YEARS TOURING THE WONDERS OF THE MULTIVERSE.
THE SIGHTS I'VE WITNESSED--GALAXIES BIRTHING, GALAXIES DYING--ARE ALMOST INDESCRIBABLE IN THEIR BEAUTY.
I'VE SEEN MOST EVERY SPECTACLE IN THE COSMOS, BUT THE MOST BEAUTIFUL THING IN IT...
...IS THIS.
NEW YORK CITY.
I'M NOT COMPLAINING. I WOULDN'T TRADE OUR TRAVELS FOR ANYTHING. BUT THERE ARE JUST SOME THINGS YOU CAN'T GET ANYWHERE ELSE BUT HOME.
THE PERFECT CUP OF COFFEE. A DECENT HAIRCUT. THE LATEST LAURA LIPPMAN BOOK.

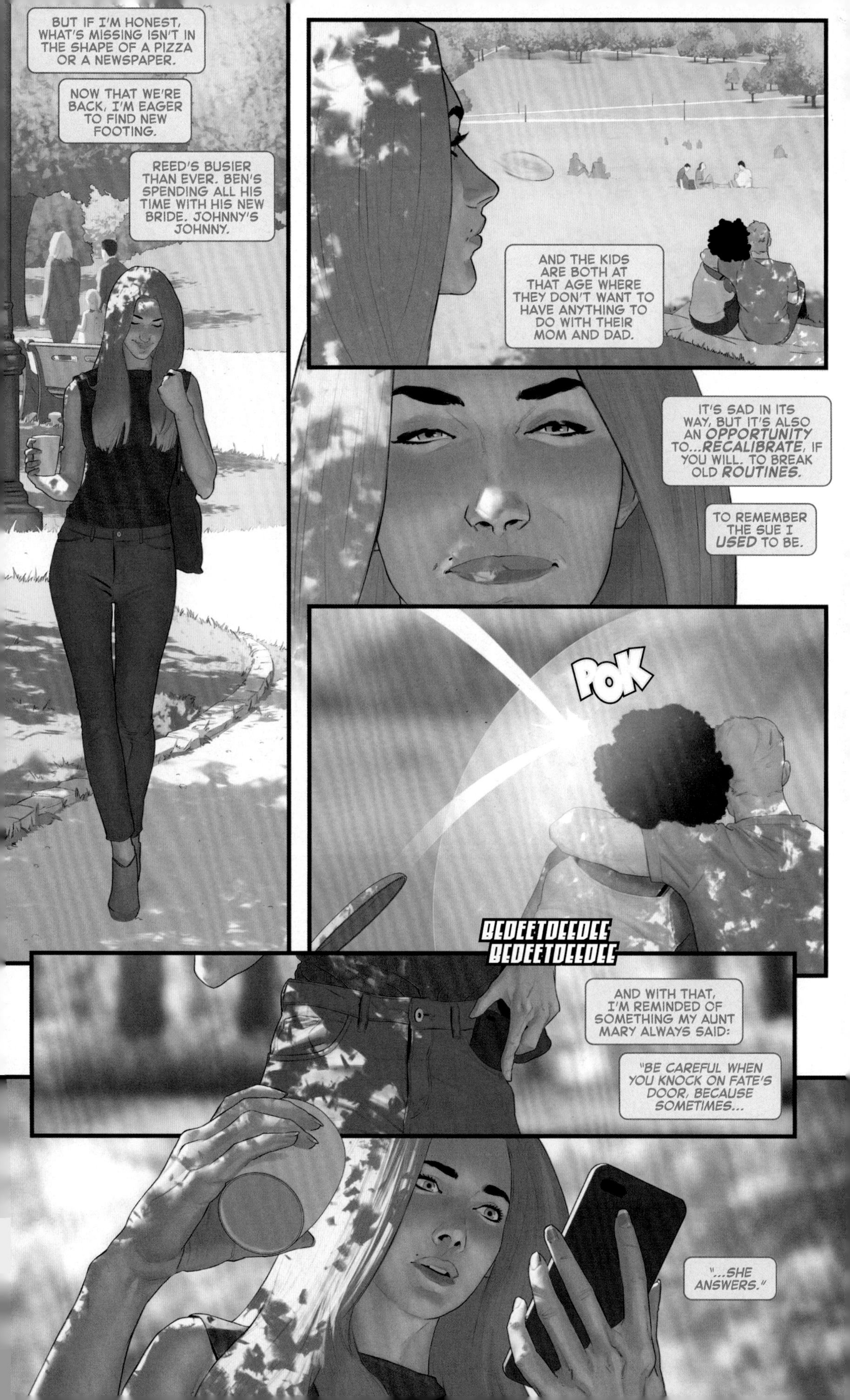
BUT IF I'M HONEST, WHAT'S MISSING ISN'T IN THE SHAPE OF A PIZZA OR A NEWSPAPER.
NOW THAT WE'RE BACK, I'M EAGER TO FIND NEW FOOTING.
REED'S BUSIER THAN EVER. BEN'S SPENDING ALL HIS TIME WITH HIS NEW BRIDE. JOHNNY'S JOHNNY.
AND THE KIDS ARE BOTH AT THAT AGE WHERE THEY DON'T WANT TO HAVE ANYTHING TO DO WITH THEIR MOM AND DAD.
IT'S SAD IN ITS WAY, BUT IT'S ALSO AN OPPORTUNITY TO...RECALIBRATE, IF YOU WILL. TO BREAK OLD ROUTINES.
TO REMEMBER THE SUE I USED TO BE.
POK
BEDEETDEEDEE BEDEETDEEDEE
AND WITH THAT, I'M REMINDED OF SOMETHING MY AUNT MARY ALWAYS SAID:
"BE CAREFUL WHEN YOU KNOCK ON FATE'S DOOR, BECAUSE SOMETIMES...
"...SHE ANSWERS."

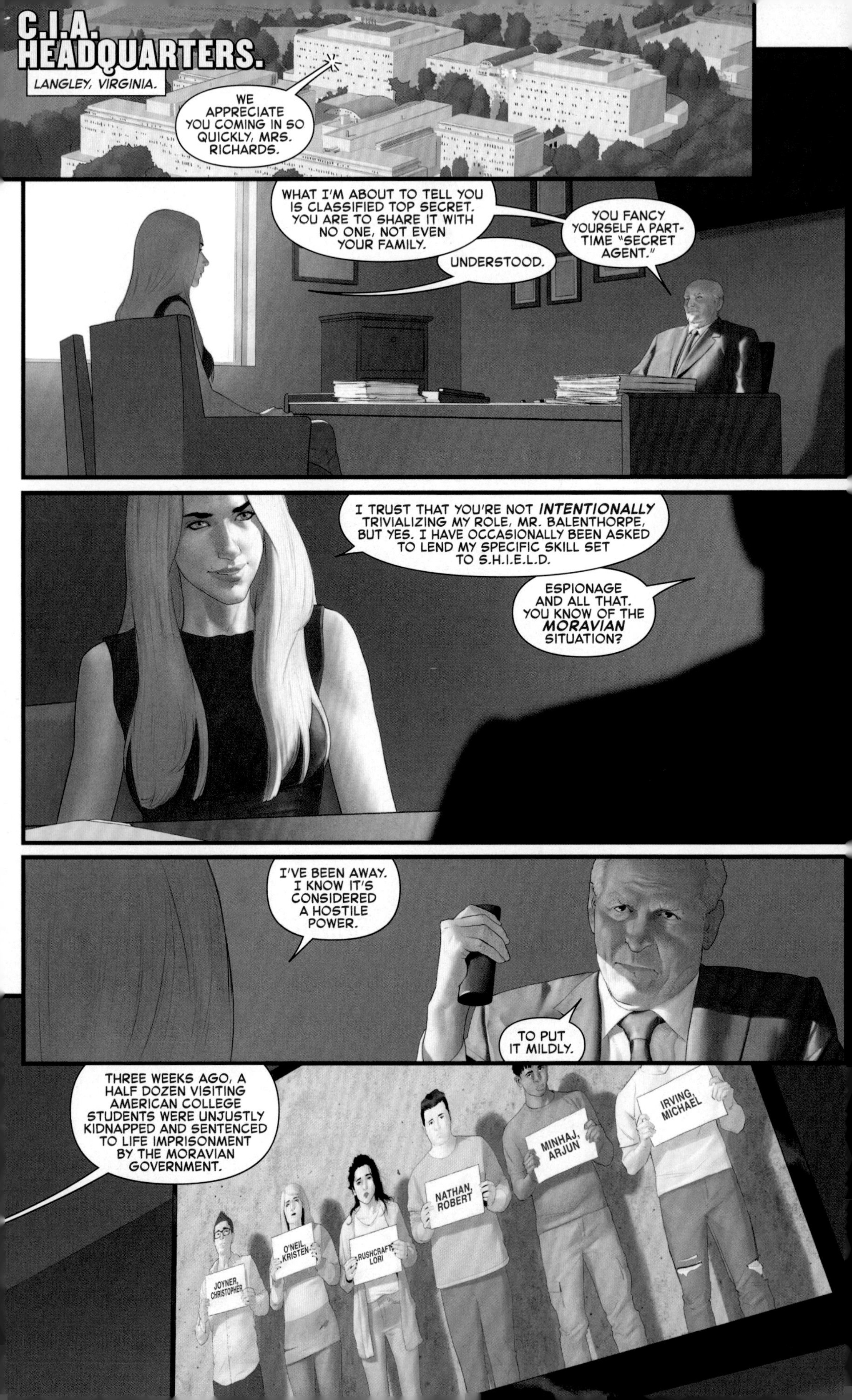
C.I.A. HEADQUARTERS.
LANGLEY, VIRGINIA.
WE APPRECIATE YOU COMING IN SO QUICKLY, MRS. RICHARDS.
WHAT I'M ABOUT TO TELL YOU IS CLASSIFIED TOP SECRET. YOU ARE TO SHARE IT WITH NO ONE, NOT EVEN YOUR FAMILY.
UNDERSTOOD.
YOU FANCY YOURSELF A PART-TIME "SECRET AGENT."
I TRUST THAT YOU'RE NOT INTENTIONALLY TRIVIALIZING MY ROLE, MR. BALENTHORPE, BUT YES. I HAVE OCCASIONALLY BEEN ASKED TO LEND MY SPECIFIC SKILL SET TO S.H.I.E.L.D.
ESPIONAGE AND ALL THAT. YOU KNOW OF THE MORAVIAN SITUATION?
I'VE BEEN AWAY. I KNOW IT'S CONSIDERED A HOSTILE POWER.
TO PUT IT MILDLY.
THREE WEEKS AGO, A HALF DOZEN VISITING AMERICAN COLLEGE STUDENTS WERE UNJUSTLY KIDNAPPED AND SENTENCED TO LIFE IMPRISONMENT BY THE MORAVIAN GOVERNMENT.
JOYNER, CHRISTOPHER
O'NEIL, KRISTEN
RUSHCRAFT, LORI
NATHAN, ROBERT
MINHAJ, ARJUN
IRVING, MICHAEL

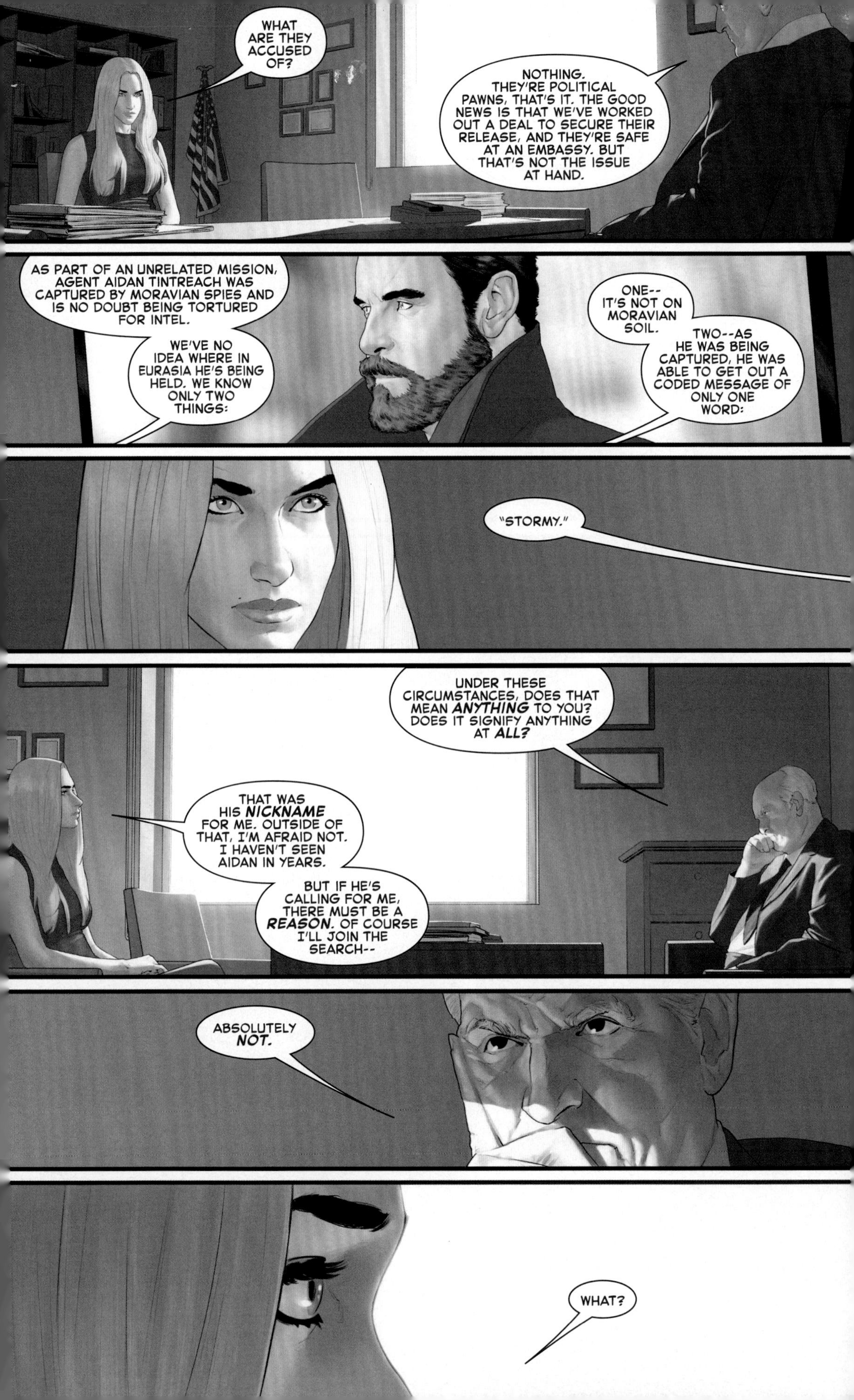
WHAT ARE THEY ACCUSED OF?
NOTHING. THEY'RE POLITICAL PAWNS, THAT'S IT. THE GOOD NEWS IS THAT WE'VE WORKED OUT A DEAL TO SECURE THEIR RELEASE, AND THEY'RE SAFE AT AN EMBASSY. BUT THAT'S NOT THE ISSUE AT HAND.
AS PART OF AN UNRELATED MISSION, AGENT AIDAN TINTREACH WAS CAPTURED BY MORAVIAN SPIES AND IS NO DOUBT BEING TORTURED FOR INTEL.
WE'VE NO IDEA WHERE IN EURASIA HE'S BEING HELD. WE KNOW ONLY TWO THINGS:
ONE-- IT'S NOT ON MORAVIAN SOIL.
TWO--AS HE WAS BEING CAPTURED, HE WAS ABLE TO GET OUT A CODED MESSAGE OF ONLY ONE WORD:
"STORMY."
UNDER THESE CIRCUMSTANCES, DOES THAT MEAN ***ANYTHING*** TO YOU? DOES IT SIGNIFY ANYTHING AT ***ALL?***
THAT WAS HIS ***NICKNAME*** FOR ME. OUTSIDE OF THAT, I'M AFRAID NOT. I HAVEN'T SEEN AIDAN IN YEARS.
BUT IF HE'S CALLING FOR ME, THERE MUST BE A ***REASON.*** OF COURSE I'LL JOIN THE SEARCH--
ABSOLUTELY ***NOT.***
WHAT?

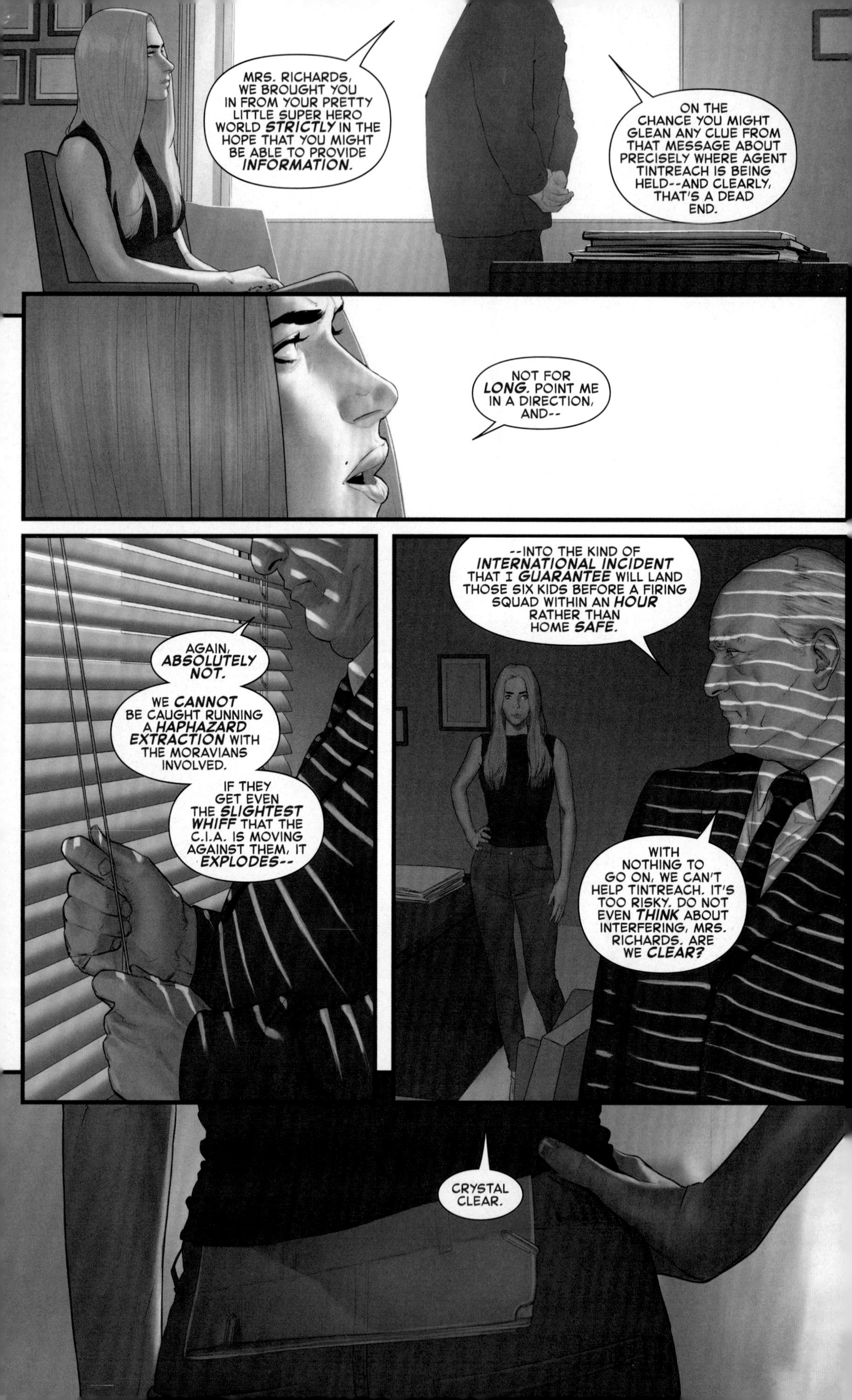
MRS. RICHARDS, WE BROUGHT YOU IN FROM YOUR PRETTY LITTLE SUPER HERO WORLD STRICTLY IN THE HOPE THAT YOU MIGHT BE ABLE TO PROVIDE INFORMATION.
ON THE CHANCE YOU MIGHT GLEAN ANY CLUE FROM THAT MESSAGE ABOUT PRECISELY WHERE AGENT TINTREACH IS BEING HELD--AND CLEARLY, THAT'S A DEAD END.
NOT FOR LONG. POINT ME IN A DIRECTION, AND--
AGAIN, ABSOLUTELY NOT.
WE CANNOT BE CAUGHT RUNNING A HAPHAZARD EXTRACTION WITH THE MORAVIANS INVOLVED.
IF THEY GET EVEN THE SLIGHTEST WHIFF THAT THE C.I.A. IS MOVING AGAINST THEM, IT EXPLODES--
--INTO THE KIND OF INTERNATIONAL INCIDENT THAT I GUARANTEE WILL LAND THOSE SIX KIDS BEFORE A FIRING SQUAD WITHIN AN HOUR RATHER THAN HOME SAFE.
WITH NOTHING TO GO ON, WE CAN'T HELP TINTREACH. IT'S TOO RISKY. DO NOT EVEN THINK ABOUT INTERFERING, MRS. RICHARDS. ARE WE CLEAR?
CRYSTAL CLEAR.

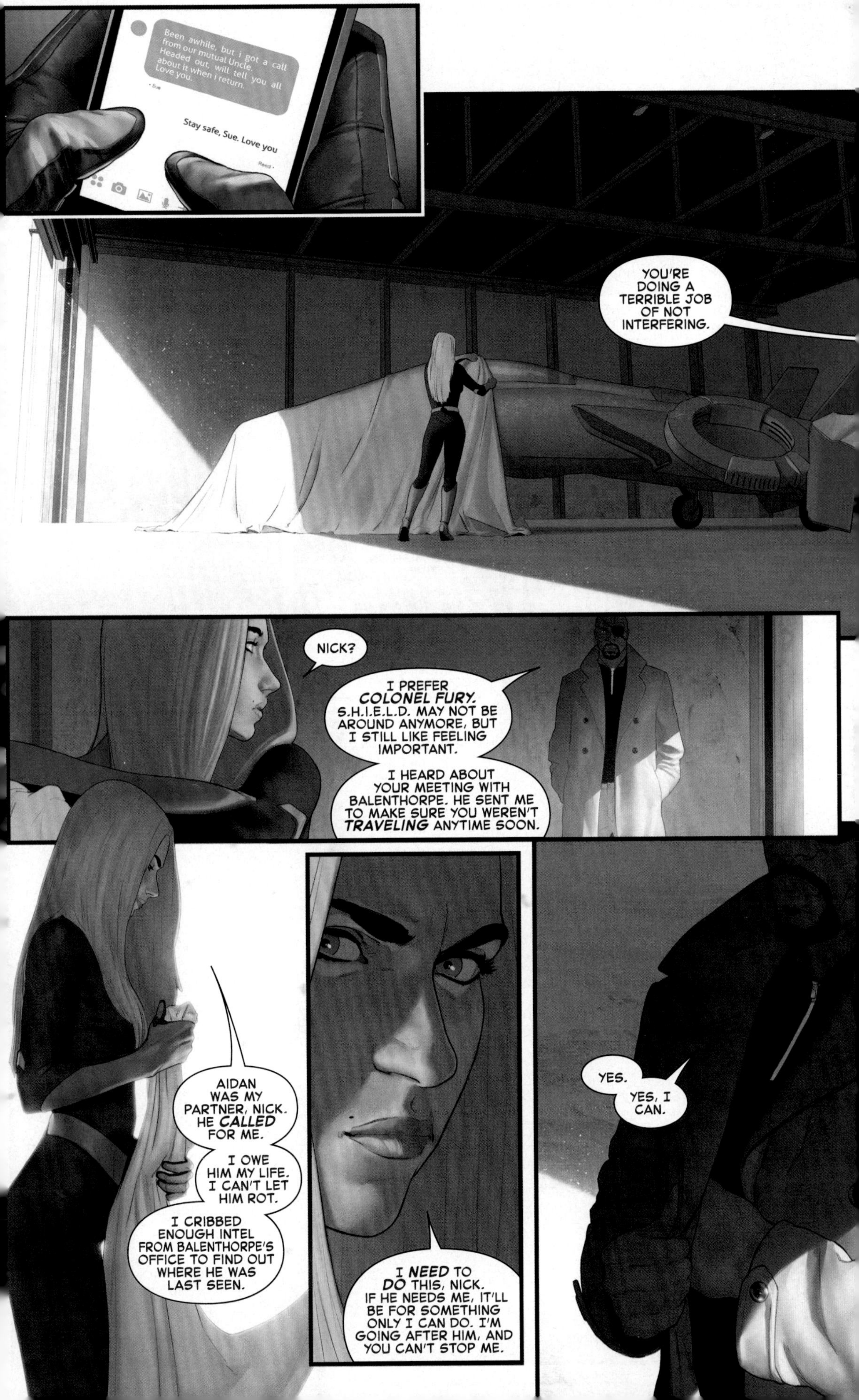

Been awhile, but i got a call from our mutual Uncle. Headed out, will tell you all about it when i return. Love you.
• Sue
Stay safe, Sue. Love you
Reed •
YOU'RE DOING A TERRIBLE JOB OF NOT INTERFERING.
NICK?
I PREFER *COLONEL FURY.* S.H.I.E.L.D. MAY NOT BE AROUND ANYMORE, BUT I STILL LIKE FEELING IMPORTANT.
I HEARD ABOUT YOUR MEETING WITH BALENTHORPE. HE SENT ME TO MAKE SURE YOU WEREN'T *TRAVELING* ANYTIME SOON.
AIDAN WAS MY PARTNER, NICK. HE *CALLED* FOR ME.
I OWE HIM MY LIFE. I CAN'T LET HIM ROT.
I CRIBBED ENOUGH INTEL FROM BALENTHORPE'S OFFICE TO FIND OUT WHERE HE WAS LAST SEEN.
I *NEED* TO DO THIS, NICK. IF HE NEEDS ME, IT'LL BE FOR SOMETHING ONLY I CAN DO. I'M GOING AFTER HIM, AND YOU CAN'T STOP ME.
YES.
YES, I CAN.

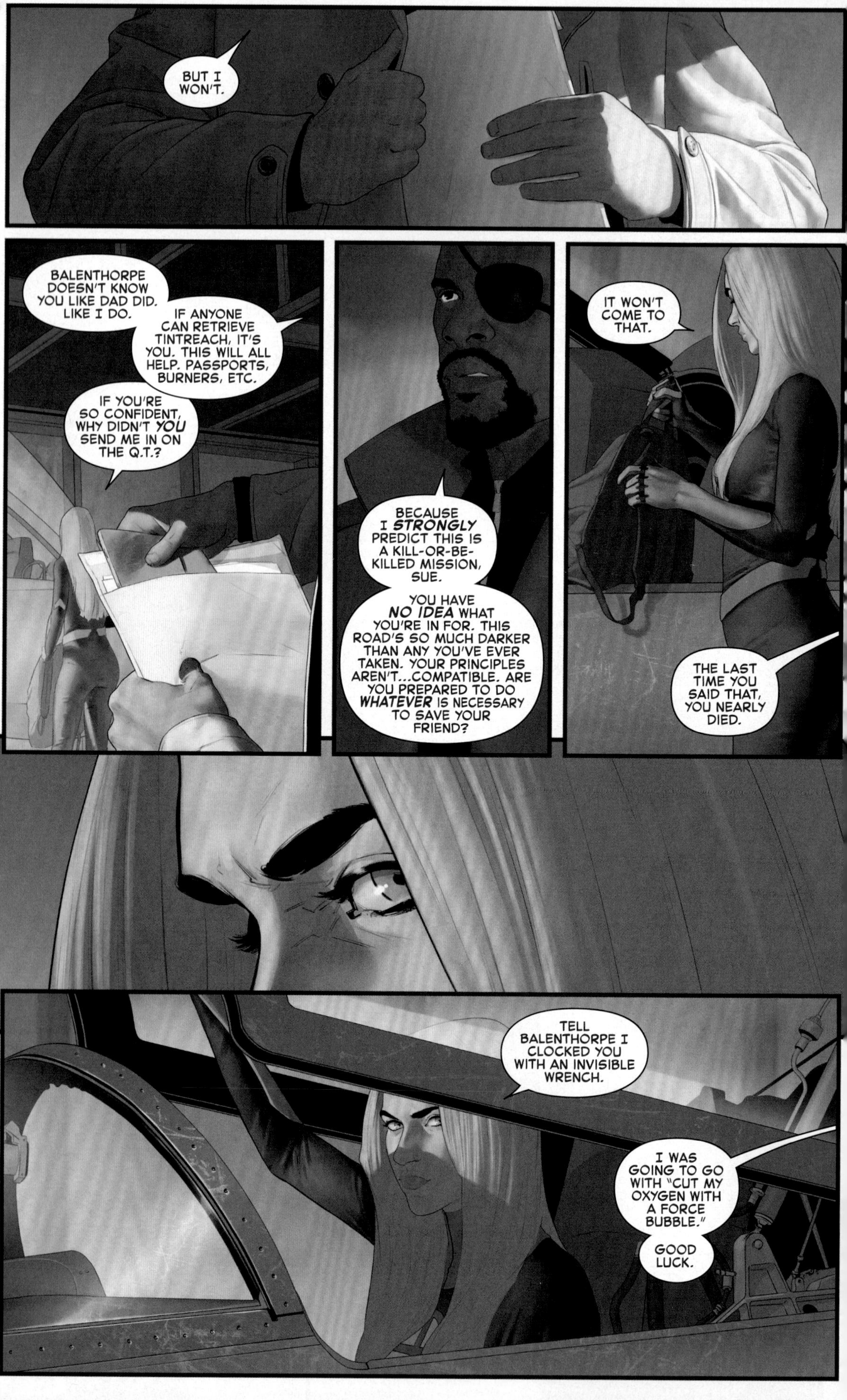
BUT I WON'T.
BALENTHORPE DOESN'T KNOW YOU LIKE DAD DID. LIKE I DO.
IF ANYONE CAN RETRIEVE TINTREACH, IT'S YOU. THIS WILL ALL HELP. PASSPORTS, BURNERS, ETC.
IF YOU'RE SO CONFIDENT, WHY DIDN'T YOU SEND ME IN ON THE Q.T.?
BECAUSE I STRONGLY PREDICT THIS IS A KILL-OR-BE-KILLED MISSION, SUE.
YOU HAVE NO IDEA WHAT YOU'RE IN FOR. THIS ROAD'S SO MUCH DARKER THAN ANY YOU'VE EVER TAKEN. YOUR PRINCIPLES AREN'T...COMPATIBLE. ARE YOU PREPARED TO DO WHATEVER IS NECESSARY TO SAVE YOUR FRIEND?
IT WON'T COME TO THAT.
THE LAST TIME YOU SAID THAT, YOU NEARLY DIED.
TELL BALENTHORPE I CLOCKED YOU WITH AN INVISIBLE WRENCH.
I WAS GOING TO GO WITH "CUT MY OXYGEN WITH A FORCE BUBBLE."
GOOD LUCK.

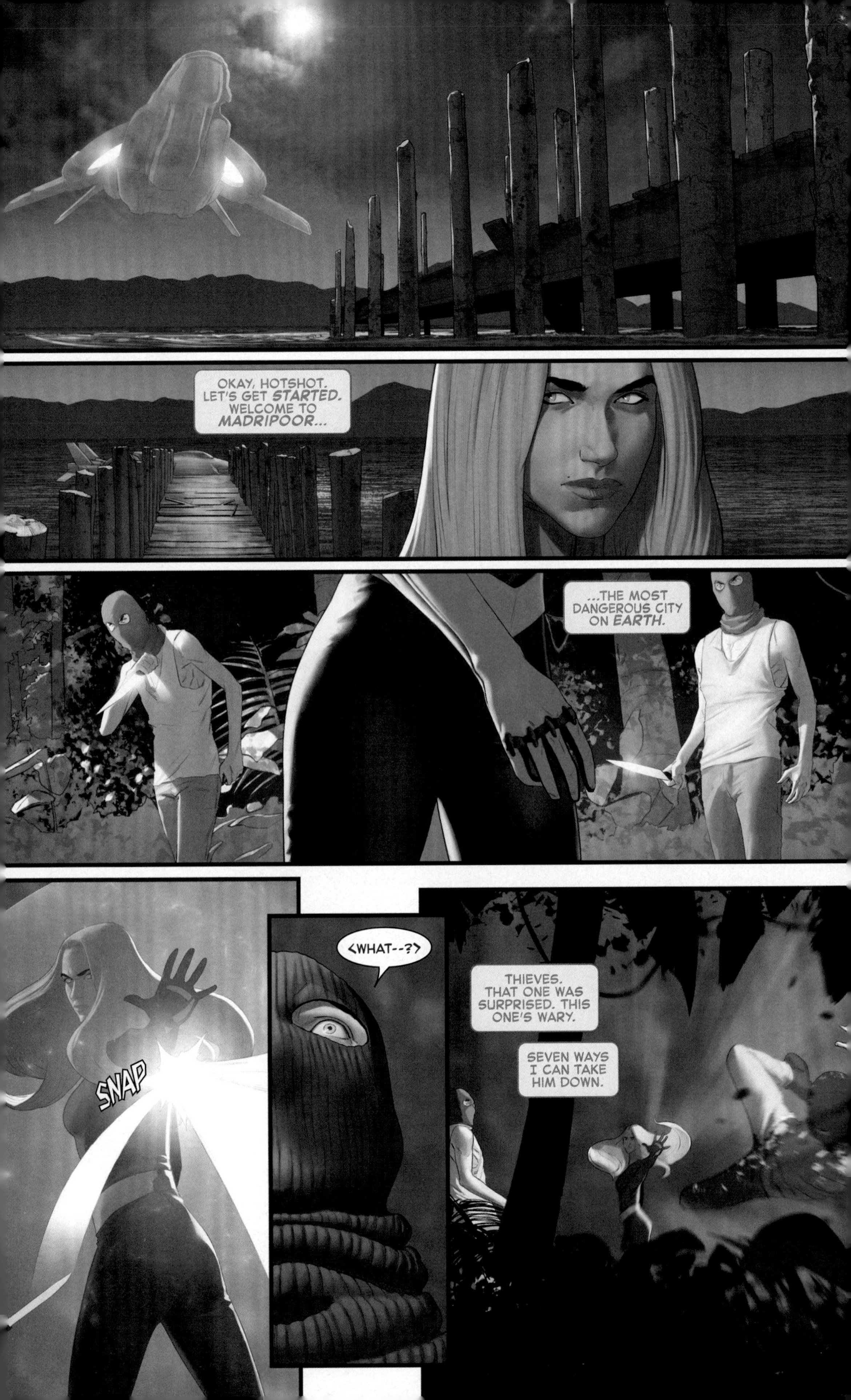
OKAY, HOTSHOT. LET'S GET STARTED. WELCOME TO MADRIPOOR...
...THE MOST DANGEROUS CITY ON EARTH.
SNAP
<WHAT--?>
THIEVES. THAT ONE WAS SURPRISED. THIS ONE'S WARY.
SEVEN WAYS I CAN TAKE HIM DOWN.

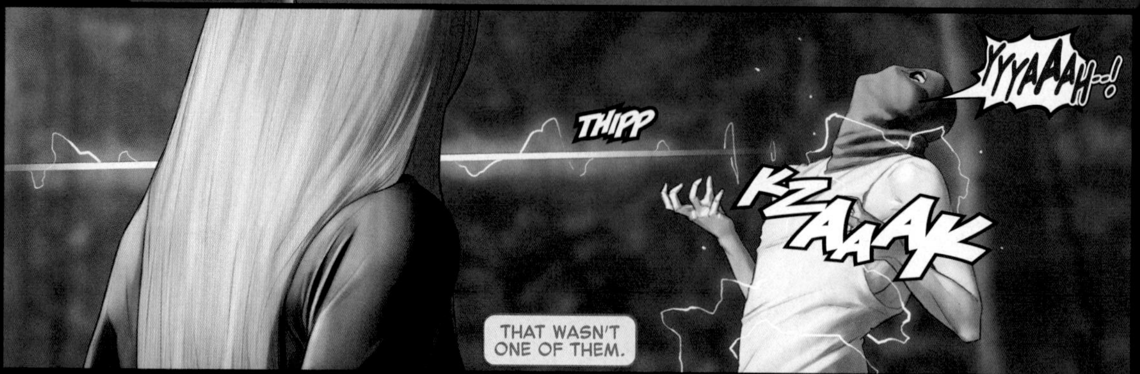
THIPP
YYYAAAH--!
KZAAAK
THAT WASN'T ONE OF THEM.

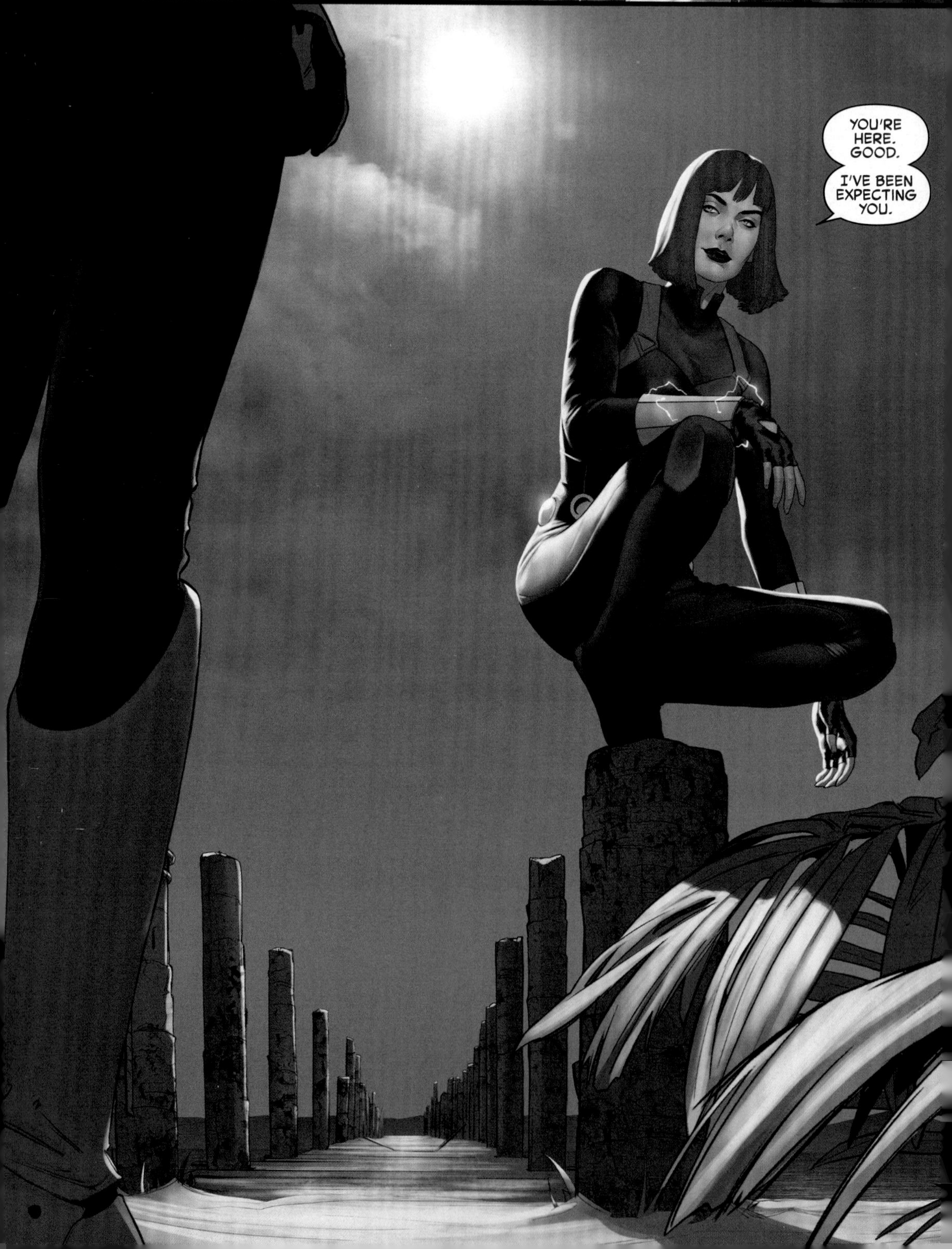
YOU'RE HERE. GOOD.
I'VE BEEN EXPECTING YOU.

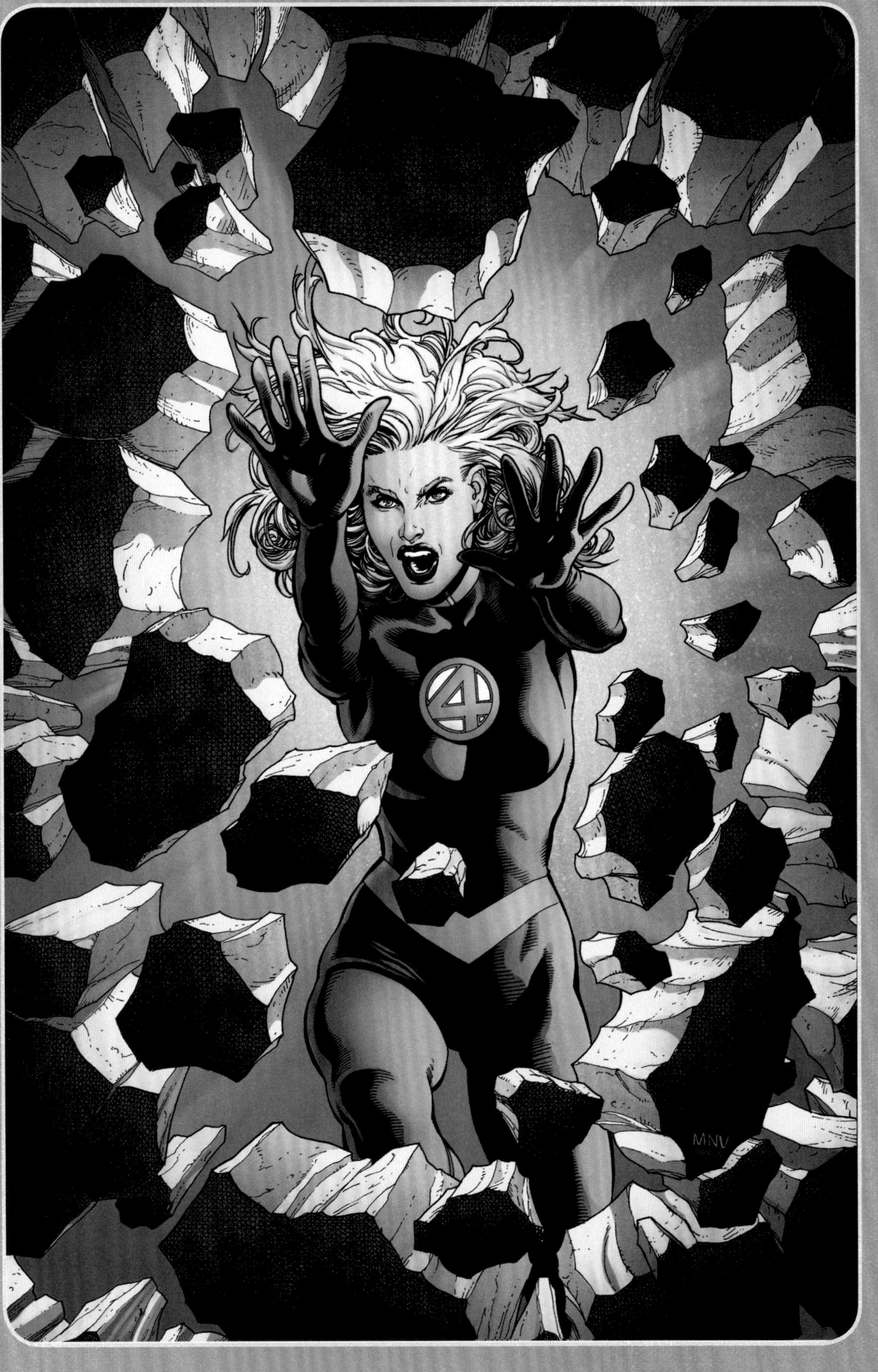
MNV

STEVE McNIVEN & RICHARD ISANOVE
1 VARIANT

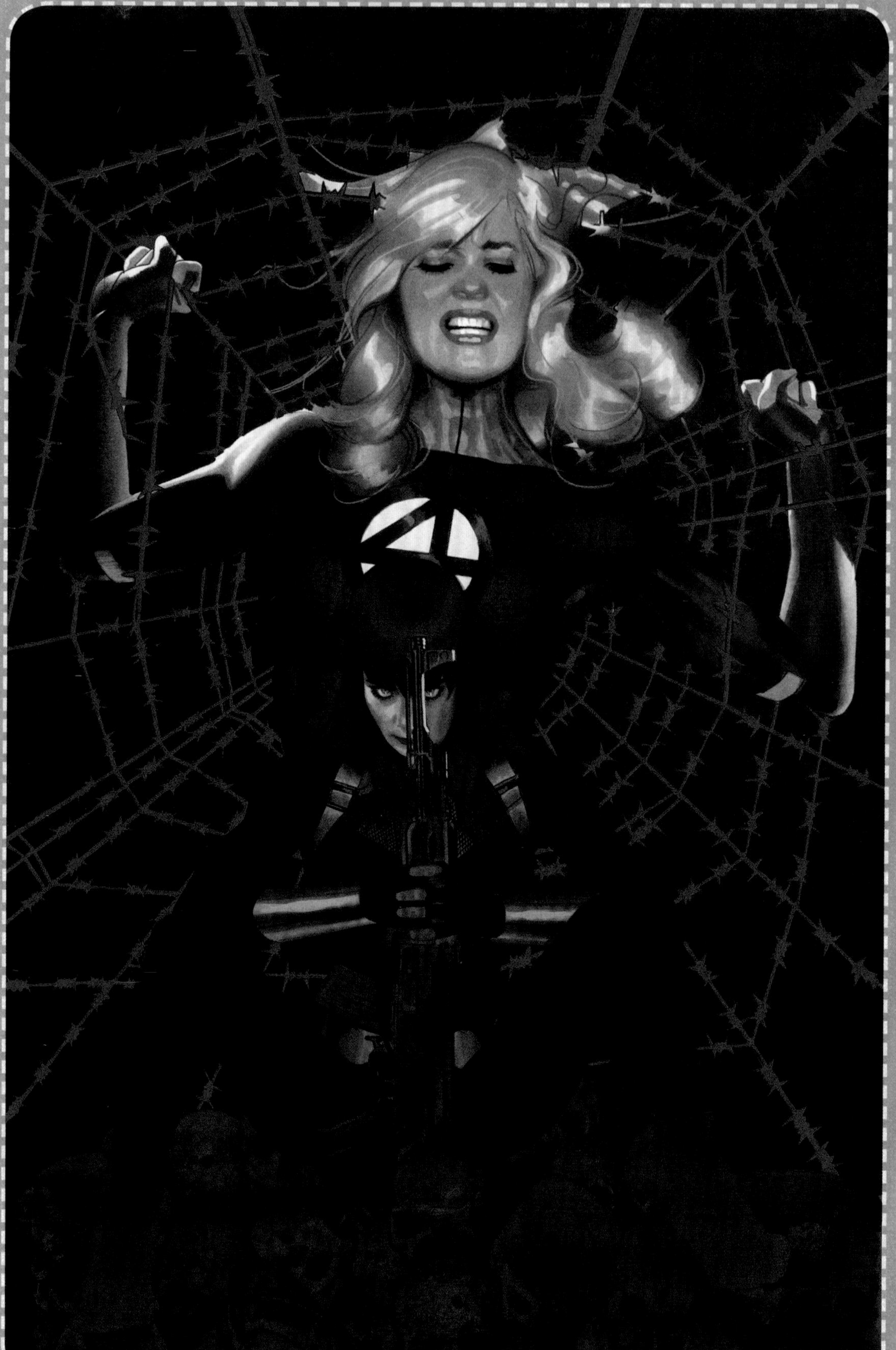

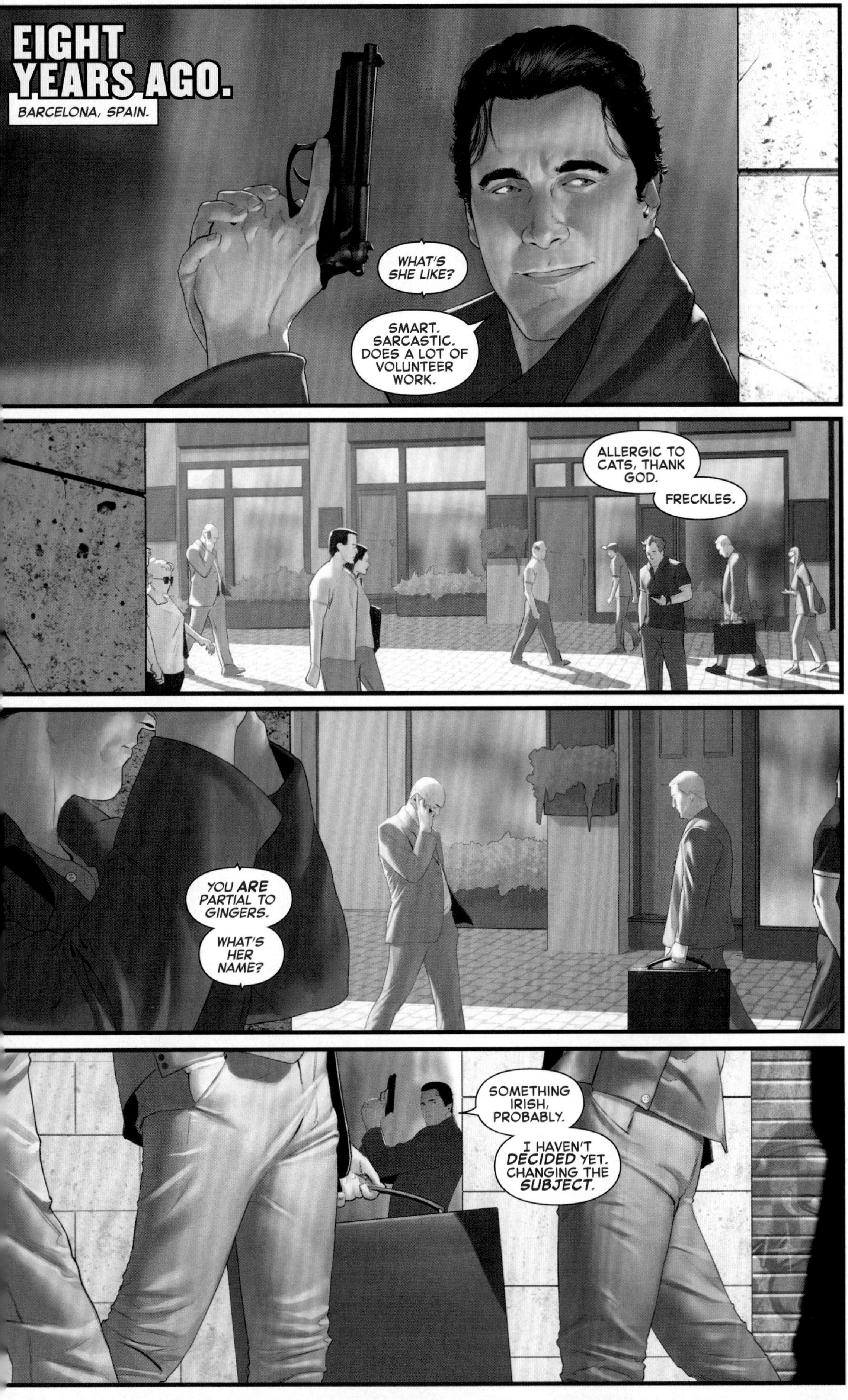
EIGHT YEARS AGO.
BARCELONA, SPAIN.
WHAT'S SHE LIKE?
SMART. SARCASTIC. DOES A LOT OF VOLUNTEER WORK.
ALLERGIC TO CATS, THANK GOD.
FRECKLES.
YOU ARE PARTIAL TO GINGERS.
WHAT'S HER NAME?
SOMETHING IRISH, PROBABLY.
I HAVEN'T DECIDED YET. CHANGING THE SUBJECT.

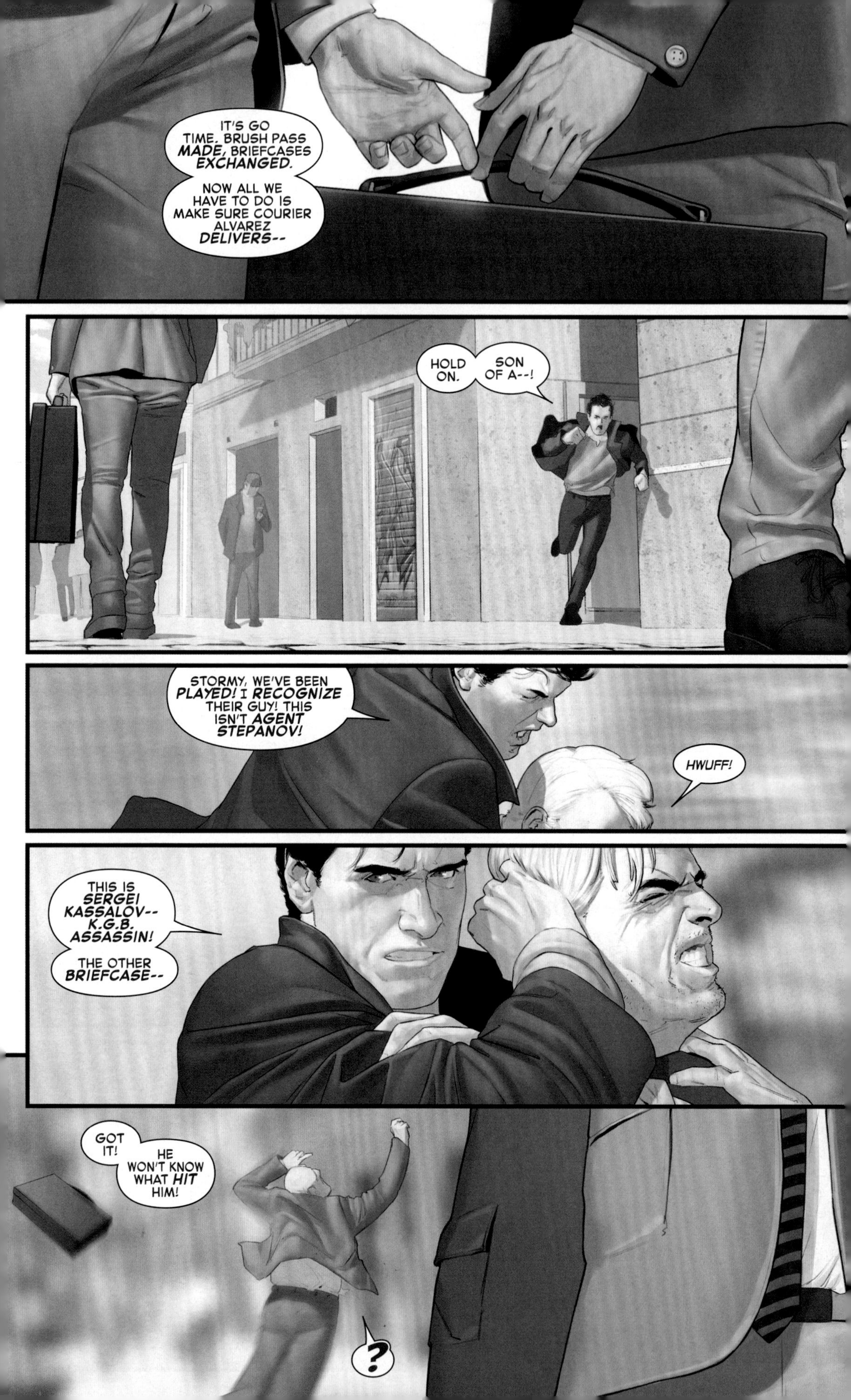

IT'S GO TIME. BRUSH PASS MADE, BRIEFCASES EXCHANGED.
NOW ALL WE HAVE TO DO IS MAKE SURE COURIER ALVAREZ DELIVERS--
HOLD ON.
SON OF A--!
STORMY, WE'VE BEEN PLAYED! I RECOGNIZE THEIR GUY! THIS ISN'T AGENT STEPANOV!
HWUFF!
THIS IS SERGEI KASSALOV-- K.G.B. ASSASSIN!
THE OTHER BRIEFCASE--
GOT IT!
HE WON'T KNOW WHAT HIT HIM!
?

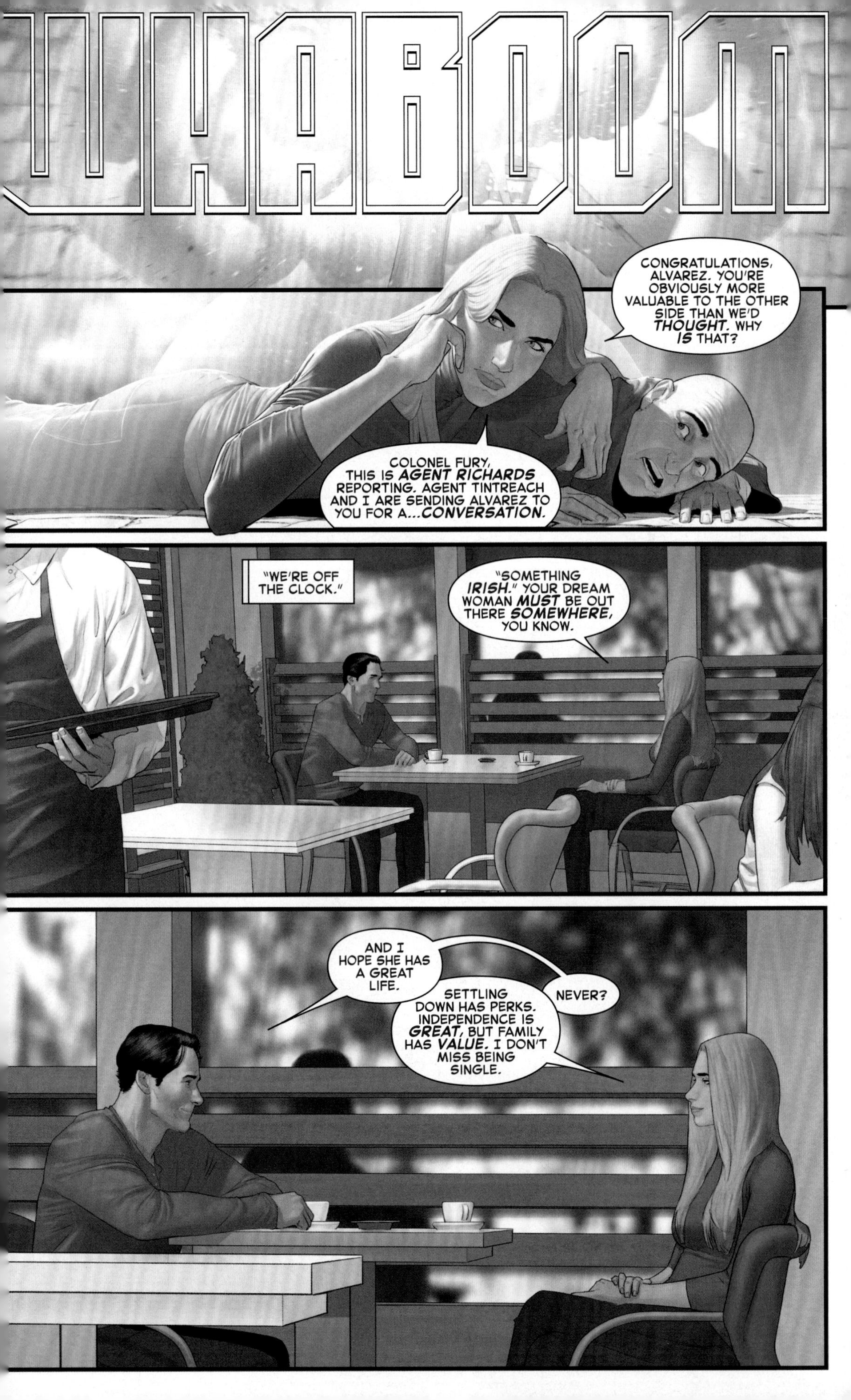
WHABOOM
CONGRATULATIONS, ALVAREZ. YOU'RE OBVIOUSLY MORE VALUABLE TO THE OTHER SIDE THAN WE'D THOUGHT. WHY IS THAT?
COLONEL FURY, THIS IS AGENT RICHARDS REPORTING. AGENT TINTREACH AND I ARE SENDING ALVAREZ TO YOU FOR A...CONVERSATION.
"WE'RE OFF THE CLOCK."
"SOMETHING IRISH." YOUR DREAM WOMAN MUST BE OUT THERE SOMEWHERE, YOU KNOW.
AND I HOPE SHE HAS A GREAT LIFE.
NEVER?
SETTLING DOWN HAS PERKS. INDEPENDENCE IS GREAT, BUT FAMILY HAS VALUE. I DON'T MISS BEING SINGLE.

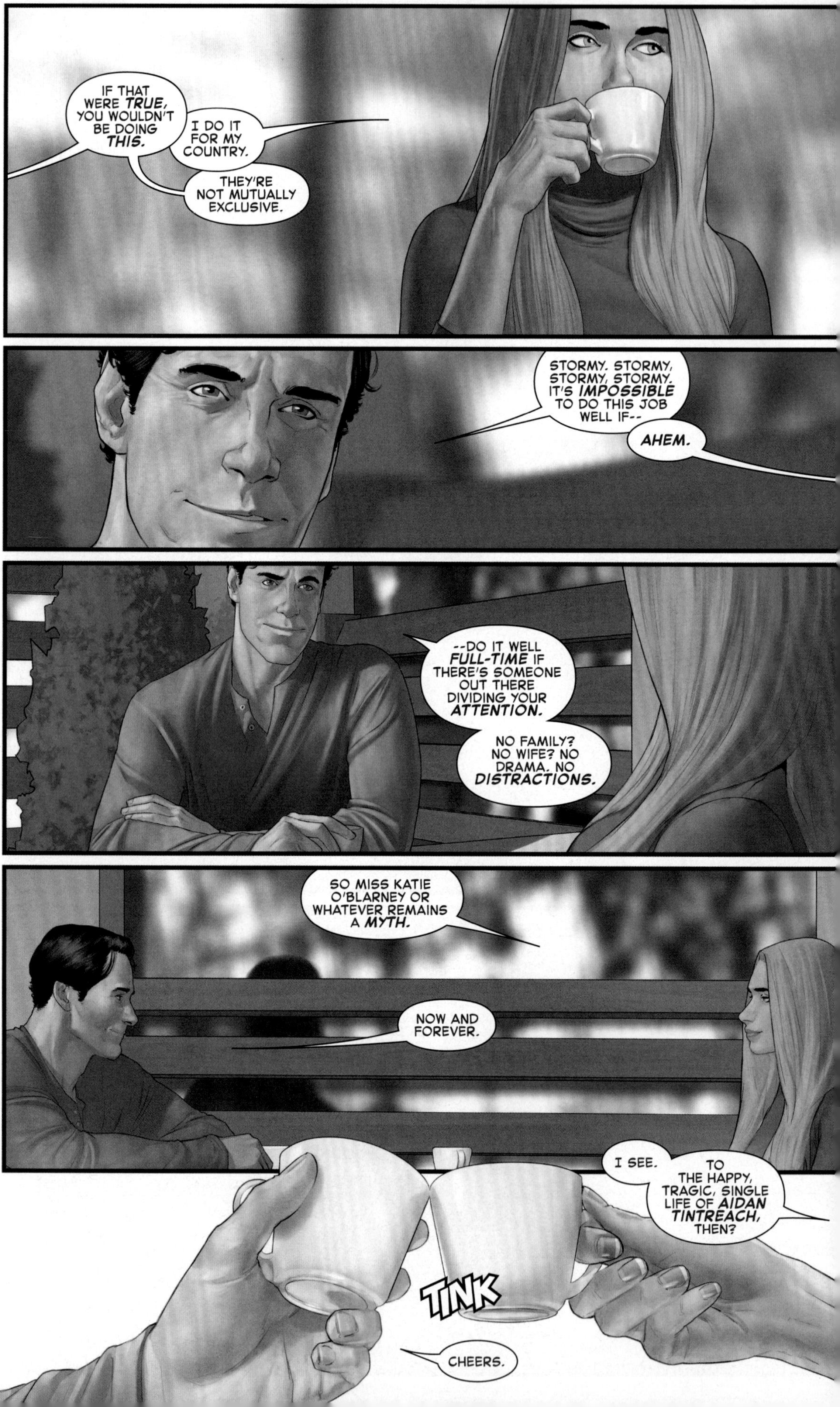
IF THAT WERE TRUE, YOU WOULDN'T BE DOING THIS.
I DO IT FOR MY COUNTRY.
THEY'RE NOT MUTUALLY EXCLUSIVE.
STORMY. STORMY, STORMY, STORMY. IT'S IMPOSSIBLE TO DO THIS JOB WELL IF--
AHEM.
--DO IT WELL FULL-TIME IF THERE'S SOMEONE OUT THERE DIVIDING YOUR ATTENTION.
NO FAMILY? NO WIFE? NO DRAMA. NO DISTRACTIONS.
SO MISS KATIE O'BLARNEY OR WHATEVER REMAINS A MYTH.
NOW AND FOREVER.
I SEE.
TO THE HAPPY, TRAGIC, SINGLE LIFE OF AIDAN TINTREACH, THEN?
TINK
CHEERS.

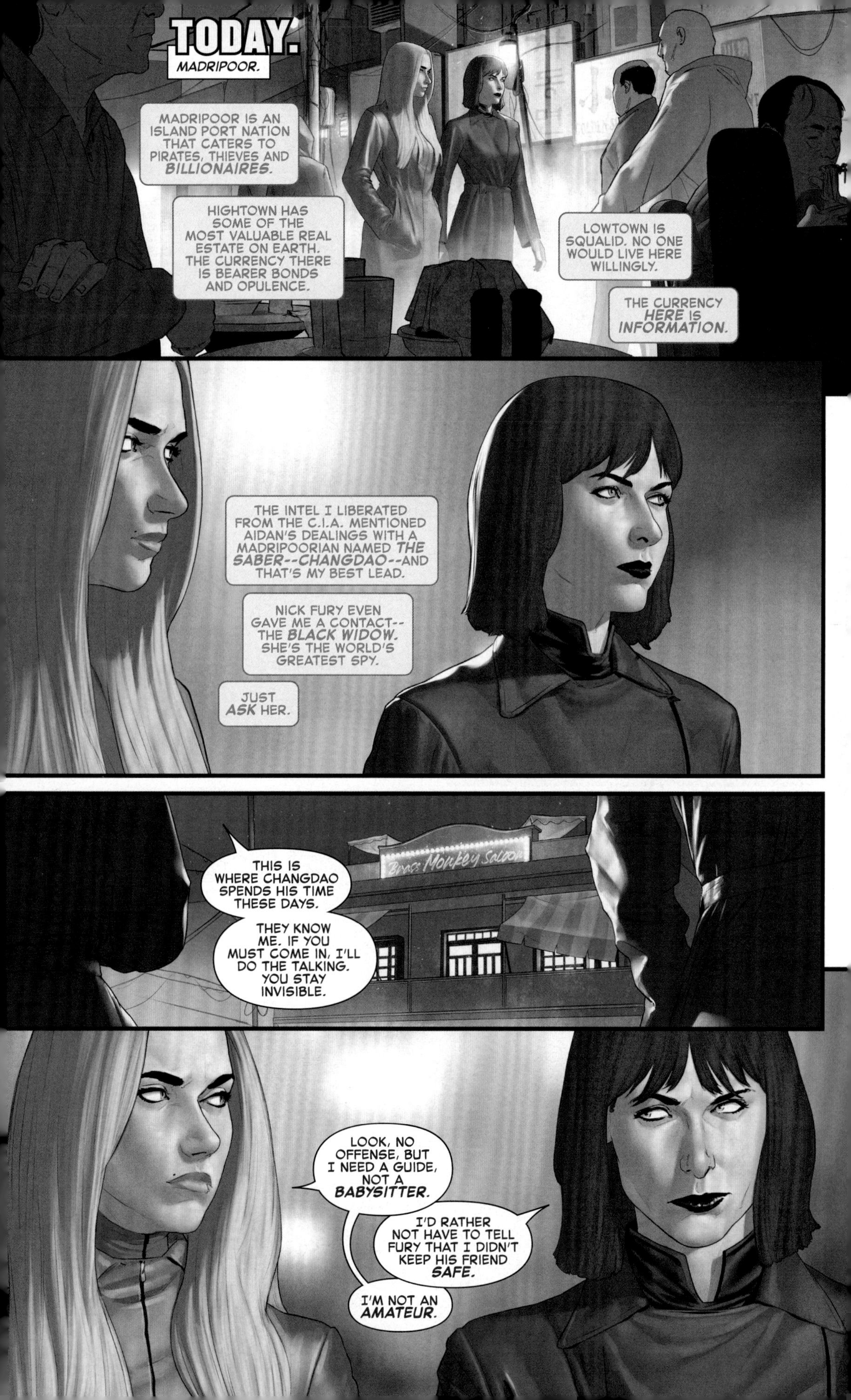
TODAY.
MADRIPOOR.
MADRIPOOR IS AN ISLAND PORT NATION THAT CATERS TO PIRATES, THIEVES AND BILLIONAIRES.
HIGHTOWN HAS SOME OF THE MOST VALUABLE REAL ESTATE ON EARTH. THE CURRENCY THERE IS BEARER BONDS AND OPULENCE.
LOWTOWN IS SQUALID. NO ONE WOULD LIVE HERE WILLINGLY.
THE CURRENCY HERE IS INFORMATION.
THE INTEL I LIBERATED FROM THE C.I.A. MENTIONED AIDAN'S DEALINGS WITH A MADRIPOORIAN NAMED THE SABER--CHANGDAO--AND THAT'S MY BEST LEAD.
NICK FURY EVEN GAVE ME A CONTACT--THE BLACK WIDOW. SHE'S THE WORLD'S GREATEST SPY.
JUST ASK HER.
THIS IS WHERE CHANGDAO SPENDS HIS TIME THESE DAYS.
Brass Monkey Saloon
THEY KNOW ME. IF YOU MUST COME IN, I'LL DO THE TALKING. YOU STAY INVISIBLE.
LOOK, NO OFFENSE, BUT I NEED A GUIDE, NOT A BABYSITTER.
I'D RATHER NOT HAVE TO TELL FURY THAT I DIDN'T KEEP HIS FRIEND SAFE.
I'M NOT AN AMATEUR.

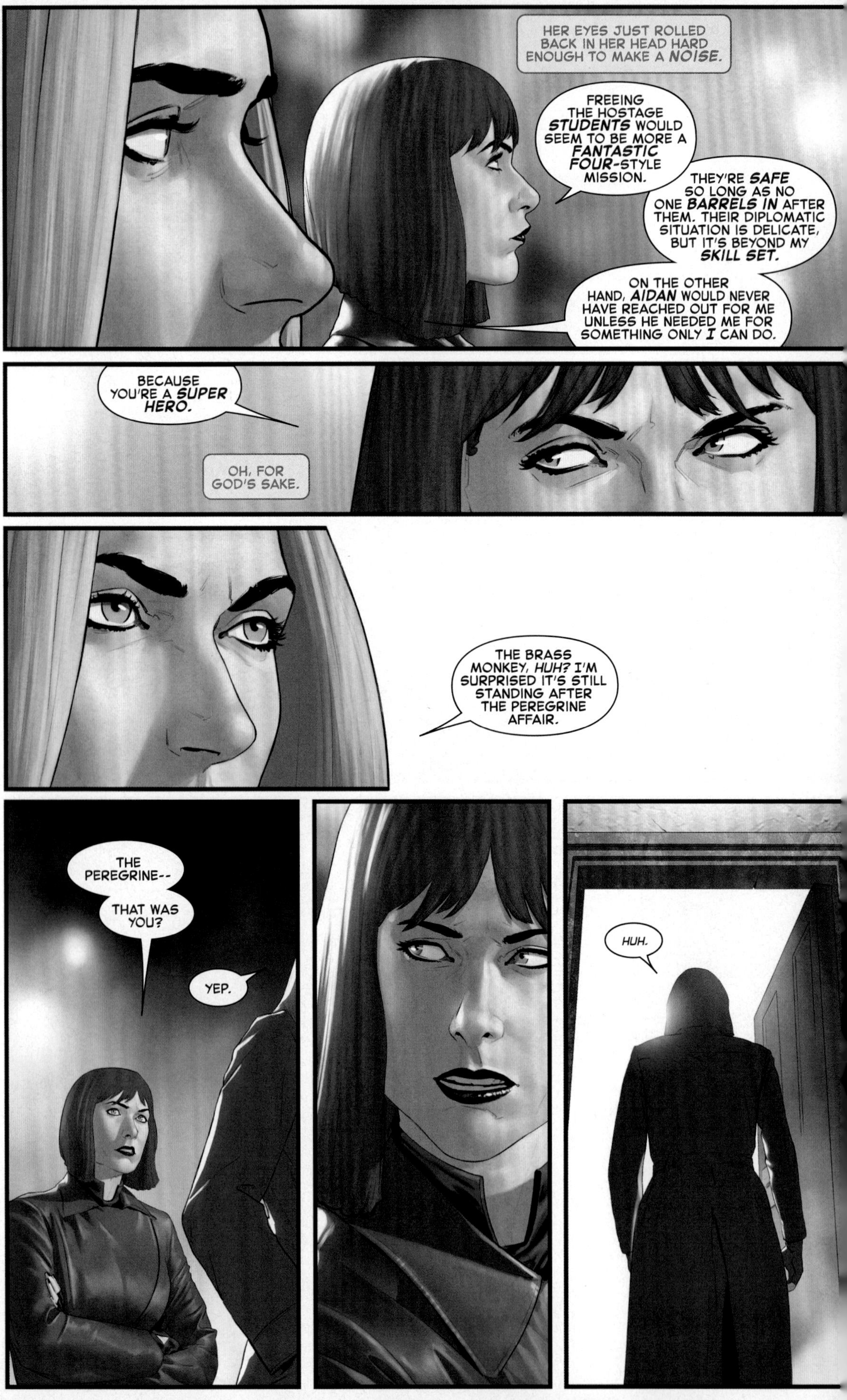

HER EYES JUST ROLLED BACK IN HER HEAD HARD ENOUGH TO MAKE A *NOISE.*
FREEING THE HOSTAGE **STUDENTS** WOULD SEEM TO BE MORE A **FANTASTIC FOUR**-STYLE MISSION.
THEY'RE **SAFE** SO LONG AS NO ONE **BARRELS IN** AFTER THEM. THEIR DIPLOMATIC SITUATION IS DELICATE, BUT IT'S BEYOND MY **SKILL SET.**
ON THE OTHER HAND, **AIDAN** WOULD NEVER HAVE REACHED OUT FOR ME UNLESS HE NEEDED ME FOR SOMETHING ONLY **I** CAN DO.
BECAUSE YOU'RE A **SUPER HERO.**
OH, FOR GOD'S SAKE.
THE BRASS MONKEY, *HUH?* I'M SURPRISED IT'S STILL STANDING AFTER THE PEREGRINE AFFAIR.
THE PEREGRINE--
THAT WAS YOU?
YEP.
HUH.

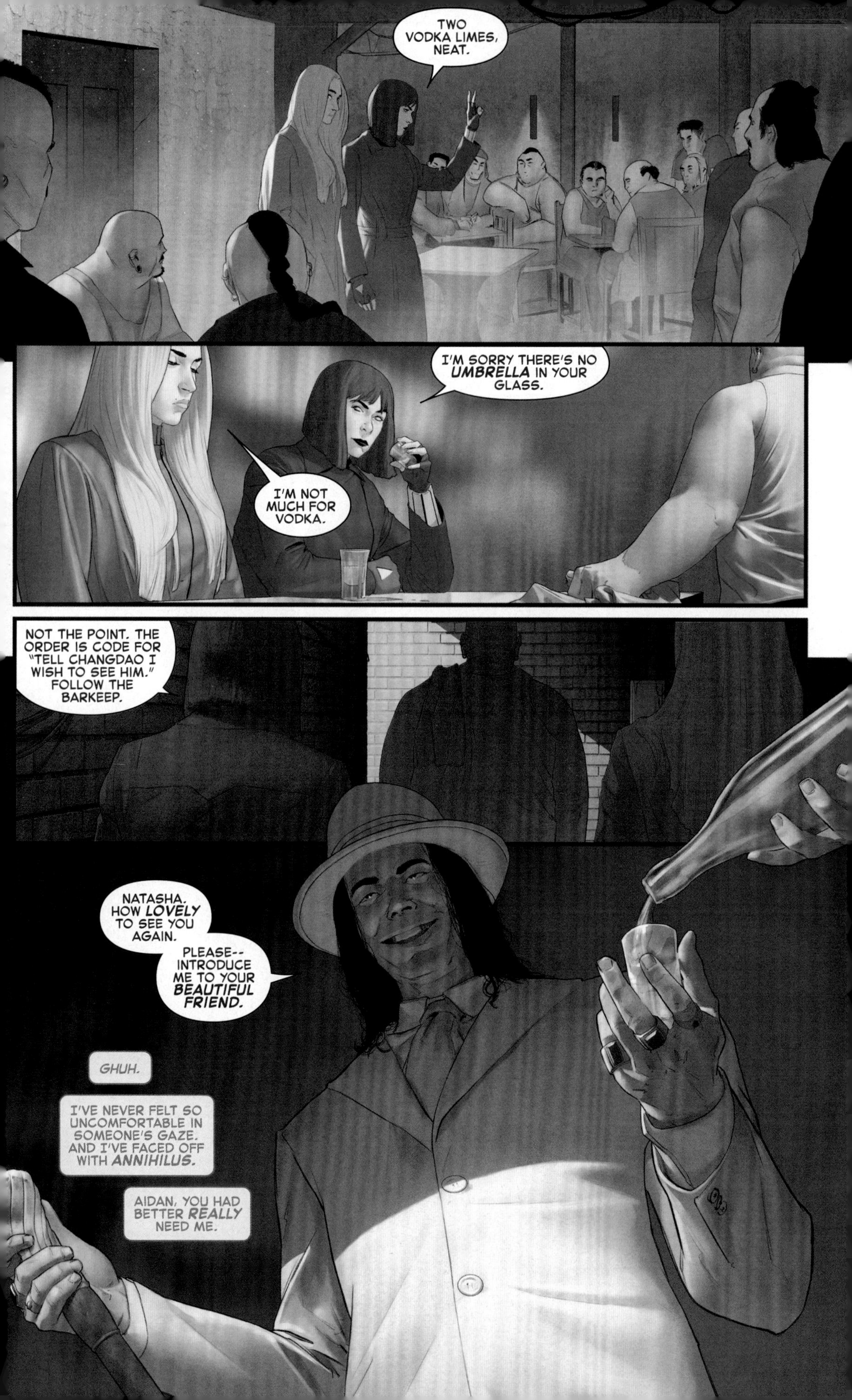
TWO VODKA LIMES, NEAT.
I'M SORRY THERE'S NO UMBRELLA IN YOUR GLASS.
I'M NOT MUCH FOR VODKA.
NOT THE POINT. THE ORDER IS CODE FOR "TELL CHANGDAO I WISH TO SEE HIM." FOLLOW THE BARKEEP.
NATASHA. HOW LOVELY TO SEE YOU AGAIN.
PLEASE-- INTRODUCE ME TO YOUR BEAUTIFUL FRIEND.
GHUH.
I'VE NEVER FELT SO UNCOMFORTABLE IN SOMEONE'S GAZE. AND I'VE FACED OFF WITH ANNIHILUS.
AIDAN, YOU HAD BETTER REALLY NEED ME.

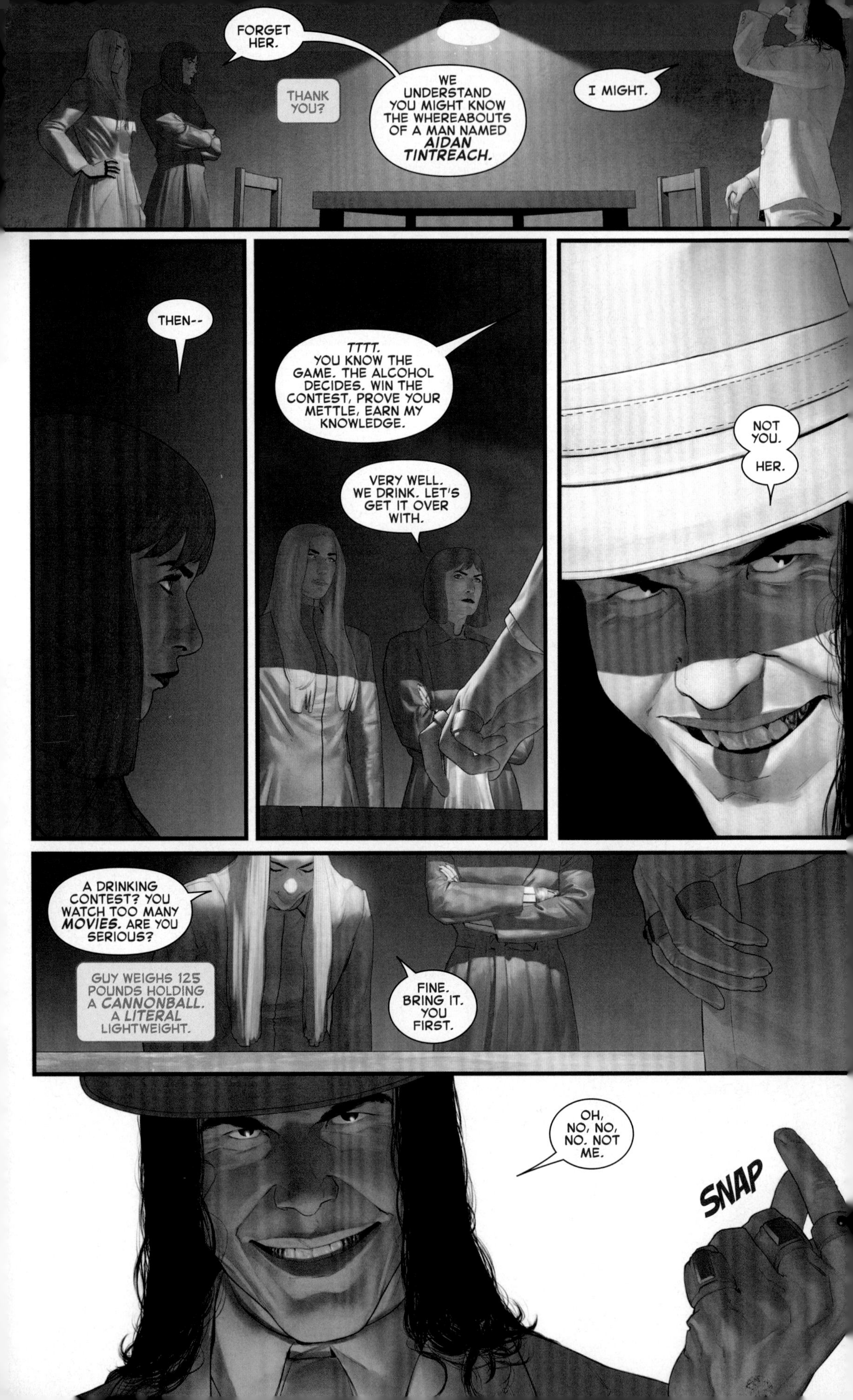
FORGET HER.
THANK YOU?
WE UNDERSTAND YOU MIGHT KNOW THE WHEREABOUTS OF A MAN NAMED *AIDAN TINTREACH.*
I MIGHT.
THEN--
TTTT. YOU KNOW THE GAME. THE ALCOHOL DECIDES. WIN THE CONTEST, PROVE YOUR METTLE, EARN MY KNOWLEDGE.
VERY WELL. WE DRINK. LET'S GET IT OVER WITH.
NOT YOU.
HER.
A DRINKING CONTEST? YOU WATCH TOO MANY *MOVIES.* ARE YOU SERIOUS?
GUY WEIGHS 125 POUNDS HOLDING A *CANNONBALL.* A *LITERAL* LIGHTWEIGHT.
FINE. BRING IT. YOU FIRST.
OH, NO, NO, NO. NOT ME.
SNAP

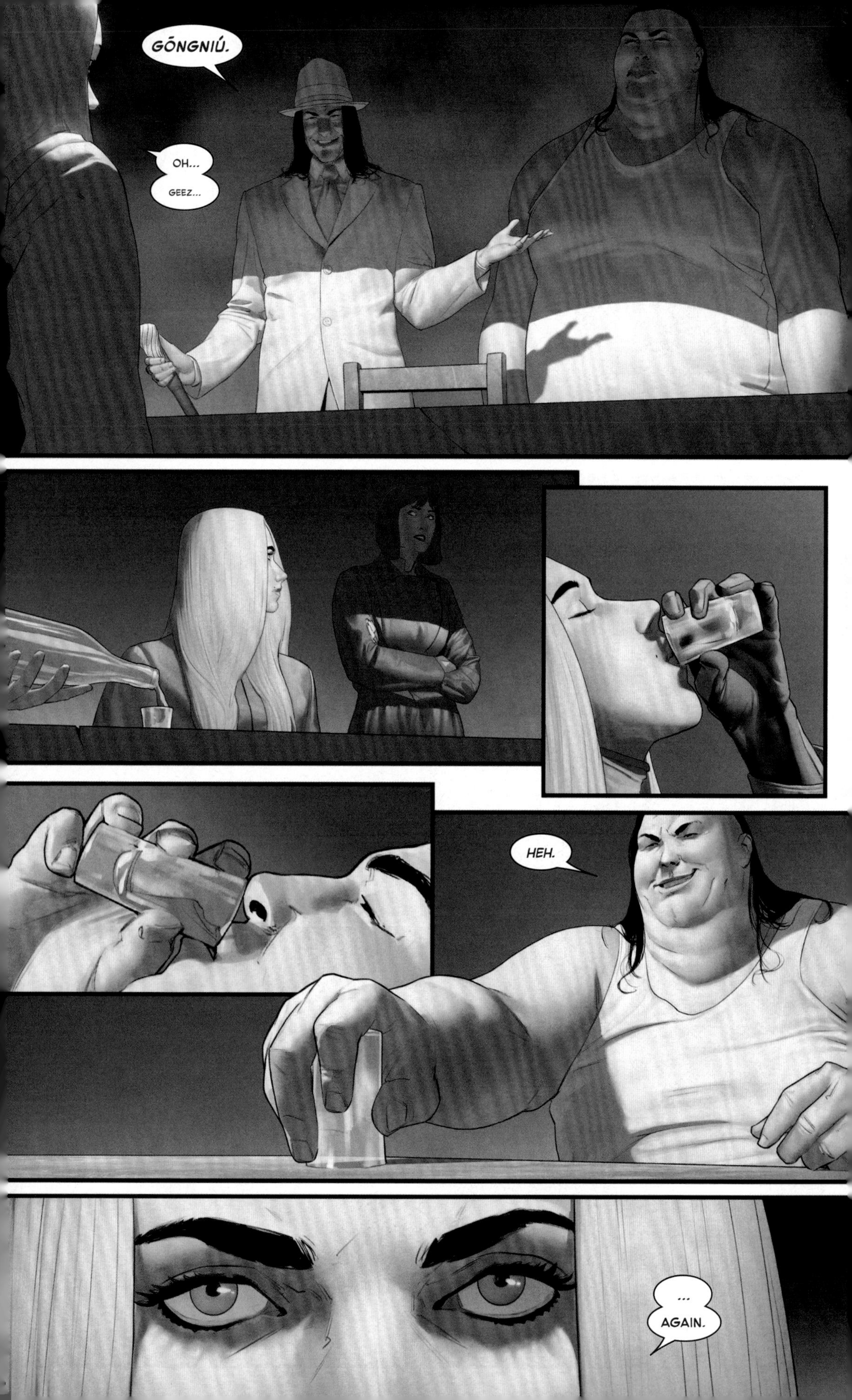
GŌNGNIÚ.
OH...
GEEZ...
HEH.
...
AGAIN.

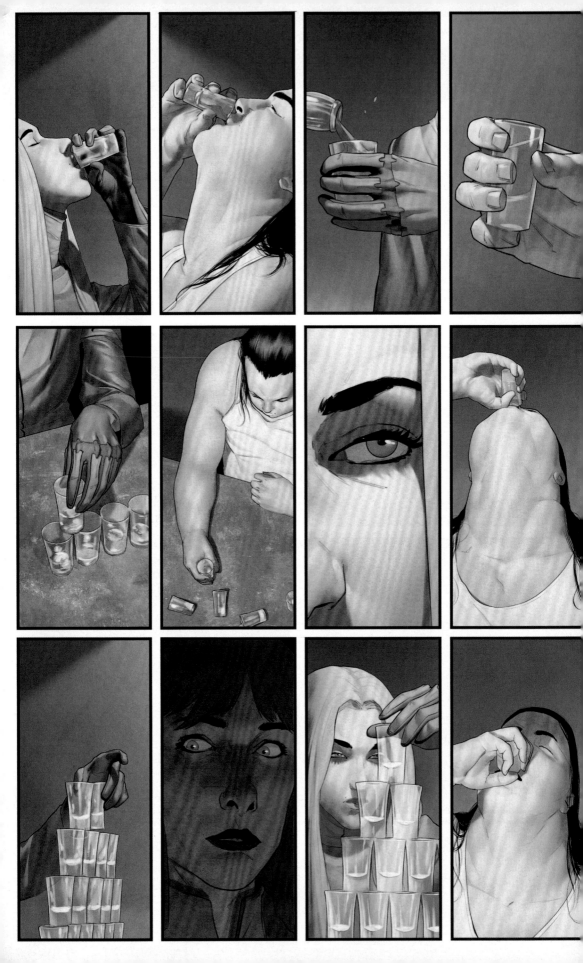

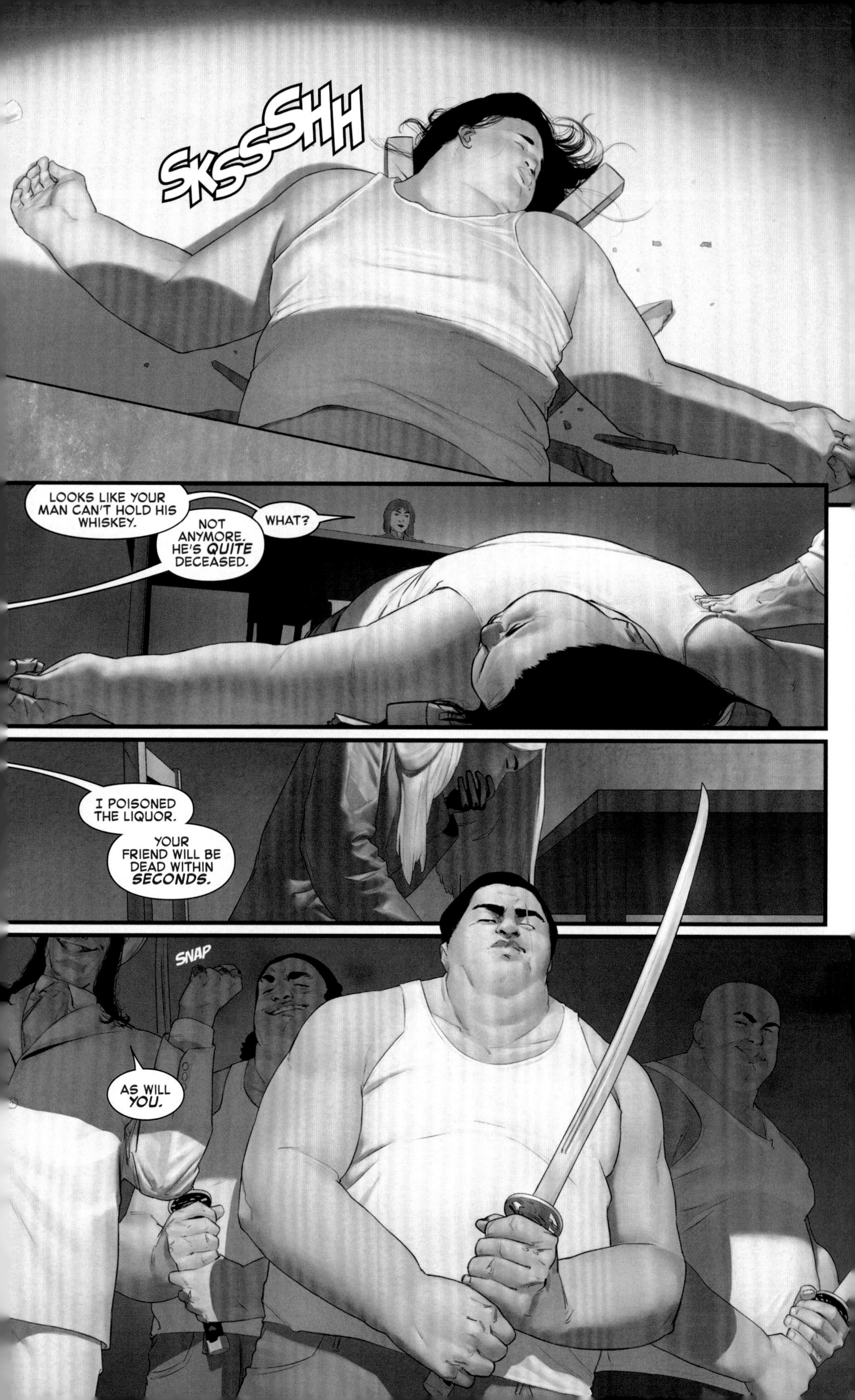
SKSSSHH
LOOKS LIKE YOUR MAN CAN'T HOLD HIS WHISKEY.
WHAT?
NOT ANYMORE. HE'S QUITE DECEASED.
I POISONED THE LIQUOR.
YOUR FRIEND WILL BE DEAD WITHIN SECONDS.
SNAP
AS WILL YOU.

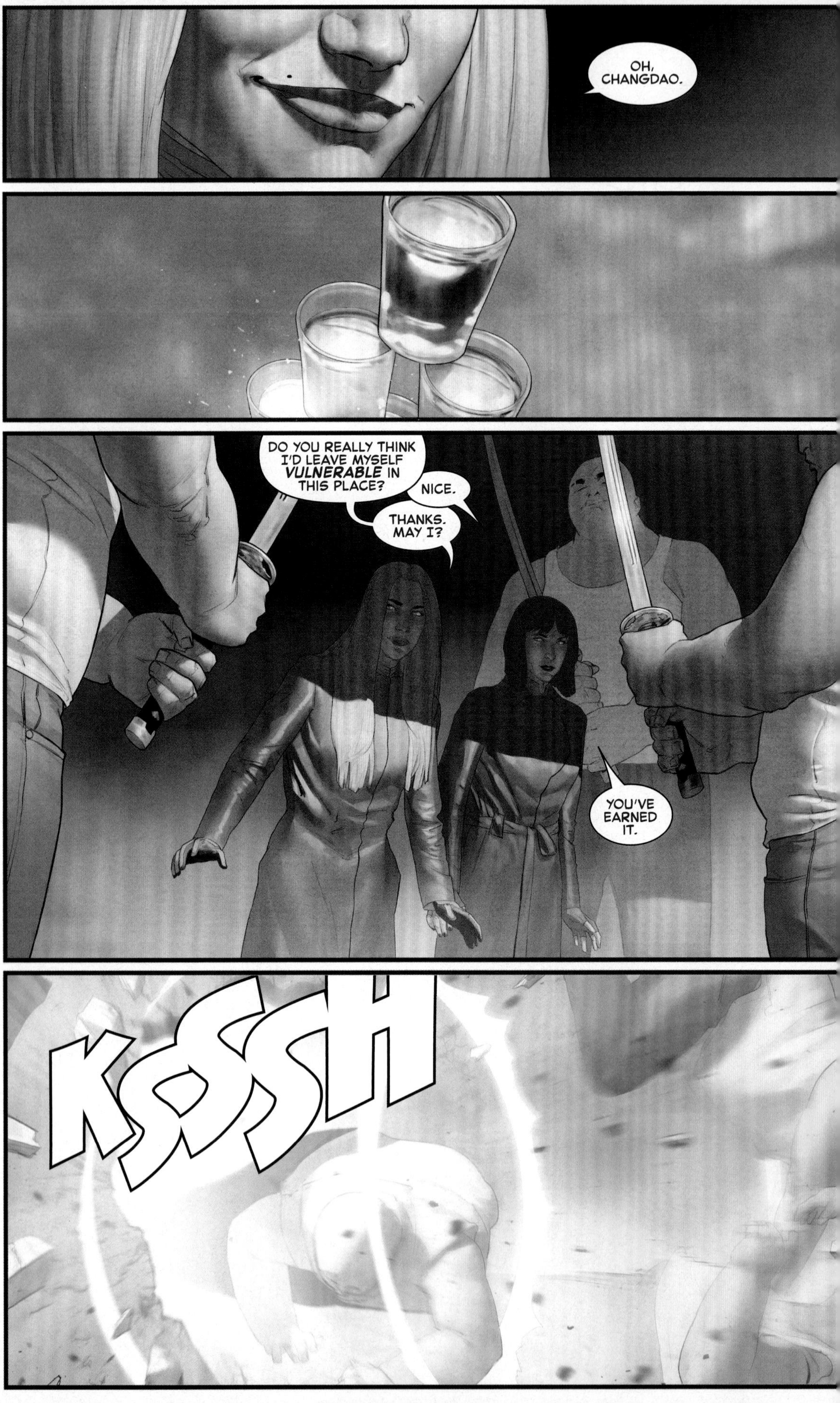
OH, CHANGDAO.
DO YOU REALLY THINK I'D LEAVE MYSELF VULNERABLE IN THIS PLACE?
NICE.
THANKS. MAY I?
YOU'VE EARNED IT.
KSSH

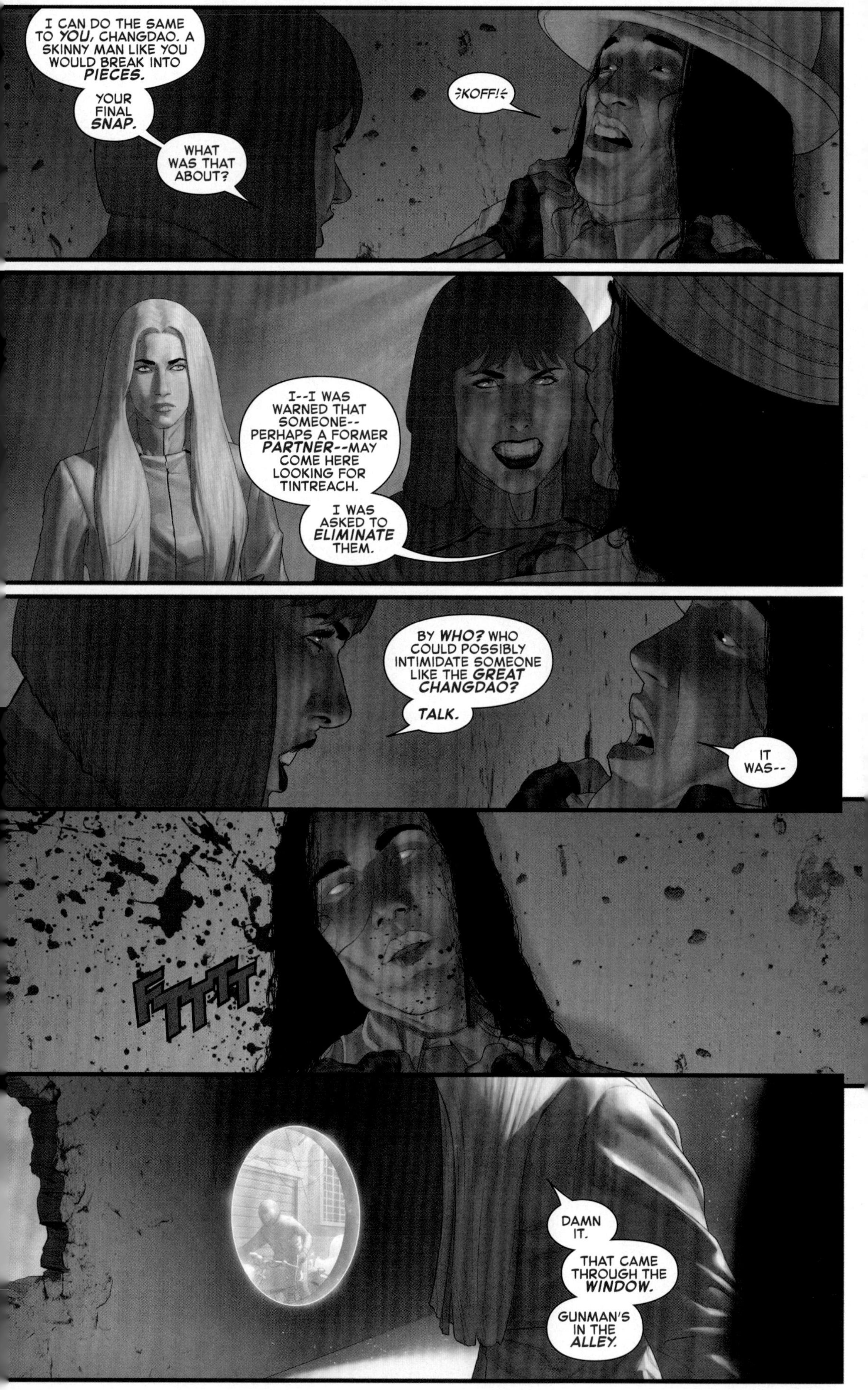

I CAN DO THE SAME TO YOU, CHANGDAO. A SKINNY MAN LIKE YOU WOULD BREAK INTO PIECES.
YOUR FINAL SNAP.
WHAT WAS THAT ABOUT?
KOFF!
I--I WAS WARNED THAT SOMEONE--PERHAPS A FORMER PARTNER--MAY COME HERE LOOKING FOR TINTREACH.
I WAS ASKED TO ELIMINATE THEM.
BY WHO? WHO COULD POSSIBLY INTIMIDATE SOMEONE LIKE THE GREAT CHANGDAO?
TALK.
IT WAS--
FTTTT
DAMN IT.
THAT CAME THROUGH THE WINDOW.
GUNMAN'S IN THE ALLEY.

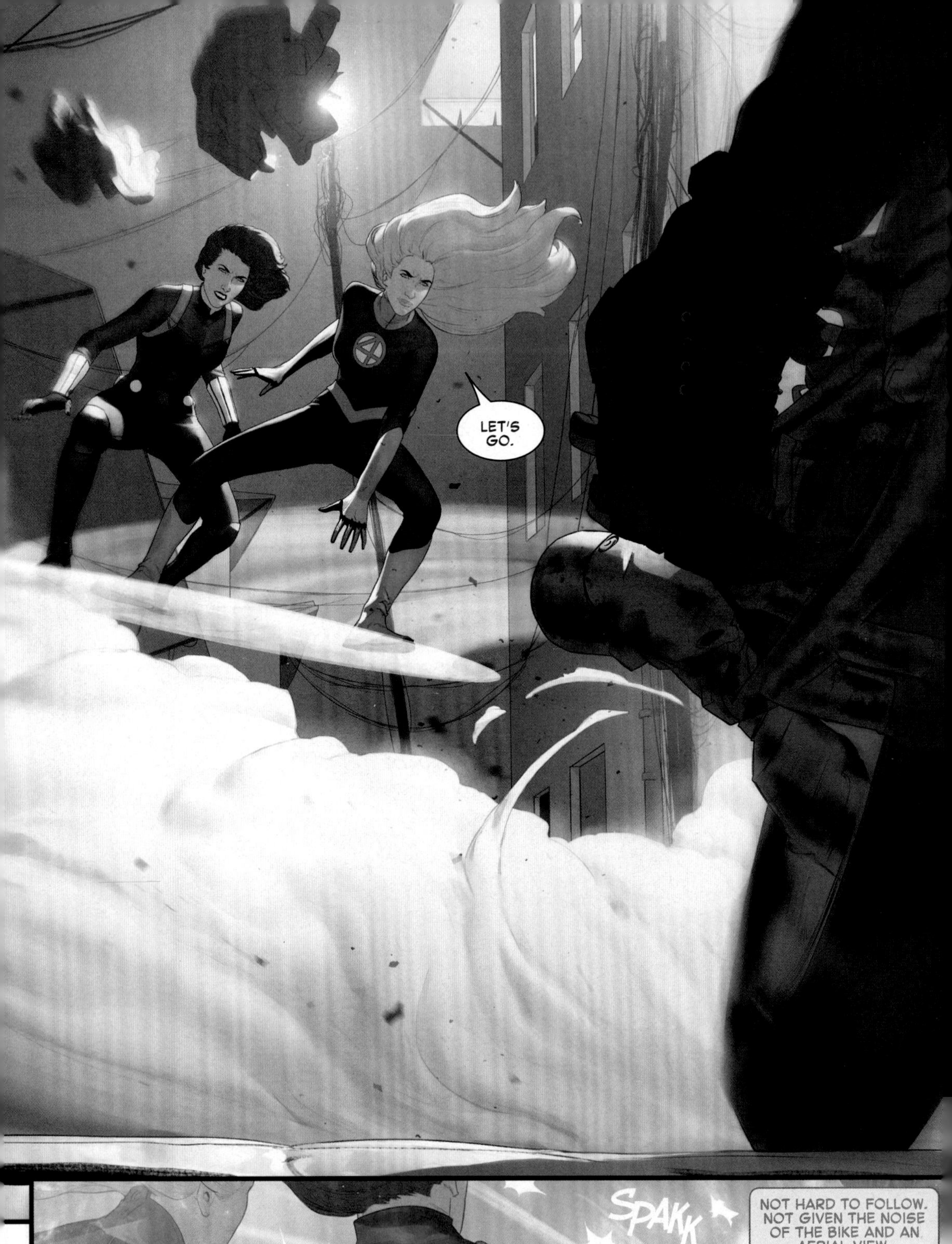
LET'S GO.

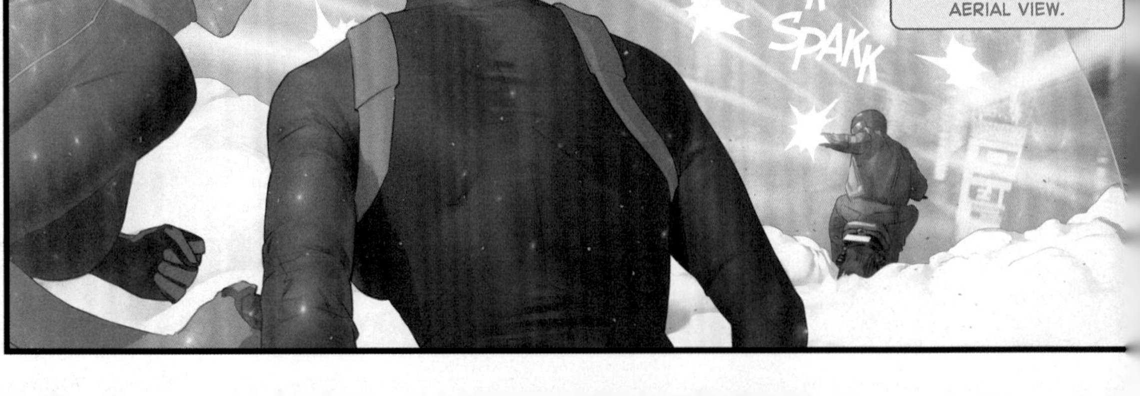
SPAKK
SPAKK
NOT HARD TO FOLLOW. NOT GIVEN THE NOISE OF THE BIKE AND AN AERIAL VIEW.

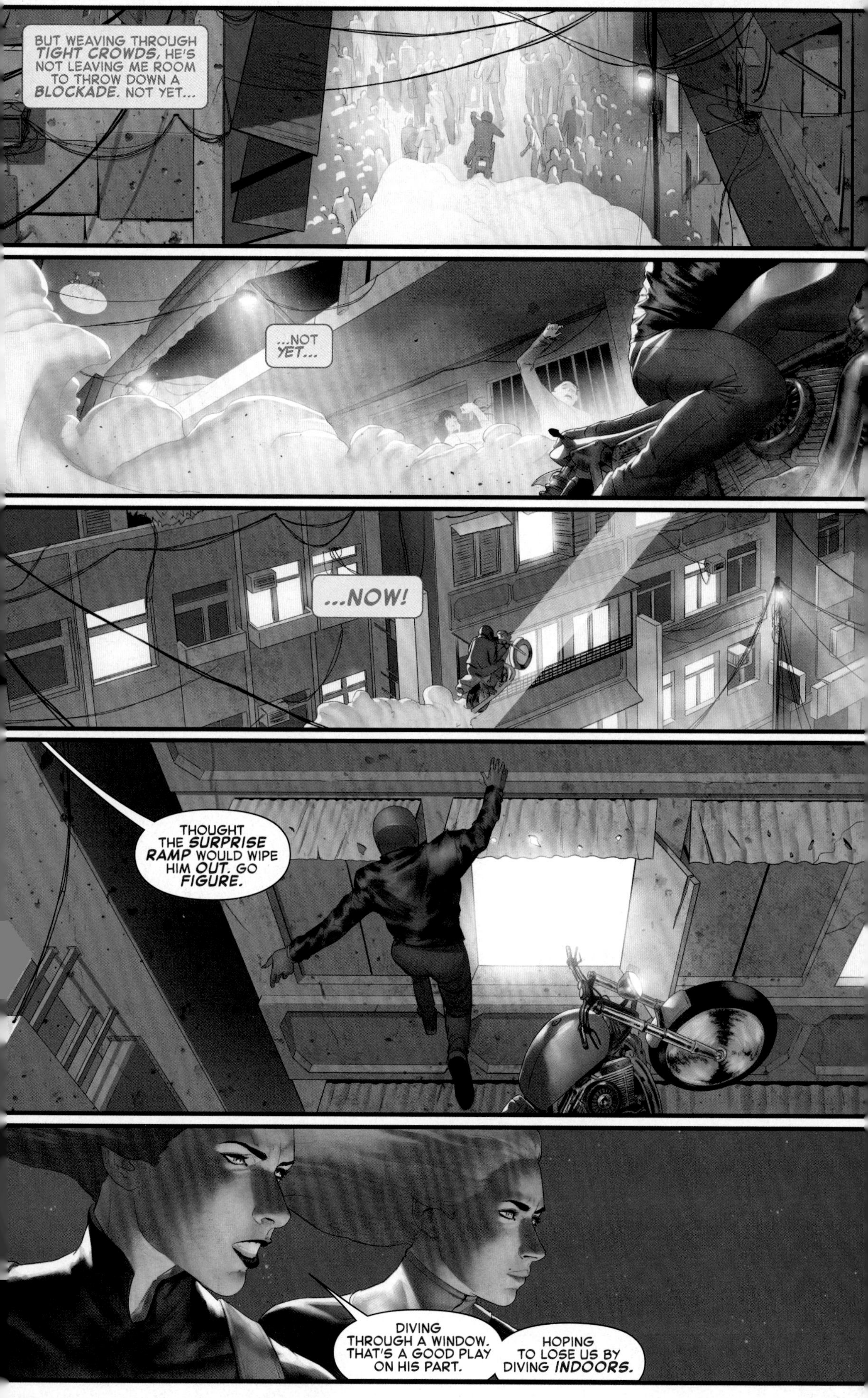
BUT WEAVING THROUGH TIGHT CROWDS, HE'S NOT LEAVING ME ROOM TO THROW DOWN A BLOCKADE. NOT YET...
...NOT YET...
...NOW!
THOUGHT THE SURPRISE RAMP WOULD WIPE HIM OUT. GO FIGURE.
DIVING THROUGH A WINDOW. THAT'S A GOOD PLAY ON HIS PART.
HOPING TO LOSE US BY DIVING INDOORS.

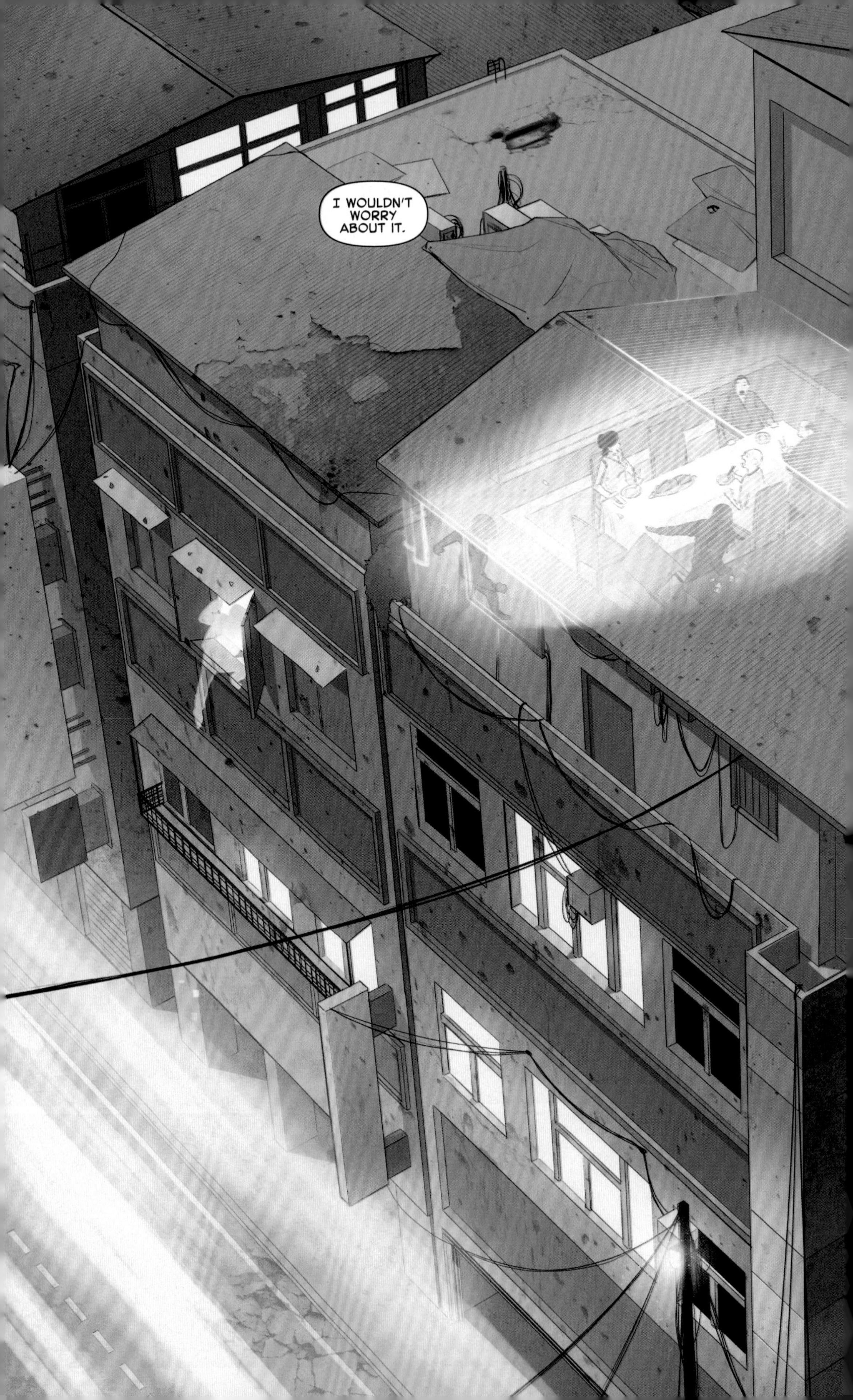
I WOULDN'T WORRY ABOUT IT.

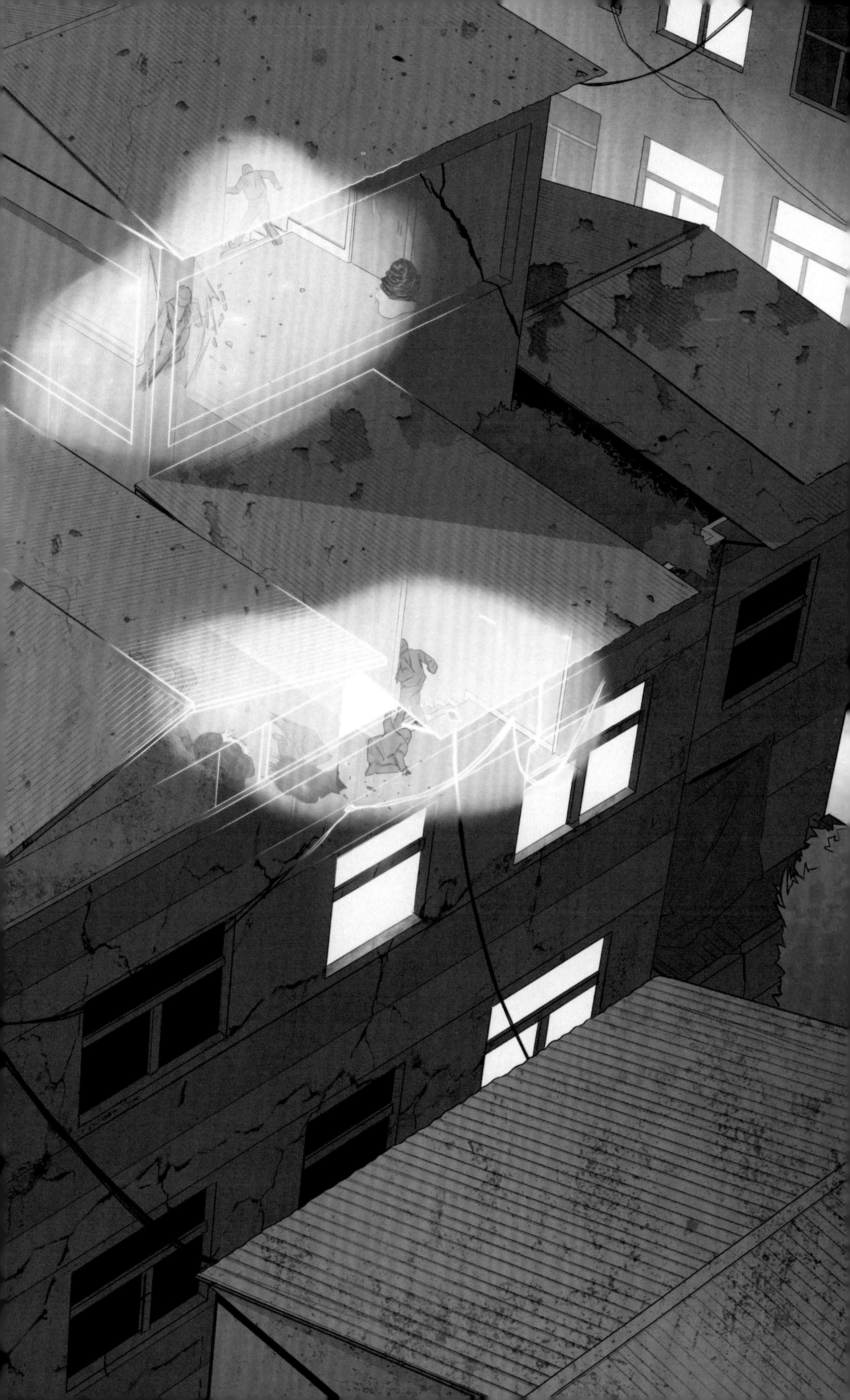

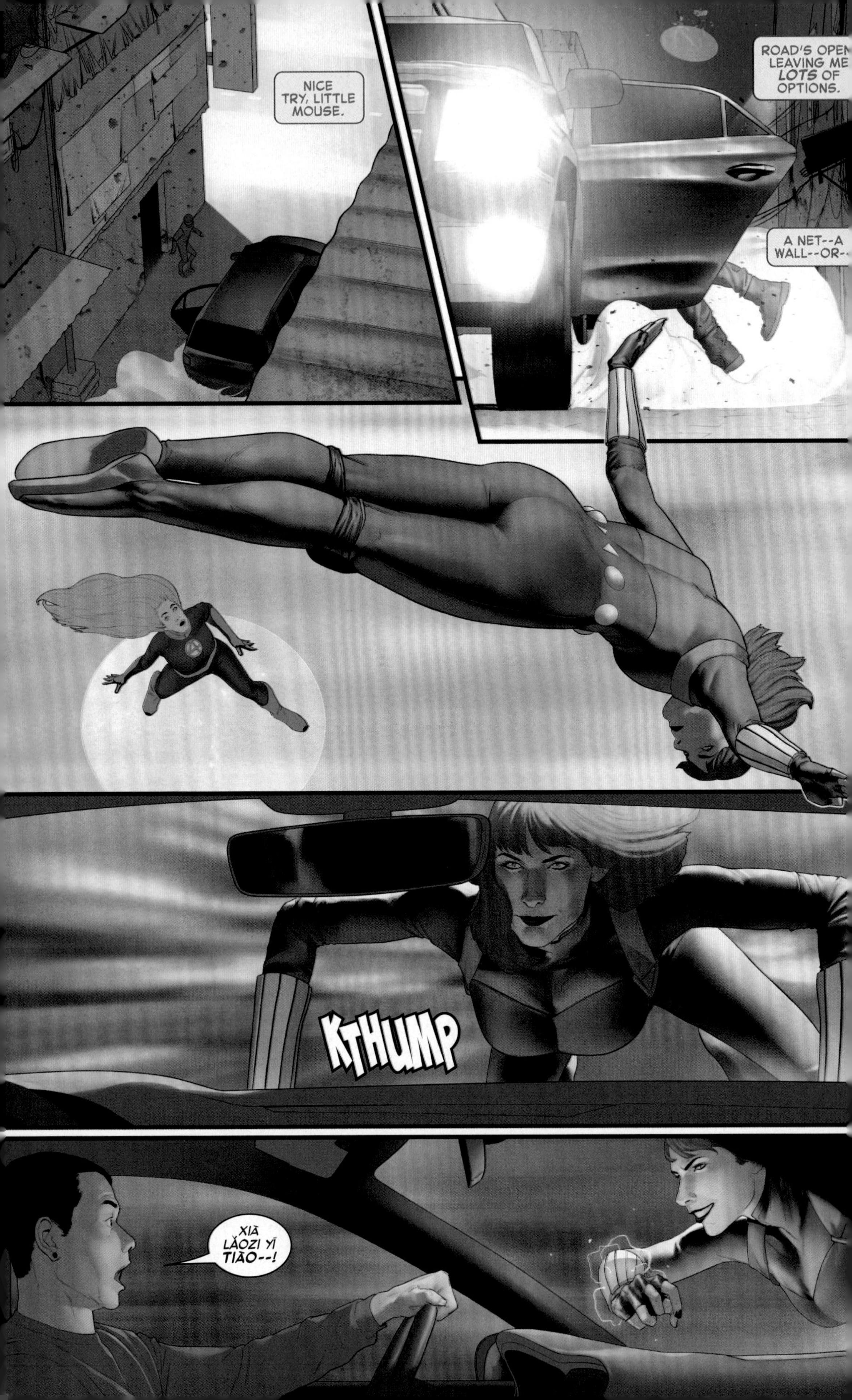
NICE TRY, LITTLE MOUSE.
ROAD'S OPEN LEAVING ME LOTS OF OPTIONS.
A NET--A WALL--OR--
KTHUMP
XIĀ LĂOZI YĪ TIÀO--!

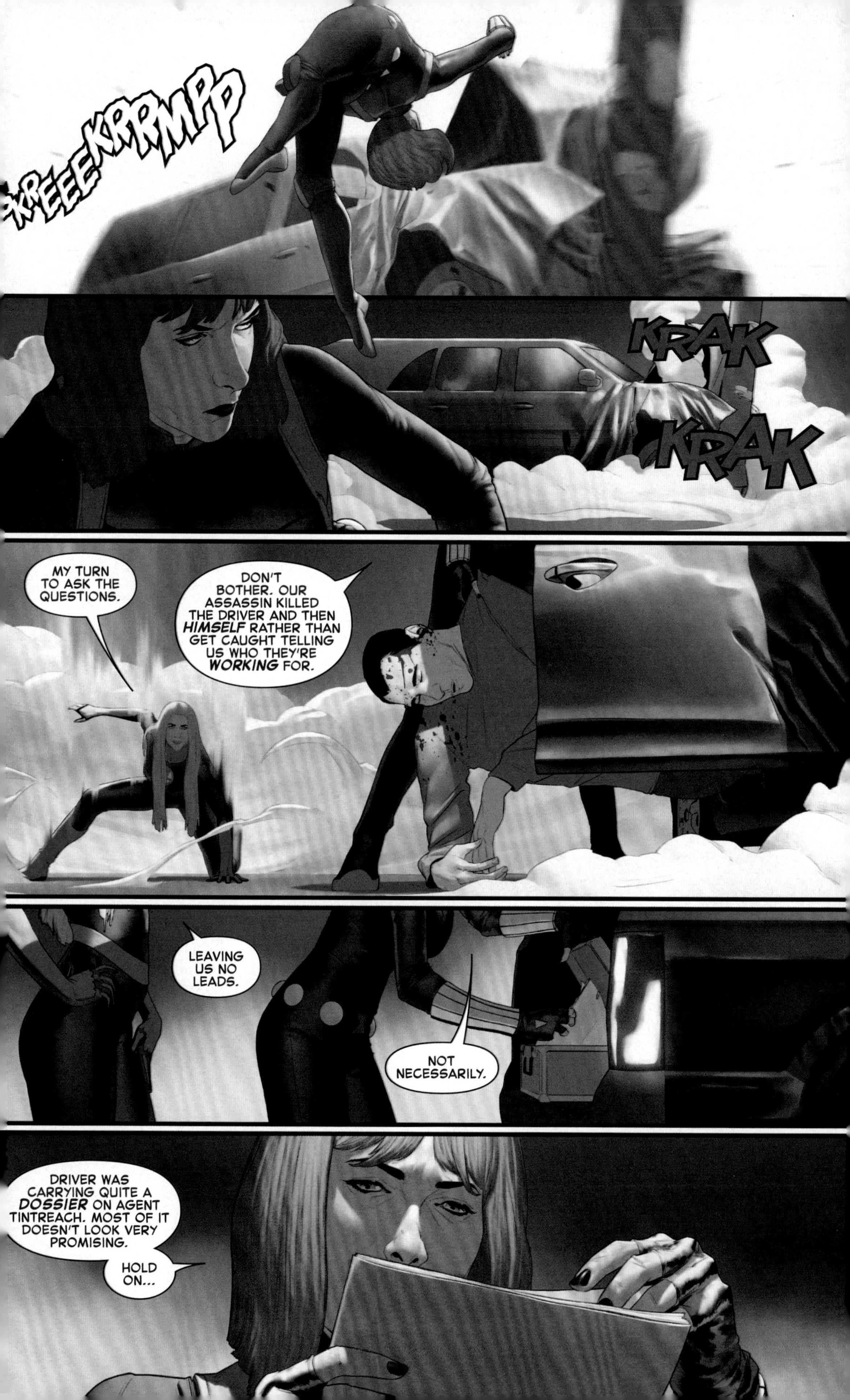
KREEEKRRMPP
KRAK
KRAK
MY TURN TO ASK THE QUESTIONS.
DON'T BOTHER. OUR ASSASSIN KILLED THE DRIVER AND THEN *HIMSELF* RATHER THAN GET CAUGHT TELLING US WHO THEY'RE *WORKING* FOR.
LEAVING US NO LEADS.
NOT NECESSARILY.
DRIVER WAS CARRYING QUITE A *DOSSIER* ON AGENT TINTREACH. MOST OF IT DOESN'T LOOK VERY PROMISING.
HOLD ON...

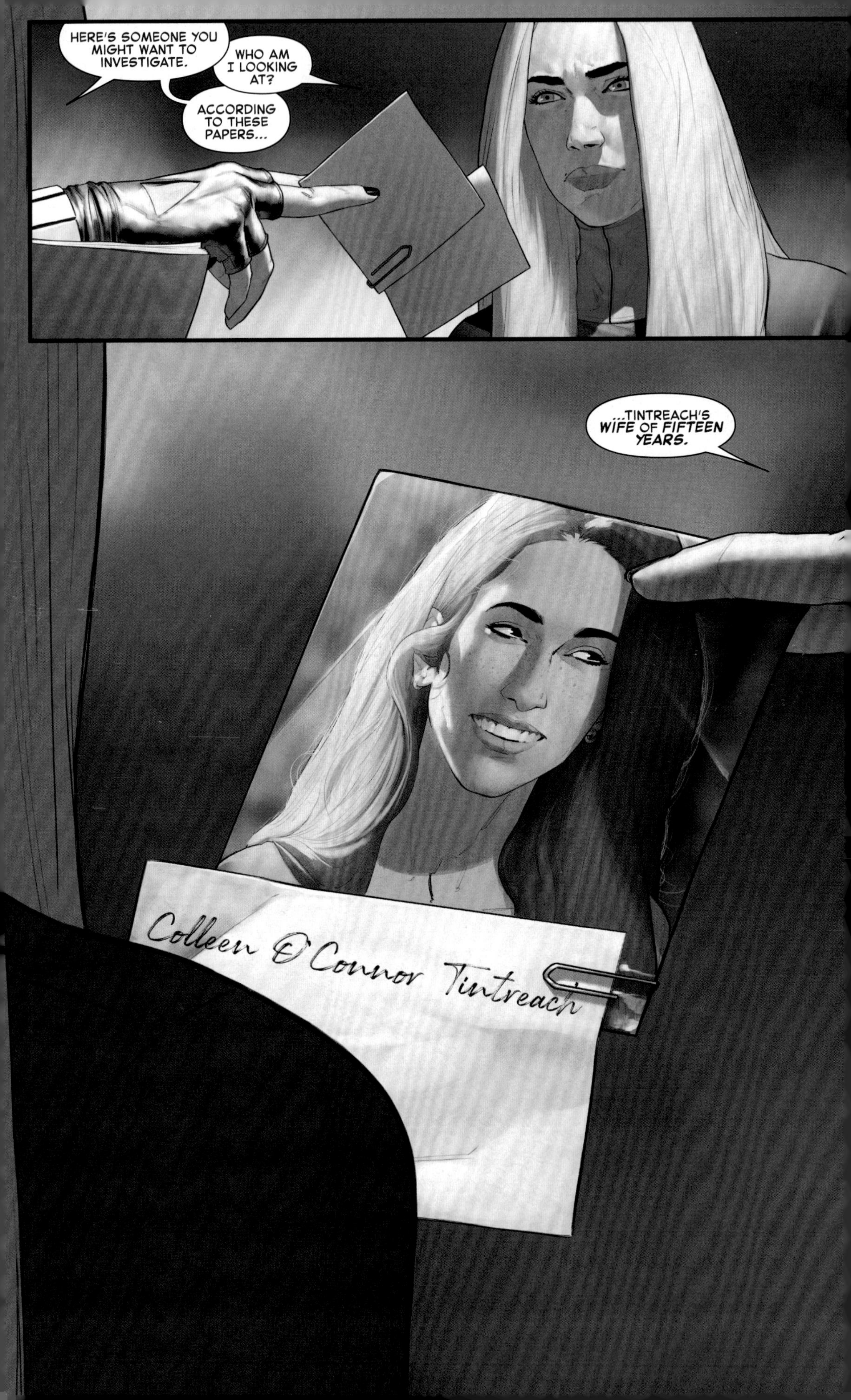
HERE'S SOMEONE YOU MIGHT WANT TO INVESTIGATE.
WHO AM I LOOKING AT?
ACCORDING TO THESE PAPERS...
...TINTREACH'S WIFE OF FIFTEEN YEARS.
Colleen O'Connor Tintreach

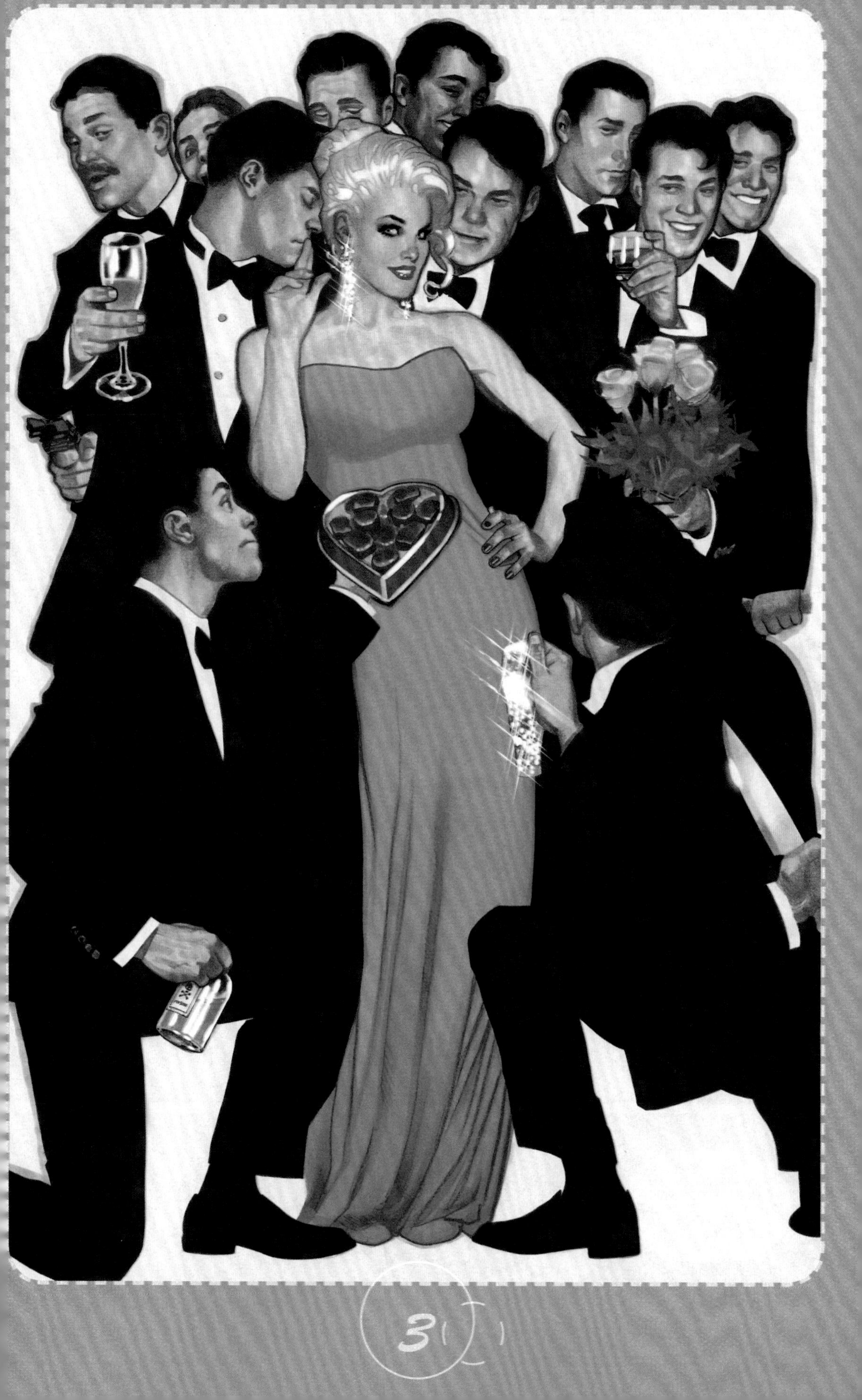

C.I.A. HEADQUARTERS.

LANGLEY, VIRGINIA.

DIRECTOR BALENTHORPE, SIR? YOU ASKED FOR ANY UPDATES ON THE MORAVIAN HOSTAGES.

PLEASE TELL ME YOUR UPDATE IS "THEY'RE HOME."

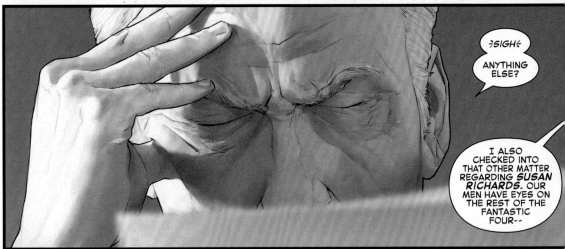

NOT QUITE YET. THEY'RE STILL SAFE IN THE EMBASSY, BUT THE MORAVIANS ARE NOW STAKING OUT THE BUILDING.

THEY'RE LOOKING FOR AN EXCUSE TO RECLAIM THOSE KIDS.

WE KEEP HAVING TO PROVE TO THEM THAT WE'RE NOT CURRENTLY INVESTIGATING THEIR ABDUCTION OF AGENT TINTREACH.

≶SIGH≶

ANYTHING ELSE?

I ALSO CHECKED INTO THAT OTHER MATTER REGARDING SUSAN RICHARDS. OUR MEN HAVE EYES ON THE REST OF THE FANTASTIC FOUR--

--BUT THE INVISIBLE WOMAN HASN'T--FORGIVE THE PUN--BEEN SEEN ANYWHERE IN THE PAST TWO DAYS.

...GET ME NICK FURY.

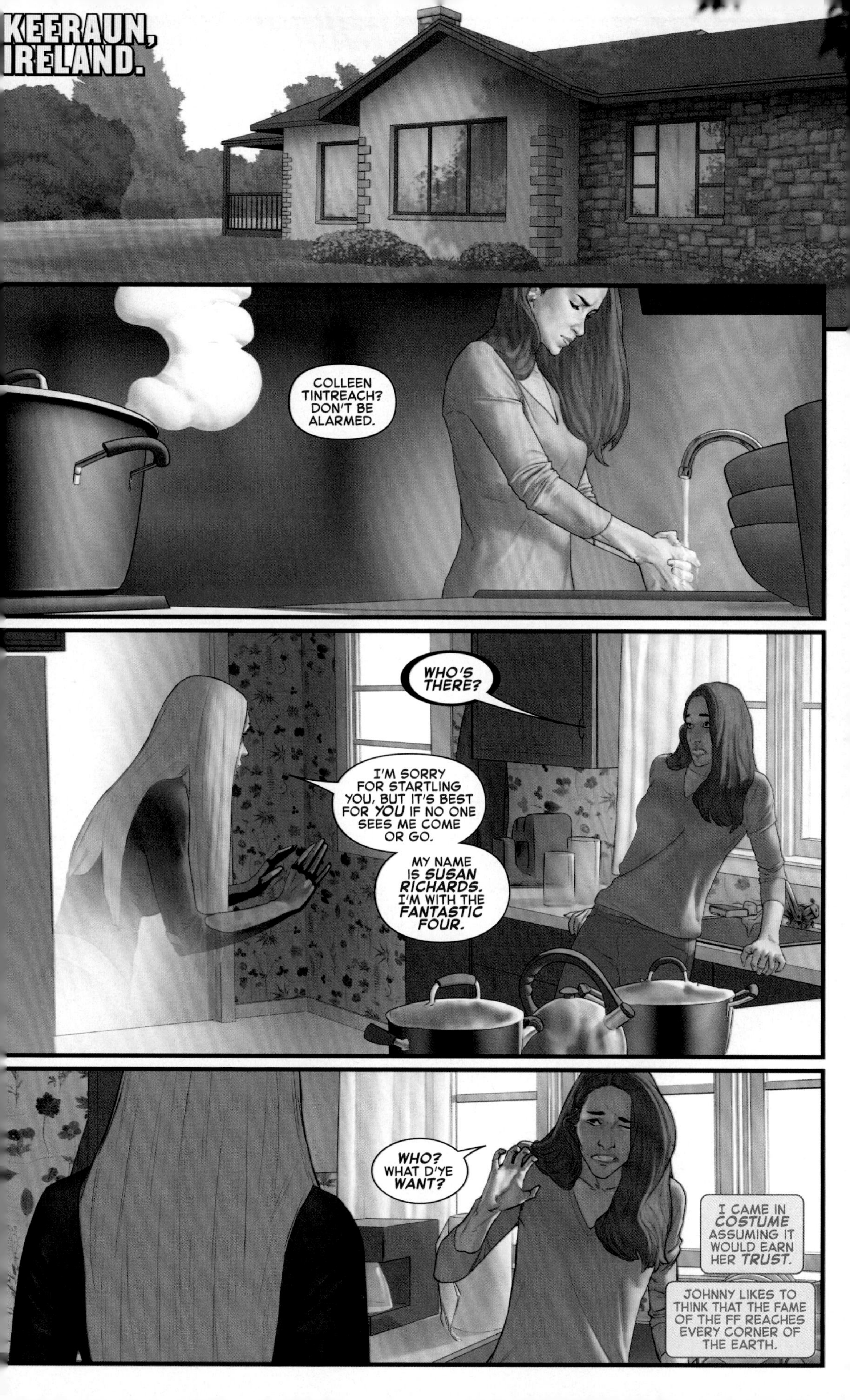

KEERAUN, IRELAND.
COLLEEN TINTREACH? DON'T BE ALARMED.
WHO'S THERE?
I'M SORRY FOR STARTLING YOU, BUT IT'S BEST FOR YOU IF NO ONE SEES ME COME OR GO.
MY NAME IS SUSAN RICHARDS. I'M WITH THE FANTASTIC FOUR.
WHO? WHAT D'YE WANT?
I CAME IN COSTUME ASSUMING IT WOULD EARN HER TRUST.
JOHNNY LIKES TO THINK THAT THE FAME OF THE FF REACHES EVERY CORNER OF THE EARTH.

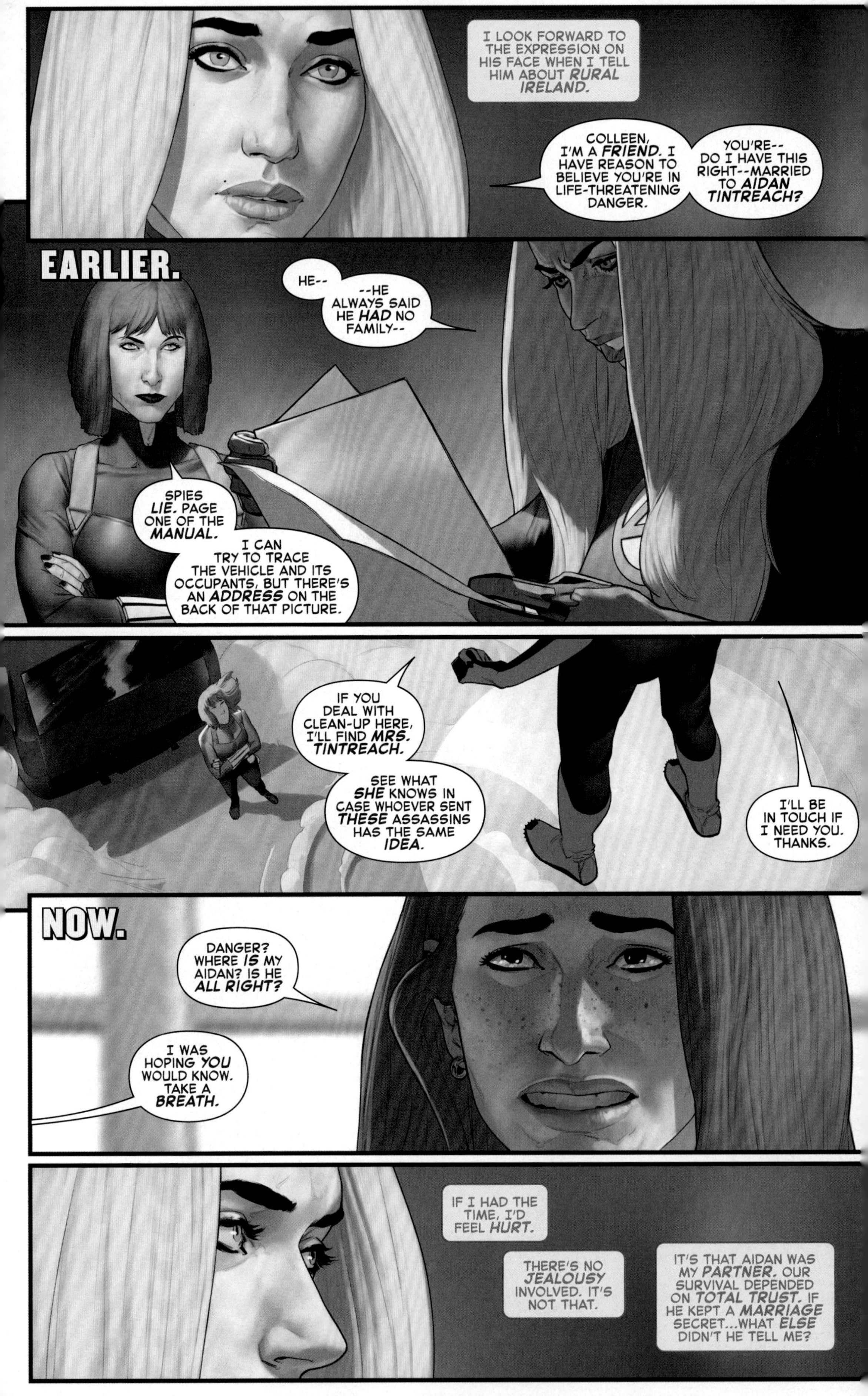

I LOOK FORWARD TO THE EXPRESSION ON HIS FACE WHEN I TELL HIM ABOUT RURAL IRELAND.
COLLEEN, I'M A FRIEND. I HAVE REASON TO BELIEVE YOU'RE IN LIFE-THREATENING DANGER.
YOU'RE-- DO I HAVE THIS RIGHT--MARRIED TO AIDAN TINTREACH?
EARLIER.
HE--
--HE ALWAYS SAID HE HAD NO FAMILY--
SPIES LIE. PAGE ONE OF THE MANUAL.
I CAN TRY TO TRACE THE VEHICLE AND ITS OCCUPANTS, BUT THERE'S AN ADDRESS ON THE BACK OF THAT PICTURE.
IF YOU DEAL WITH CLEAN-UP HERE, I'LL FIND MRS. TINTREACH.
SEE WHAT SHE KNOWS IN CASE WHOEVER SENT THESE ASSASSINS HAS THE SAME IDEA.
I'LL BE IN TOUCH IF I NEED YOU. THANKS.
NOW.
DANGER? WHERE IS MY AIDAN? IS HE ALL RIGHT?
I WAS HOPING YOU WOULD KNOW. TAKE A BREATH.
IF I HAD THE TIME, I'D FEEL HURT.
THERE'S NO JEALOUSY INVOLVED. IT'S NOT THAT.
IT'S THAT AIDAN WAS MY PARTNER. OUR SURVIVAL DEPENDED ON TOTAL TRUST. IF HE KEPT A MARRIAGE SECRET...WHAT ELSE DIDN'T HE TELL ME?

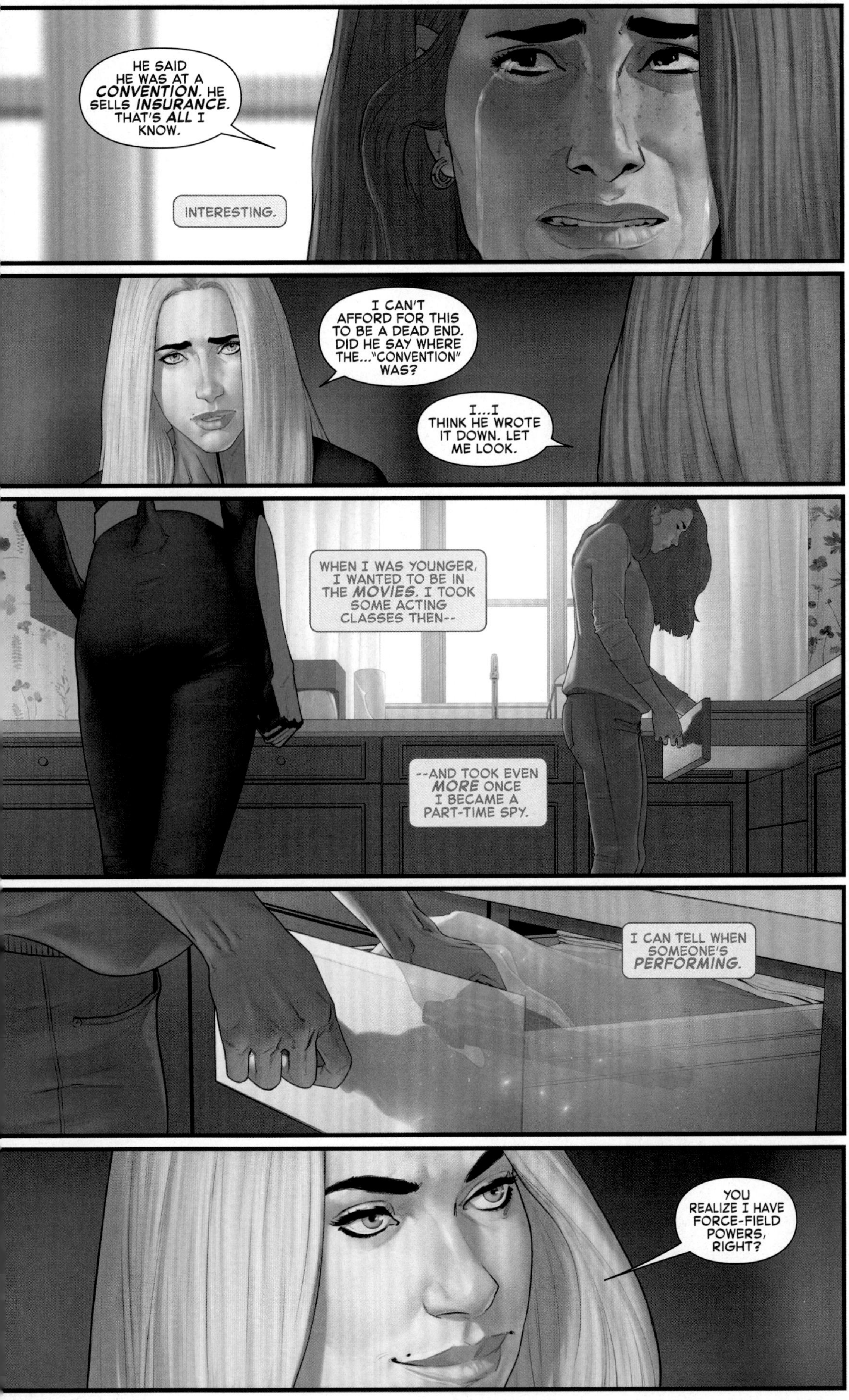
HE SAID HE WAS AT A *CONVENTION.* HE SELLS *INSURANCE.* THAT'S *ALL* I KNOW.
INTERESTING.
I CAN'T AFFORD FOR THIS TO BE A DEAD END. DID HE SAY WHERE THE..."CONVENTION" WAS?
I...I THINK HE WROTE IT DOWN. LET ME LOOK.
WHEN I WAS YOUNGER, I WANTED TO BE IN THE *MOVIES.* I TOOK SOME ACTING CLASSES THEN--
--AND TOOK EVEN *MORE* ONCE I BECAME A PART-TIME SPY.
I CAN TELL WHEN SOMEONE'S *PERFORMING.*
YOU REALIZE I HAVE FORCE-FIELD POWERS, RIGHT?

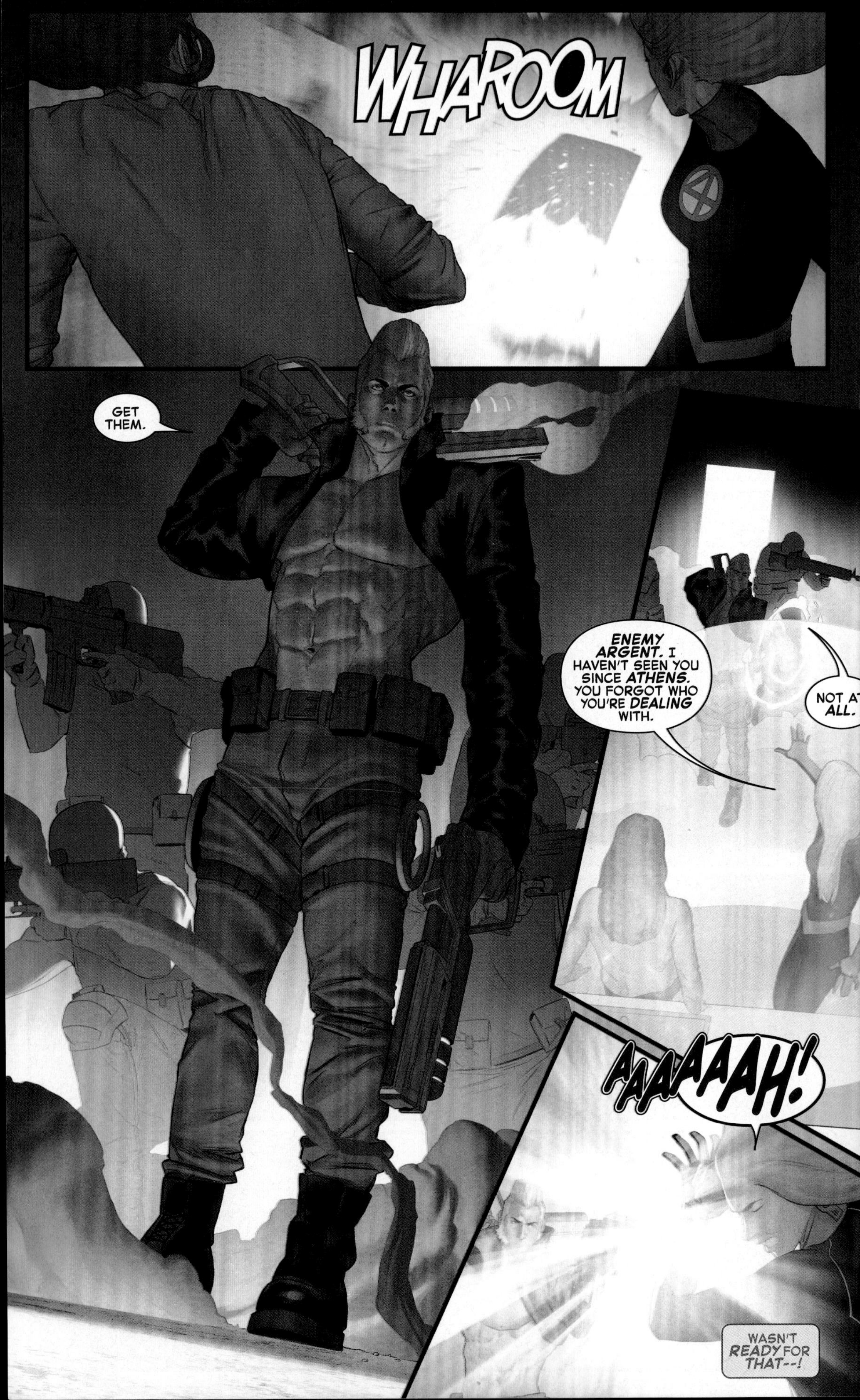
WHAROOM
GET THEM.
ENEMY ARGENT. I HAVEN'T SEEN YOU SINCE ATHENS. YOU FORGOT WHO YOU'RE DEALING WITH.
NOT AT ALL.
AAAAAAAH!
WASN'T READY FOR THAT--!

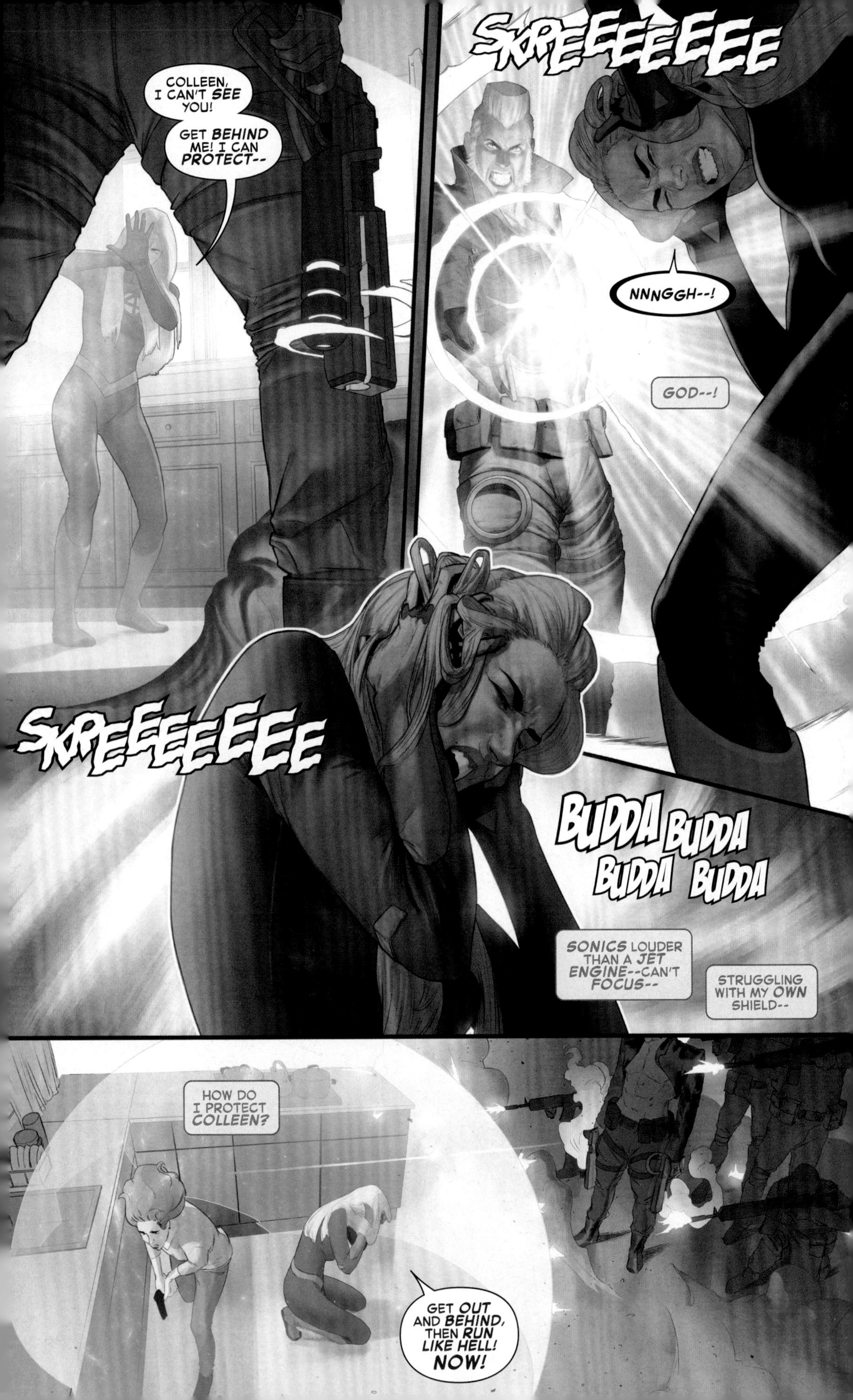

COLLEEN, I CAN'T SEE YOU!
GET BEHIND ME! I CAN PROTECT--
SKREEEEEEEEE
NNNGGH--!
GOD--!
SKREEEEEEEEEE
BUDDA BUDDA BUDDA BUDDA
SONICS LOUDER THAN A JET ENGINE--CAN'T FOCUS--
STRUGGLING WITH MY OWN SHIELD--
HOW DO I PROTECT COLLEEN?
GET OUT AND BEHIND, THEN RUN LIKE HELL! NOW!

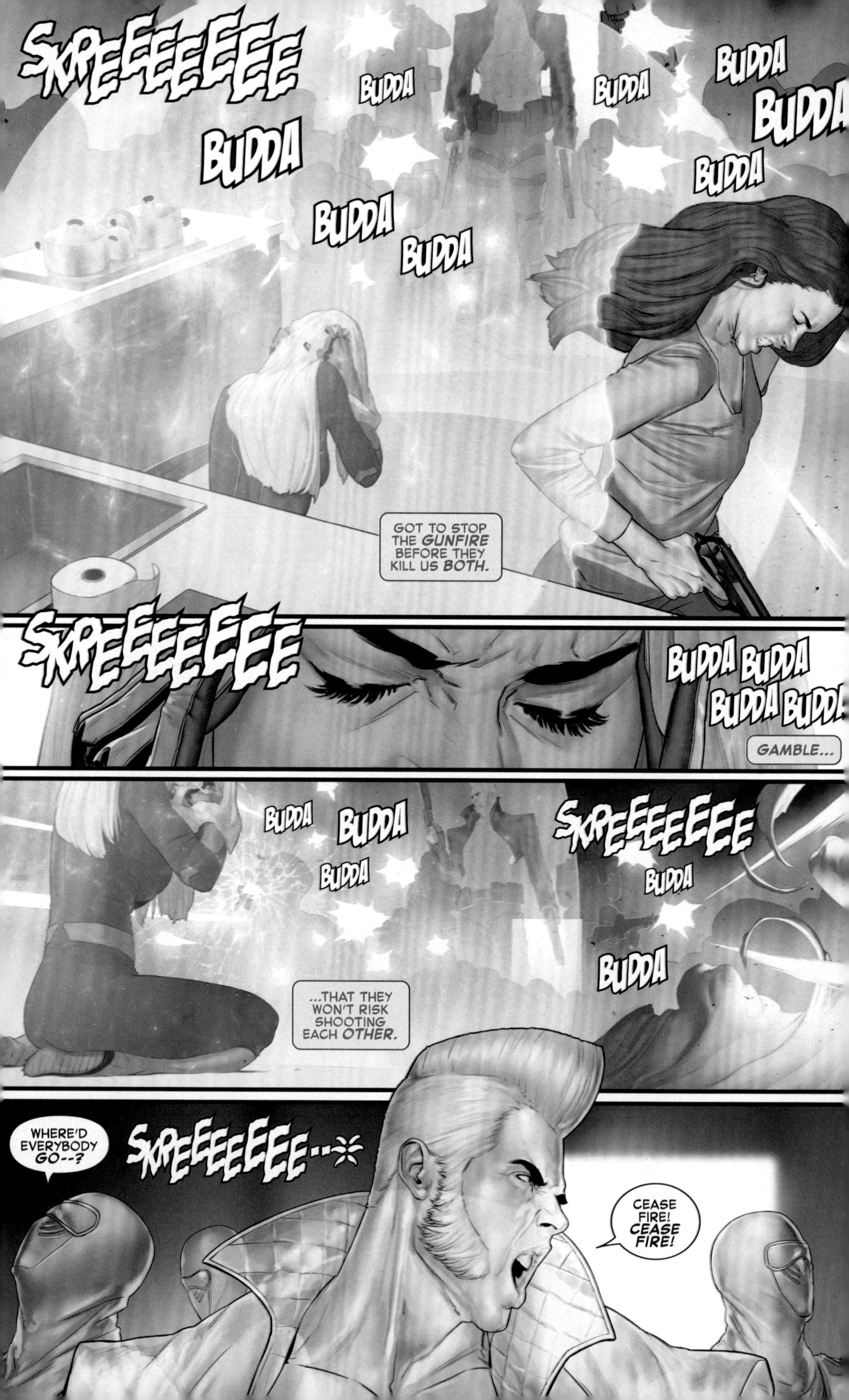
SKREEEEEEEE
BUDDA
BUDDA
BUDDA
BUDDA
BUDDA
BUDDA
BUDDA
BUDDA
GOT TO STOP THE GUNFIRE BEFORE THEY KILL US BOTH.
SKREEEEEEE
BUDDA BUDDA
BUDDA
GAMBLE...
BUDDA
BUDDA
BUDDA
SKREEEEEEEE
BUDDA
BUDDA
...THAT THEY WON'T RISK SHOOTING EACH OTHER.
WHERE'D EVERYBODY GO--?
SKREEEEEEE--
CEASE FIRE! CEASE FIRE!

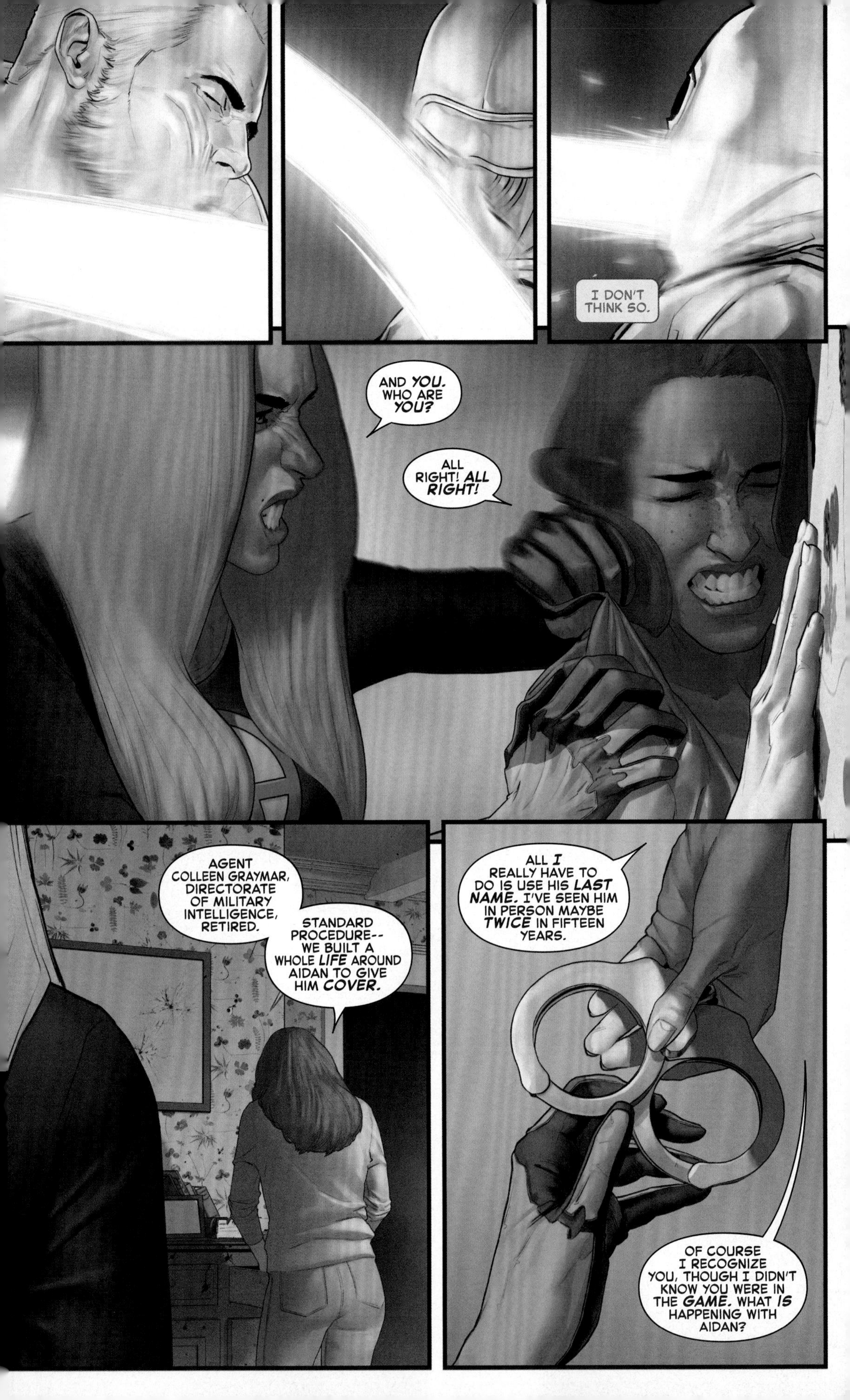
I DON'T THINK SO.
AND YOU. WHO ARE YOU?
ALL RIGHT! ALL RIGHT!
AGENT COLLEEN GRAYMAR, DIRECTORATE OF MILITARY INTELLIGENCE, RETIRED.
STANDARD PROCEDURE-- WE BUILT A WHOLE LIFE AROUND AIDAN TO GIVE HIM COVER.
ALL I REALLY HAVE TO DO IS USE HIS LAST NAME. I'VE SEEN HIM IN PERSON MAYBE TWICE IN FIFTEEN YEARS.
OF COURSE I RECOGNIZE YOU, THOUGH I DIDN'T KNOW YOU WERE IN THE GAME. WHAT IS HAPPENING WITH AIDAN?

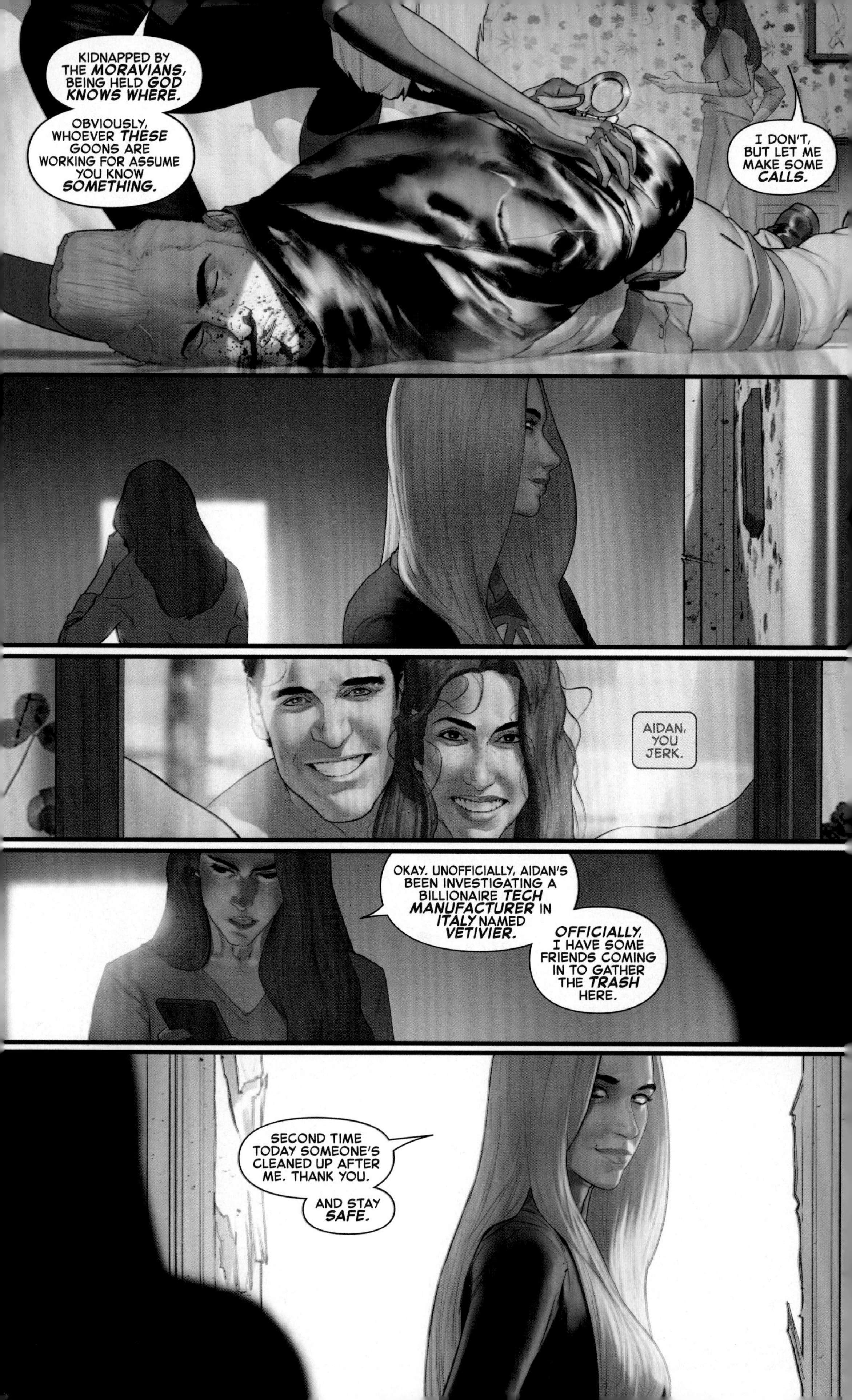
KIDNAPPED BY THE MORAVIANS, BEING HELD GOD KNOWS WHERE.
OBVIOUSLY, WHOEVER THESE GOONS ARE WORKING FOR ASSUME YOU KNOW SOMETHING.
I DON'T, BUT LET ME MAKE SOME CALLS.
AIDAN, YOU JERK.
OKAY. UNOFFICIALLY, AIDAN'S BEEN INVESTIGATING A BILLIONAIRE TECH MANUFACTURER IN ITALY NAMED VETIVIER.
OFFICIALLY, I HAVE SOME FRIENDS COMING IN TO GATHER THE TRASH HERE.
SECOND TIME TODAY SOMEONE'S CLEANED UP AFTER ME. THANK YOU.
AND STAY SAFE.

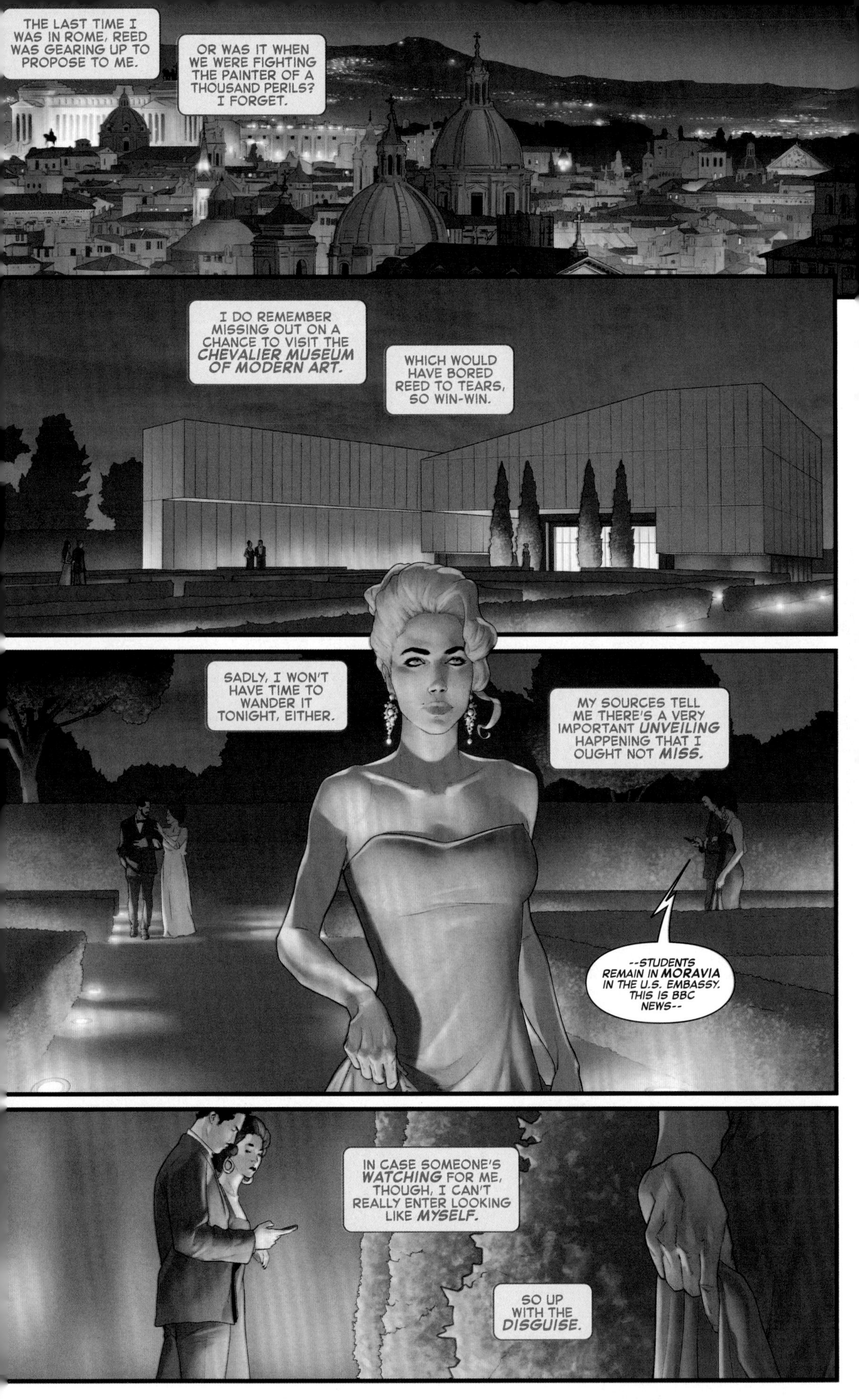
THE LAST TIME I WAS IN ROME, REED WAS GEARING UP TO PROPOSE TO ME.
OR WAS IT WHEN WE WERE FIGHTING THE PAINTER OF A THOUSAND PERILS? I FORGET.
I DO REMEMBER MISSING OUT ON A CHANCE TO VISIT THE CHEVALIER MUSEUM OF MODERN ART.
WHICH WOULD HAVE BORED REED TO TEARS, SO WIN-WIN.
SADLY, I WON'T HAVE TIME TO WANDER IT TONIGHT, EITHER.
MY SOURCES TELL ME THERE'S A VERY IMPORTANT UNVEILING HAPPENING THAT I OUGHT NOT MISS.
--STUDENTS REMAIN IN MORAVIA IN THE U.S. EMBASSY. THIS IS BBC NEWS--
IN CASE SOMEONE'S WATCHING FOR ME, THOUGH, I CAN'T REALLY ENTER LOOKING LIKE MYSELF.
SO UP WITH THE DISGUISE.

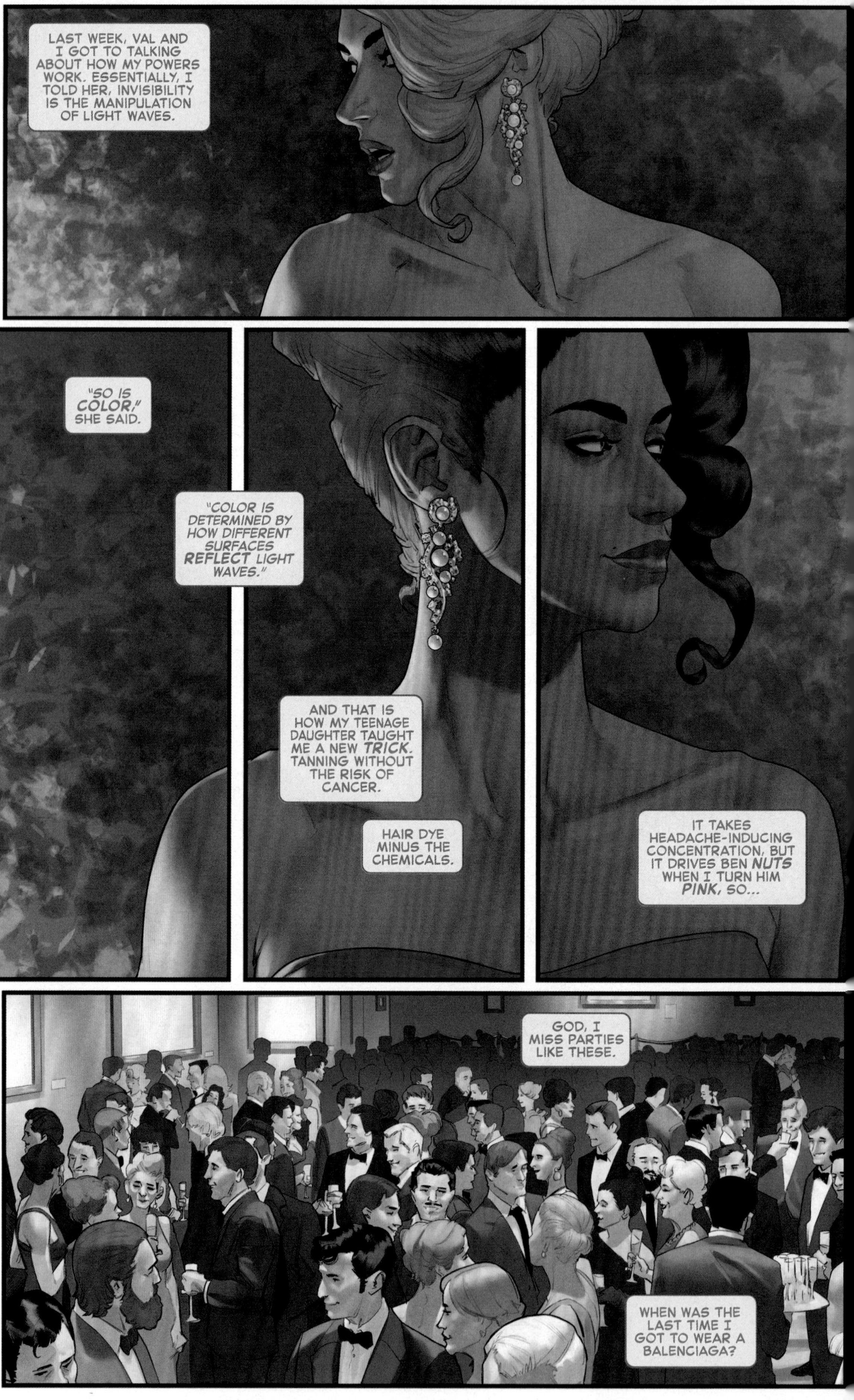
LAST WEEK, VAL AND I GOT TO TALKING ABOUT HOW MY POWERS WORK. ESSENTIALLY, I TOLD HER, INVISIBILITY IS THE MANIPULATION OF LIGHT WAVES.
"SO IS COLOR," SHE SAID.
"COLOR IS DETERMINED BY HOW DIFFERENT SURFACES REFLECT LIGHT WAVES."
AND THAT IS HOW MY TEENAGE DAUGHTER TAUGHT ME A NEW TRICK. TANNING WITHOUT THE RISK OF CANCER.
HAIR DYE MINUS THE CHEMICALS.
IT TAKES HEADACHE-INDUCING CONCENTRATION, BUT IT DRIVES BEN NUTS WHEN I TURN HIM PINK, SO...
GOD, I MISS PARTIES LIKE THESE.
WHEN WAS THE LAST TIME I GOT TO WEAR A BALENCIAGA?

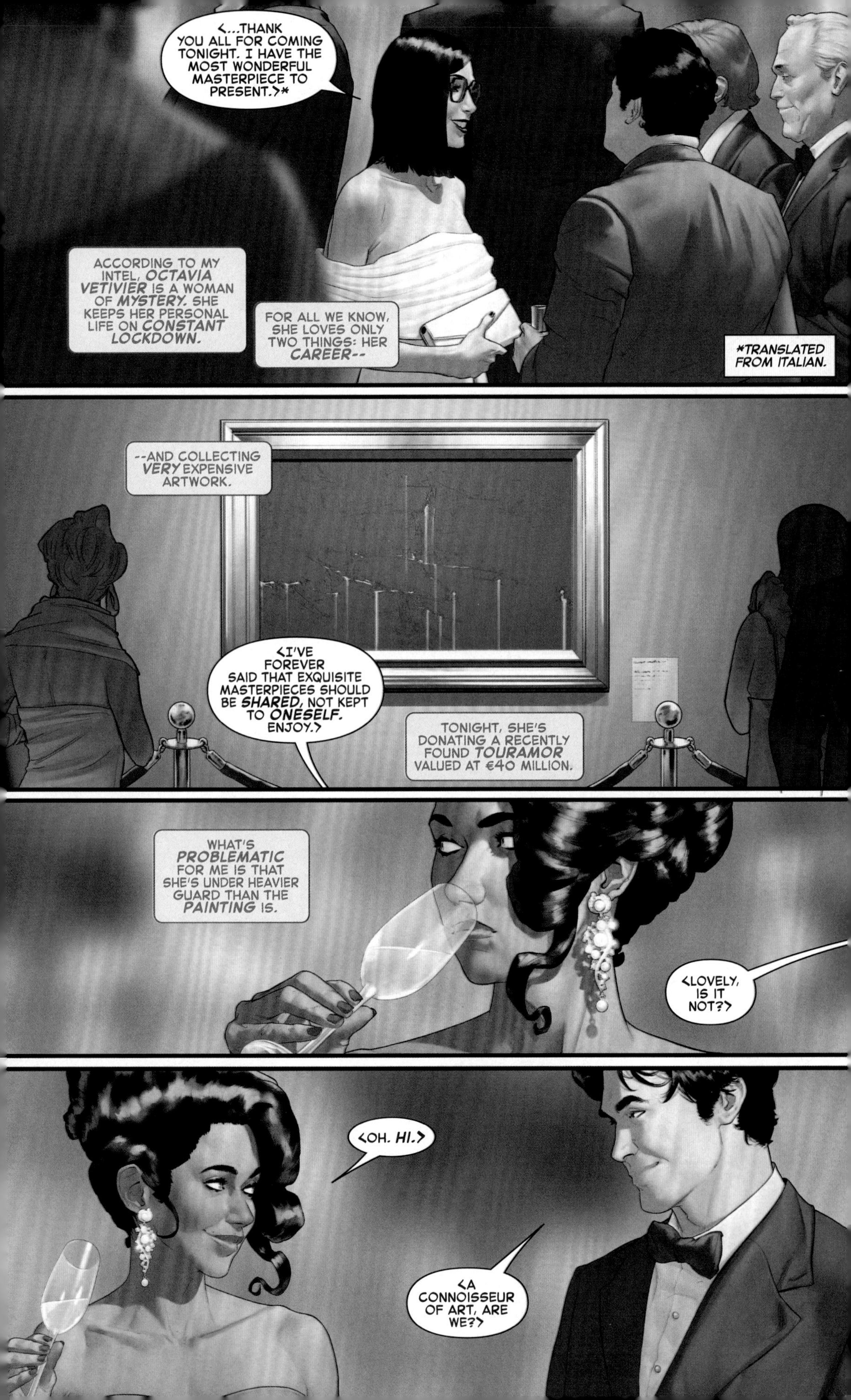
<...THANK YOU ALL FOR COMING TONIGHT. I HAVE THE MOST WONDERFUL MASTERPIECE TO PRESENT.>*
ACCORDING TO MY INTEL, OCTAVIA VETIVIER IS A WOMAN OF MYSTERY. SHE KEEPS HER PERSONAL LIFE ON CONSTANT LOCKDOWN.
FOR ALL WE KNOW, SHE LOVES ONLY TWO THINGS: HER CAREER--
*TRANSLATED FROM ITALIAN.
--AND COLLECTING VERY EXPENSIVE ARTWORK.
<I'VE FOREVER SAID THAT EXQUISITE MASTERPIECES SHOULD BE SHARED, NOT KEPT TO ONESELF. ENJOY.>
TONIGHT, SHE'S DONATING A RECENTLY FOUND TOURAMOR VALUED AT €40 MILLION.
WHAT'S PROBLEMATIC FOR ME IS THAT SHE'S UNDER HEAVIER GUARD THAN THE PAINTING IS.
<LOVELY, IS IT NOT?>
<OH. HI.>
<A CONNOISSEUR OF ART, ARE WE?>

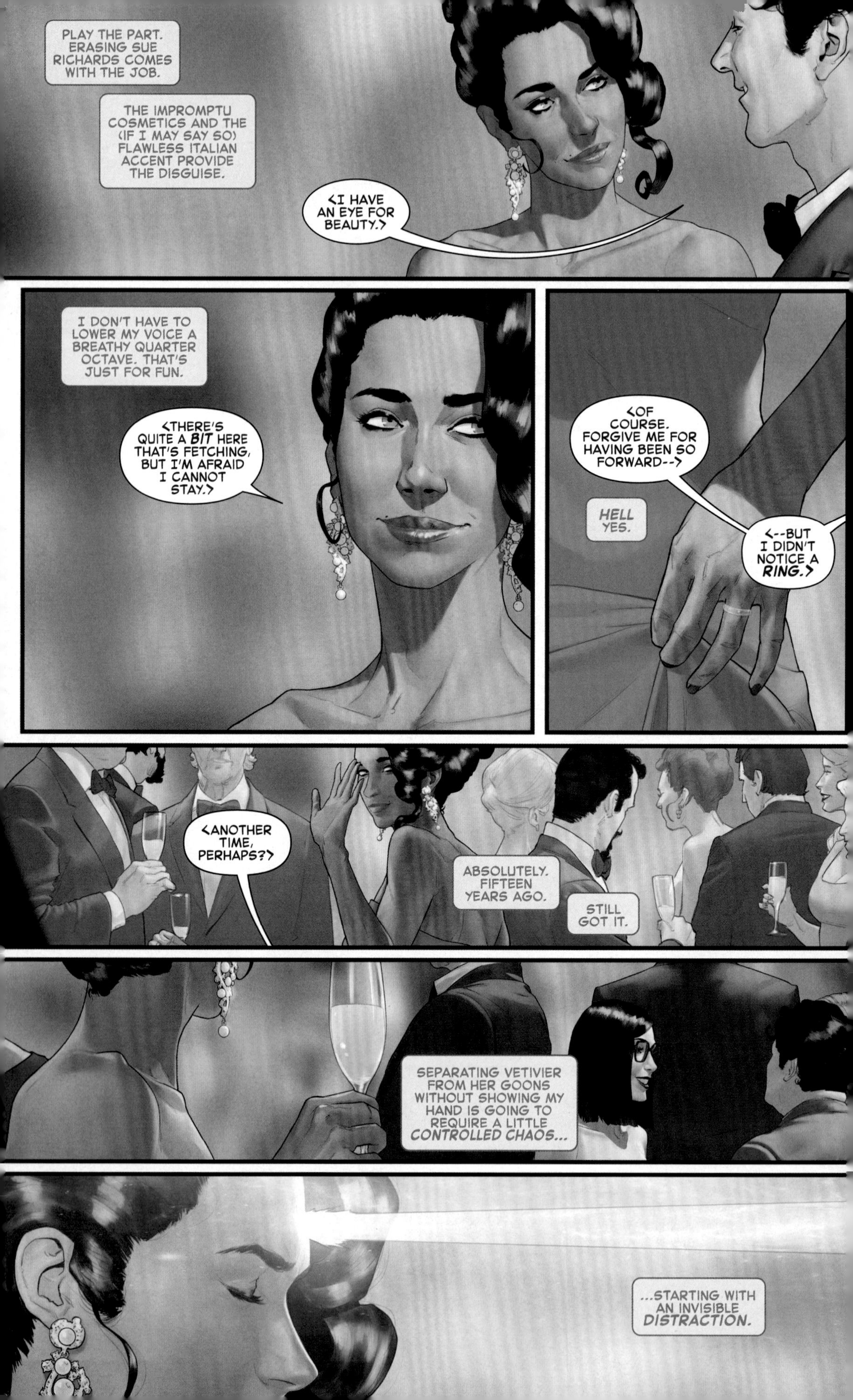
PLAY THE PART. ERASING SUE RICHARDS COMES WITH THE JOB.
THE IMPROMPTU COSMETICS AND THE (IF I MAY SAY SO) FLAWLESS ITALIAN ACCENT PROVIDE THE DISGUISE.
<I HAVE AN EYE FOR BEAUTY.>
I DON'T HAVE TO LOWER MY VOICE A BREATHY QUARTER OCTAVE. THAT'S JUST FOR FUN.
<THERE'S QUITE A *BIT* HERE THAT'S FETCHING, BUT I'M AFRAID I CANNOT STAY.>
<OF COURSE. FORGIVE ME FOR HAVING BEEN SO FORWARD-->
HELL YES.
<--BUT I DIDN'T NOTICE A *RING.*>
<ANOTHER TIME, PERHAPS?>
ABSOLUTELY. FIFTEEN YEARS AGO.
STILL GOT IT.
SEPARATING VETIVIER FROM HER GOONS WITHOUT SHOWING MY HAND IS GOING TO REQUIRE A LITTLE *CONTROLLED CHAOS...*
...STARTING WITH AN INVISIBLE *DISTRACTION.*

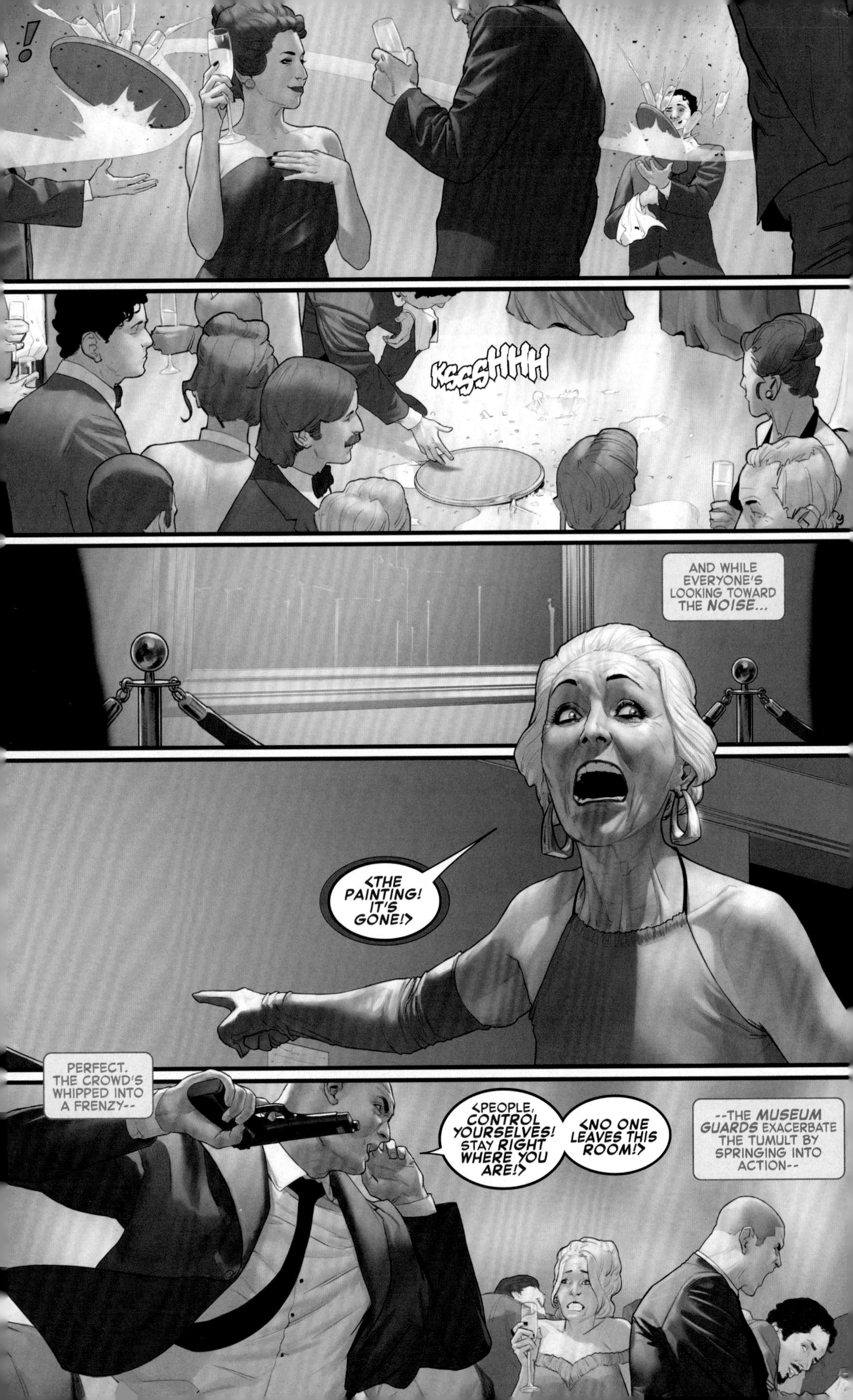
!
KSSSHHH
AND WHILE EVERYONE'S LOOKING TOWARD THE NOISE...
<THE PAINTING! IT'S GONE!>
PERFECT. THE CROWD'S WHIPPED INTO A FRENZY--
<PEOPLE, CONTROL YOURSELVES! STAY RIGHT WHERE YOU ARE!>
<NO ONE LEAVES THIS ROOM!>
--THE MUSEUM GUARDS EXACERBATE THE TUMULT BY SPRINGING INTO ACTION--

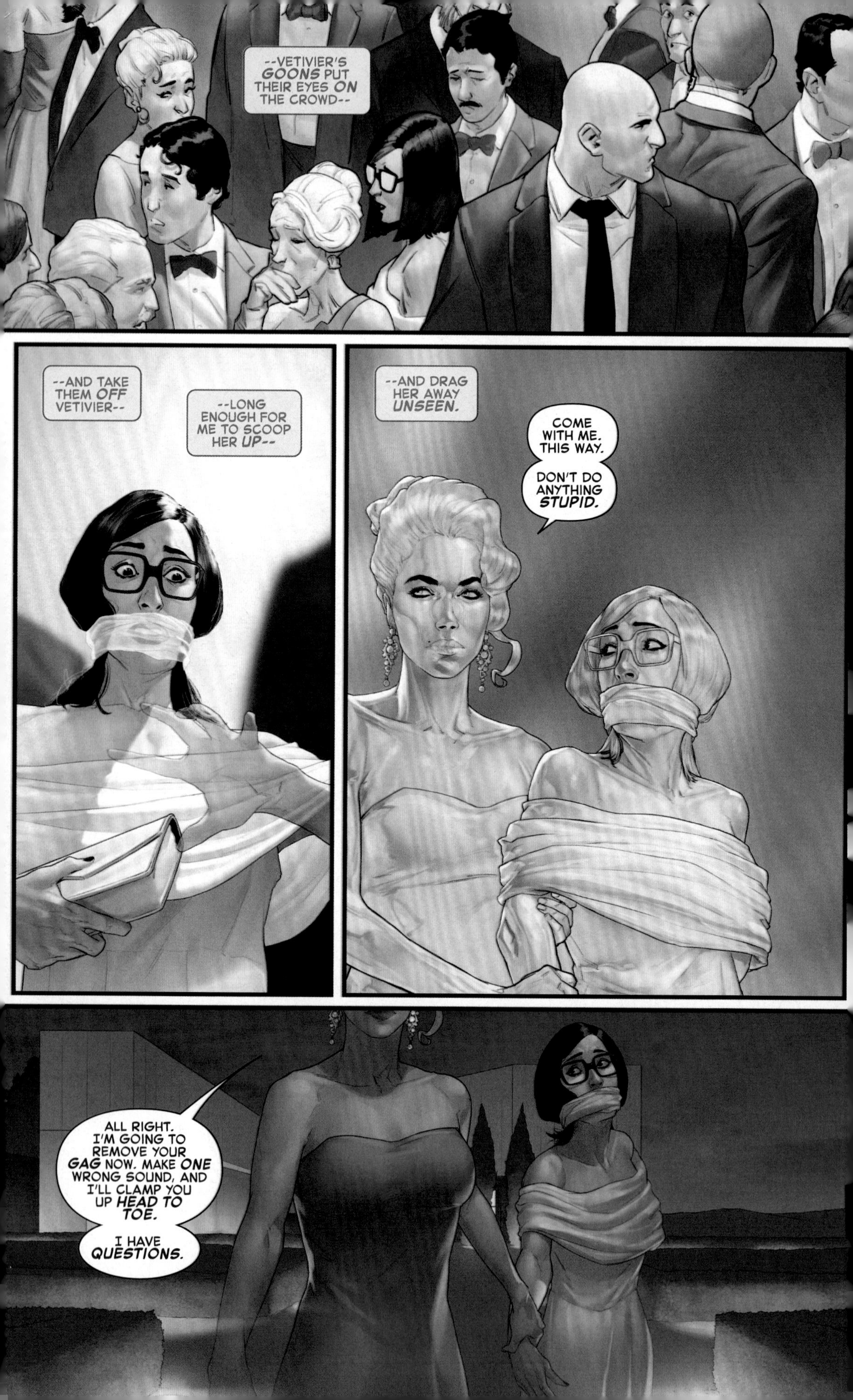
--VETIVIER'S GOONS PUT THEIR EYES ON THE CROWD--
--AND TAKE THEM OFF VETIVIER--
--LONG ENOUGH FOR ME TO SCOOP HER UP--
--AND DRAG HER AWAY UNSEEN.
COME WITH ME. THIS WAY.
DON'T DO ANYTHING STUPID.
ALL RIGHT. I'M GOING TO REMOVE YOUR GAG NOW. MAKE ONE WRONG SOUND, AND I'LL CLAMP YOU UP HEAD TO TOE.
I HAVE QUESTIONS.

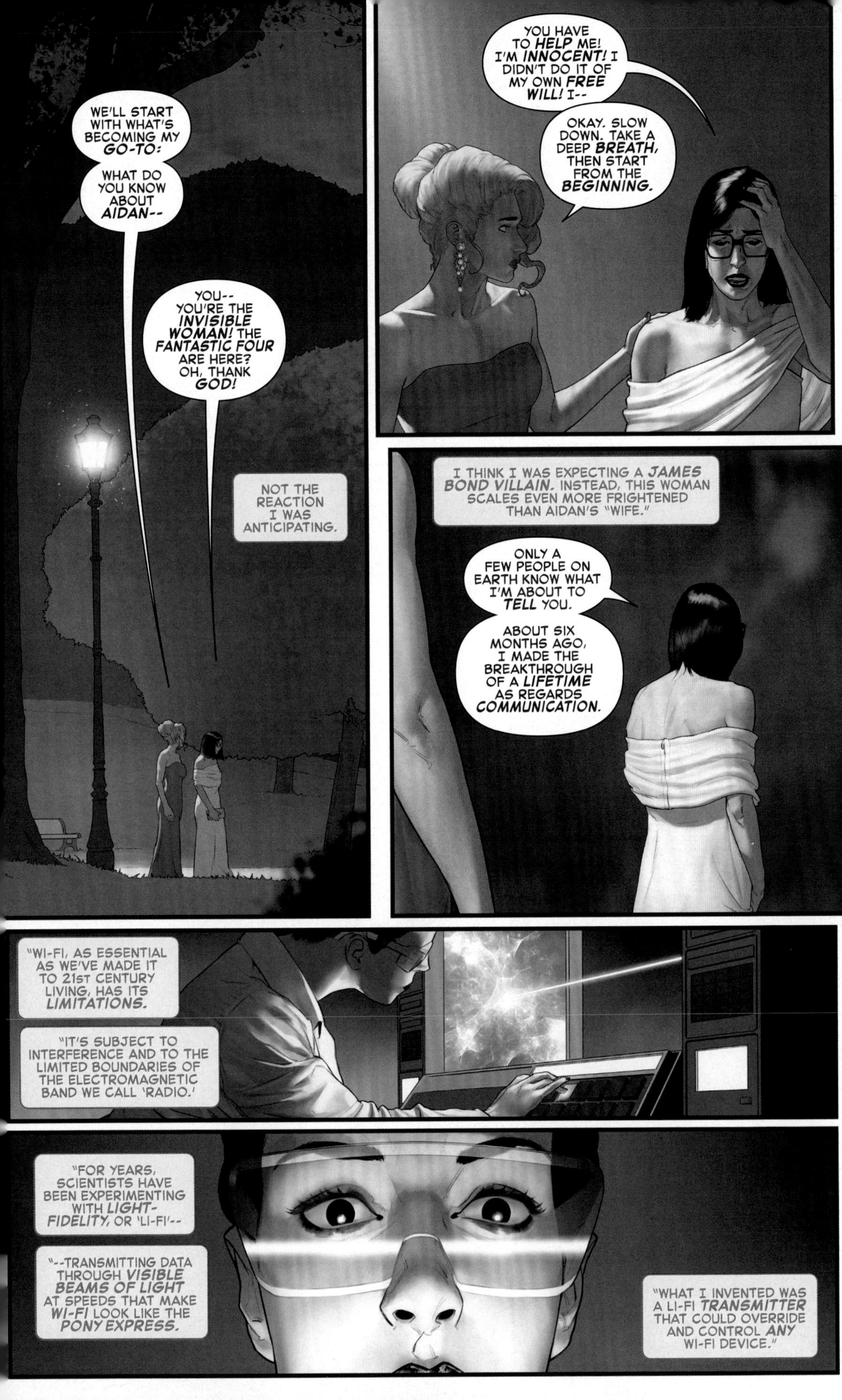
WE'LL START WITH WHAT'S BECOMING MY GO-TO:
WHAT DO YOU KNOW ABOUT AIDAN--
YOU-- YOU'RE THE INVISIBLE WOMAN! THE FANTASTIC FOUR ARE HERE? OH, THANK GOD!
NOT THE REACTION I WAS ANTICIPATING.
YOU HAVE TO HELP ME! I'M INNOCENT! I DIDN'T DO IT OF MY OWN FREE WILL! I--
OKAY. SLOW DOWN. TAKE A DEEP BREATH, THEN START FROM THE BEGINNING.
I THINK I WAS EXPECTING A JAMES BOND VILLAIN. INSTEAD, THIS WOMAN SCALES EVEN MORE FRIGHTENED THAN AIDAN'S "WIFE."
ONLY A FEW PEOPLE ON EARTH KNOW WHAT I'M ABOUT TO TELL YOU.
ABOUT SIX MONTHS AGO, I MADE THE BREAKTHROUGH OF A LIFETIME AS REGARDS COMMUNICATION.
"WI-FI, AS ESSENTIAL AS WE'VE MADE IT TO 21ST CENTURY LIVING, HAS ITS LIMITATIONS.
"IT'S SUBJECT TO INTERFERENCE AND TO THE LIMITED BOUNDARIES OF THE ELECTROMAGNETIC BAND WE CALL 'RADIO.'
"FOR YEARS, SCIENTISTS HAVE BEEN EXPERIMENTING WITH LIGHT-FIDELITY, OR 'LI-FI'--
"--TRANSMITTING DATA THROUGH VISIBLE BEAMS OF LIGHT AT SPEEDS THAT MAKE WI-FI LOOK LIKE THE PONY EXPRESS.
"WHAT I INVENTED WAS A LI-FI TRANSMITTER THAT COULD OVERRIDE AND CONTROL ANY WI-FI DEVICE."

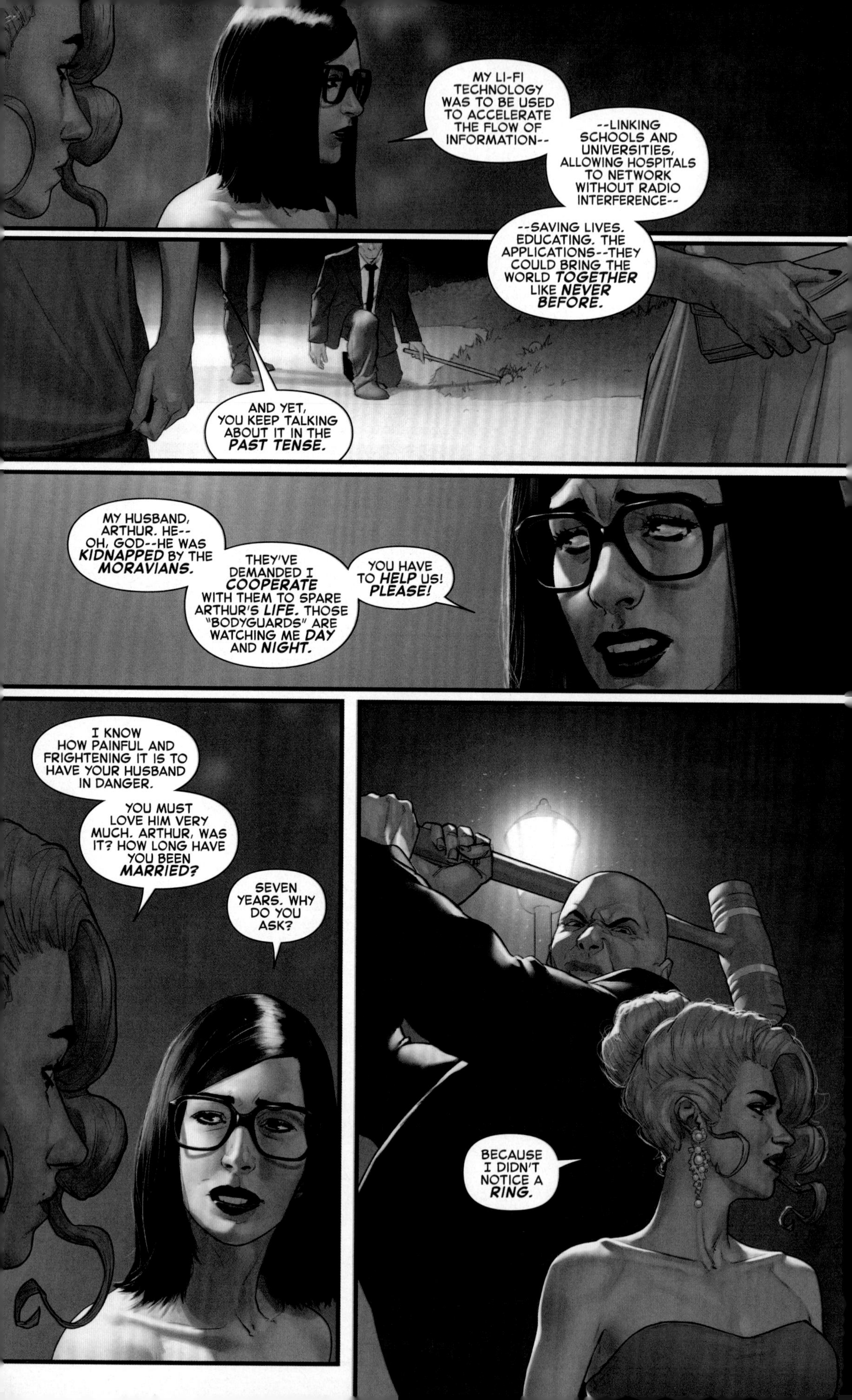
MY LI-FI TECHNOLOGY WAS TO BE USED TO ACCELERATE THE FLOW OF INFORMATION--
--LINKING SCHOOLS AND UNIVERSITIES, ALLOWING HOSPITALS TO NETWORK WITHOUT RADIO INTERFERENCE--
--SAVING LIVES. EDUCATING. THE APPLICATIONS--THEY COULD BRING THE WORLD TOGETHER LIKE NEVER BEFORE.
AND YET, YOU KEEP TALKING ABOUT IT IN THE PAST TENSE.
MY HUSBAND, ARTHUR. HE--OH, GOD--HE WAS KIDNAPPED BY THE MORAVIANS.
THEY'VE DEMANDED I COOPERATE WITH THEM TO SPARE ARTHUR'S LIFE. THOSE "BODYGUARDS" ARE WATCHING ME DAY AND NIGHT.
YOU HAVE TO HELP US! PLEASE!
I KNOW HOW PAINFUL AND FRIGHTENING IT IS TO HAVE YOUR HUSBAND IN DANGER.
YOU MUST LOVE HIM VERY MUCH. ARTHUR, WAS IT? HOW LONG HAVE YOU BEEN MARRIED?
SEVEN YEARS. WHY DO YOU ASK?
BECAUSE I DIDN'T NOTICE A RING.

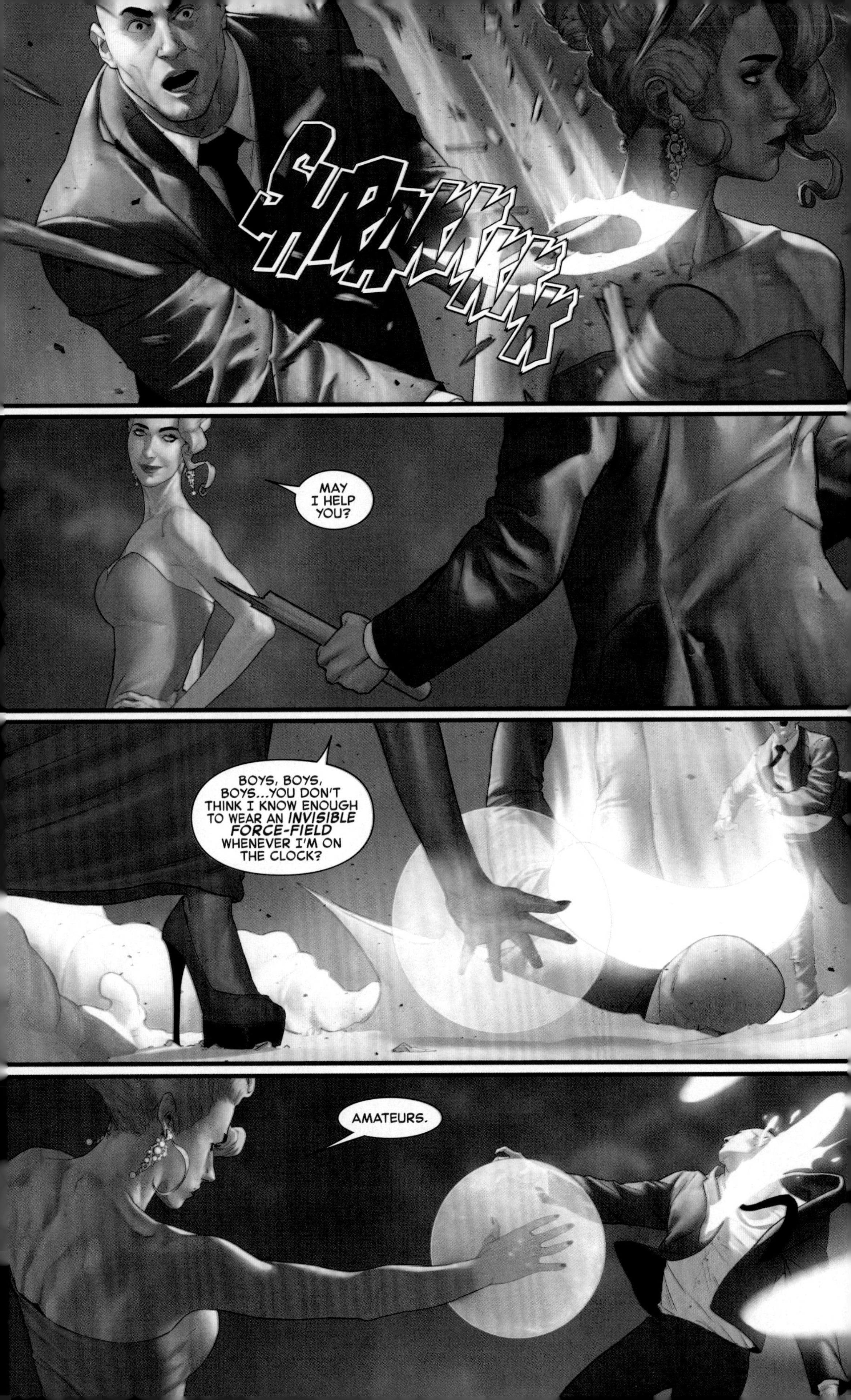

MAY I HELP YOU?
BOYS, BOYS, BOYS...YOU DON'T THINK I KNOW ENOUGH TO WEAR AN *INVISIBLE FORCE-FIELD* WHENEVER I'M ON THE CLOCK?
AMATEURS.

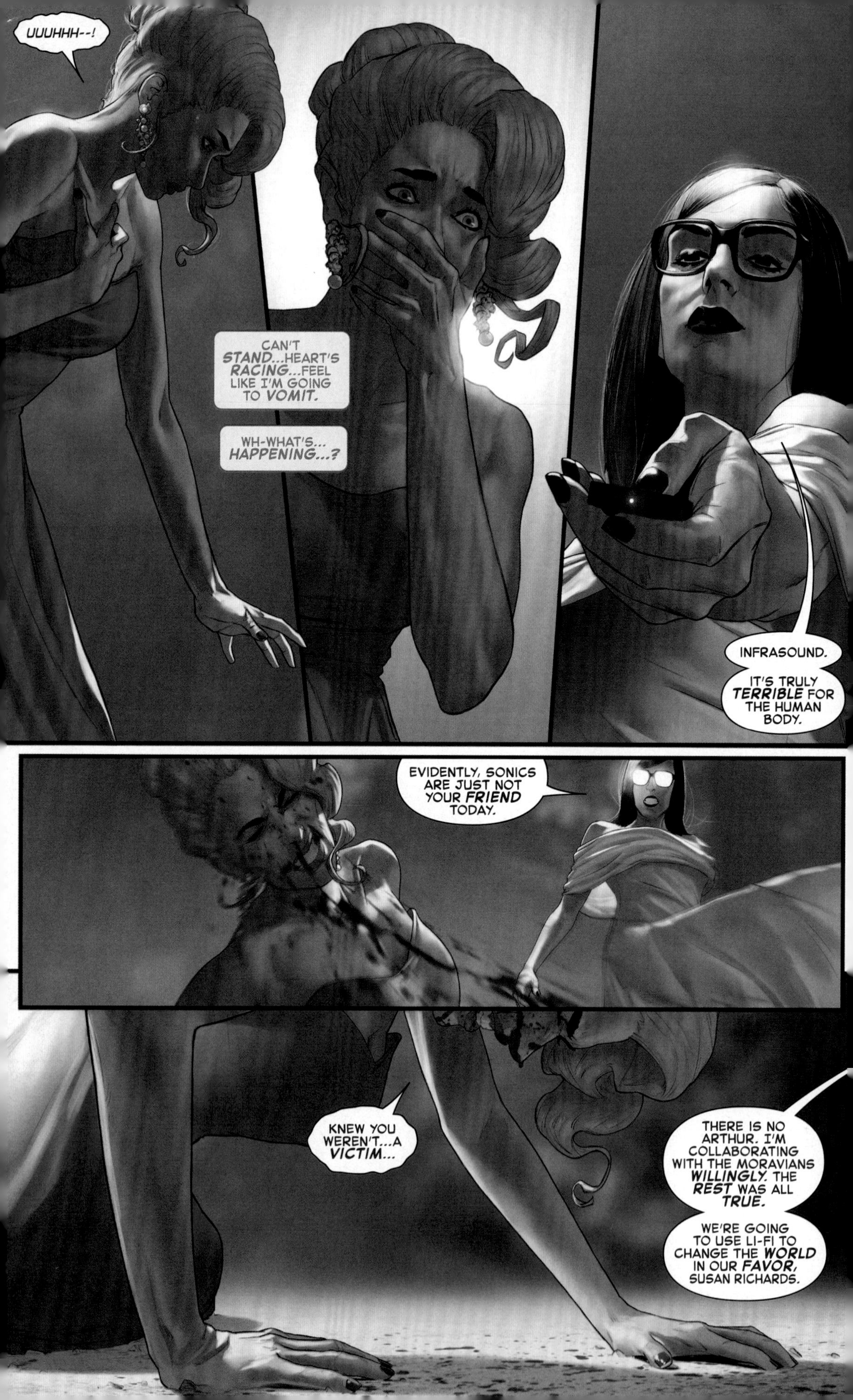
UUUHHH--!
CAN'T STAND...HEART'S RACING...FEEL LIKE I'M GOING TO VOMIT.
WH-WHAT'S... HAPPENING...?
INFRASOUND.
IT'S TRULY TERRIBLE FOR THE HUMAN BODY.
EVIDENTLY, SONICS ARE JUST NOT YOUR FRIEND TODAY.
KNEW YOU WEREN'T...A VICTIM...
THERE IS NO ARTHUR. I'M COLLABORATING WITH THE MORAVIANS WILLINGLY. THE REST WAS ALL TRUE.
WE'RE GOING TO USE LI-FI TO CHANGE THE WORLD IN OUR FAVOR, SUSAN RICHARDS.

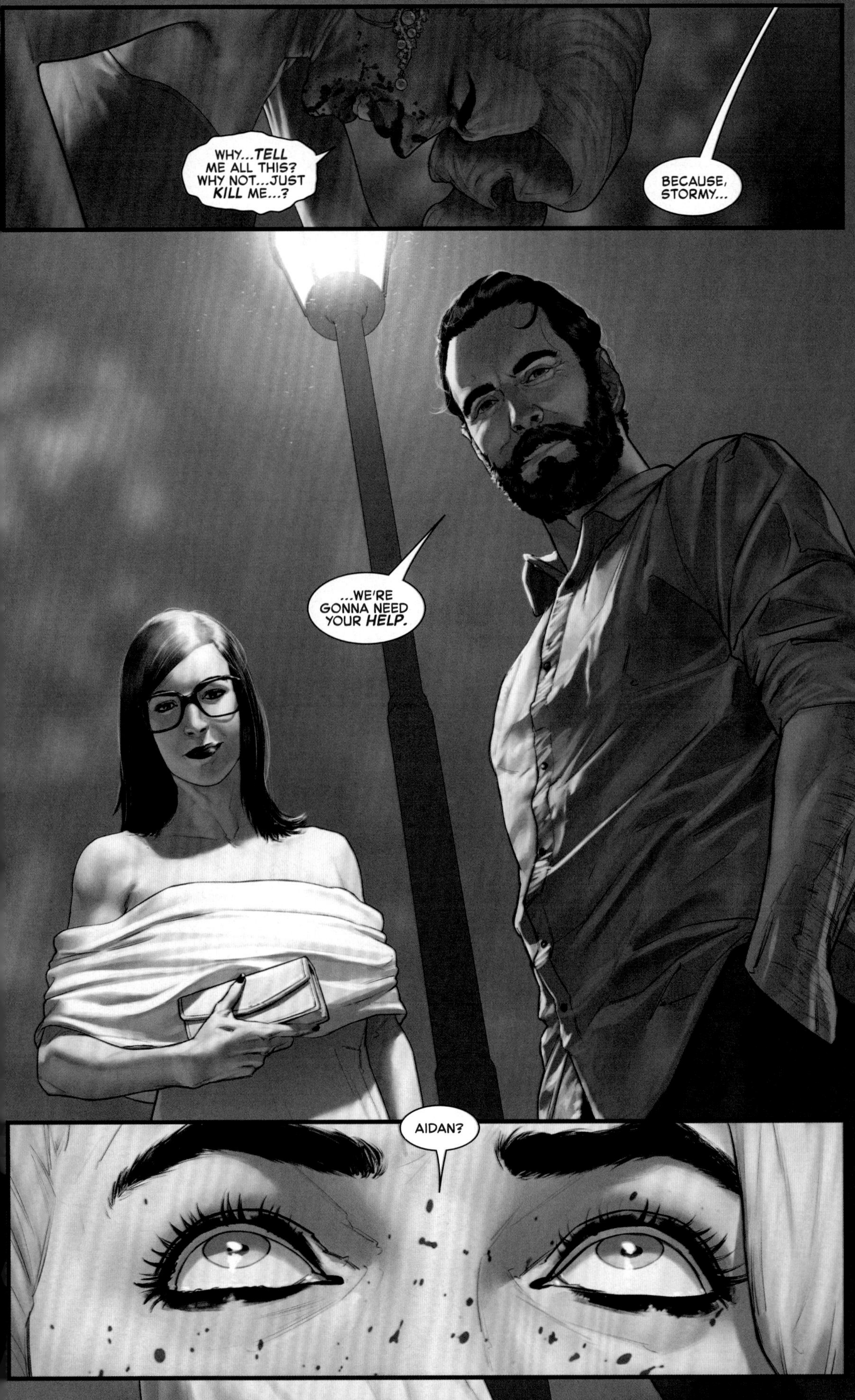
WHY...TELL ME ALL THIS? WHY NOT...JUST KILL ME...?
BECAUSE, STORMY...
...WE'RE GONNA NEED YOUR HELP.
AIDAN?

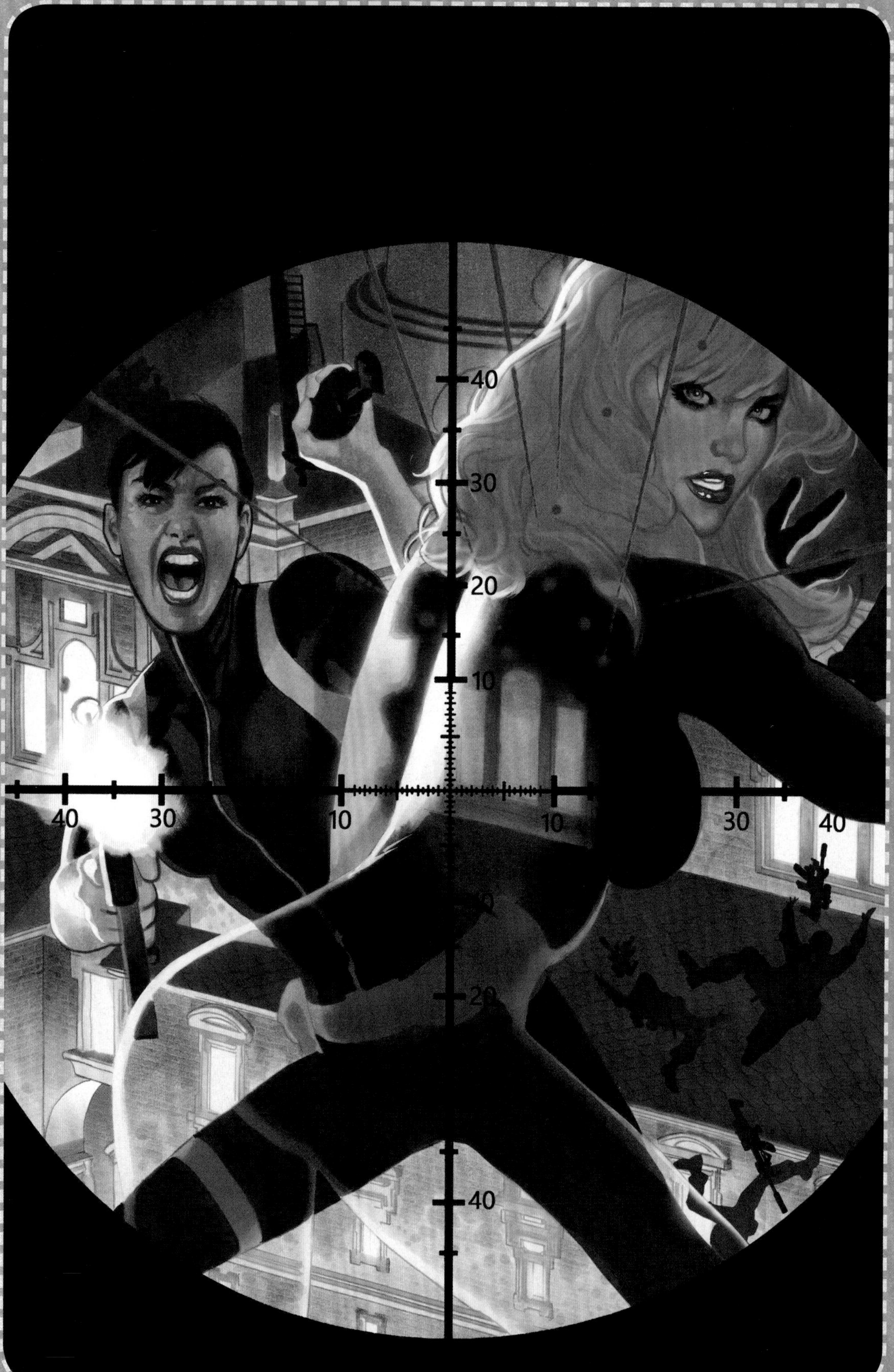

4

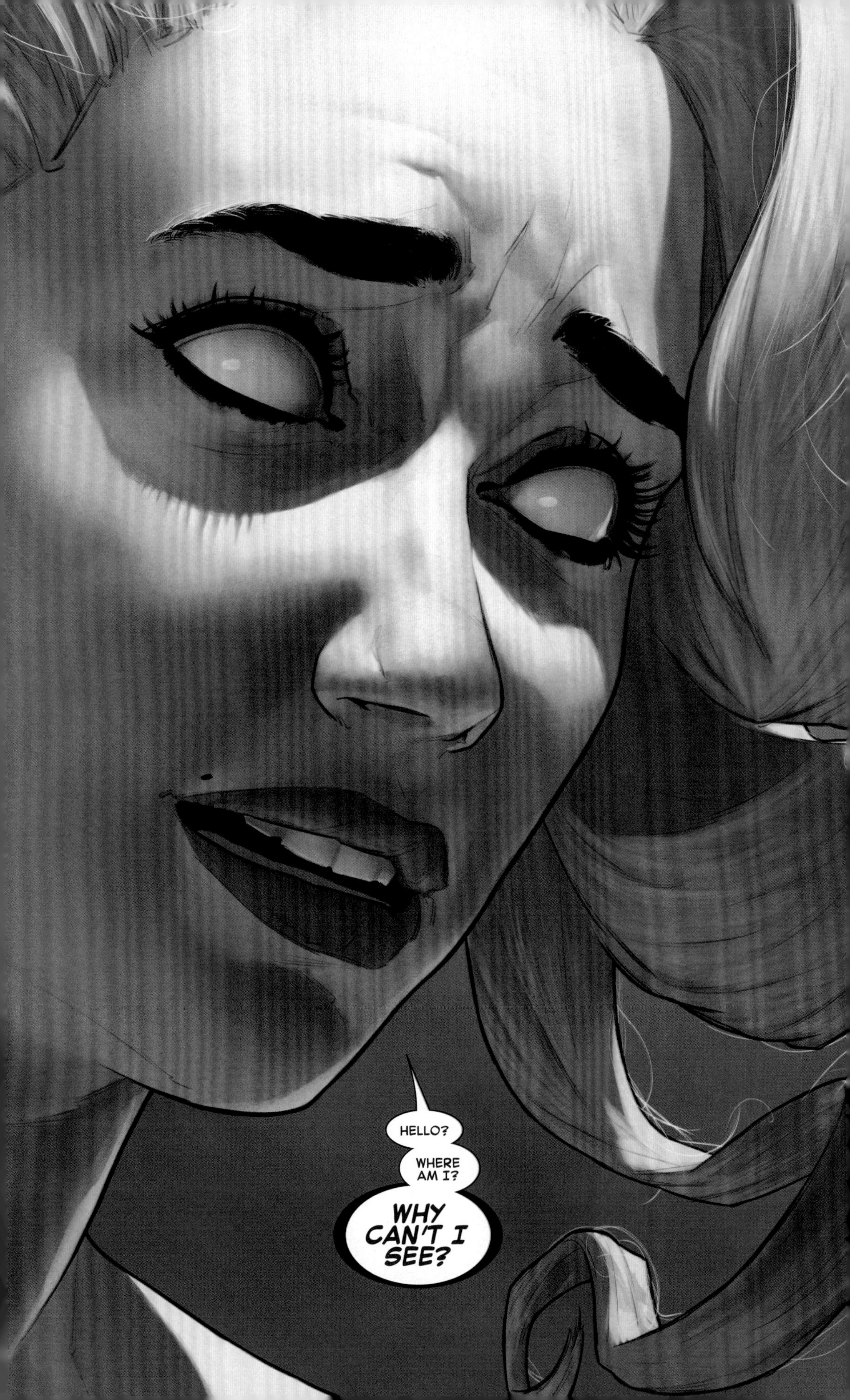
HELLO?
WHERE AM I?
WHY CAN'T I SEE?

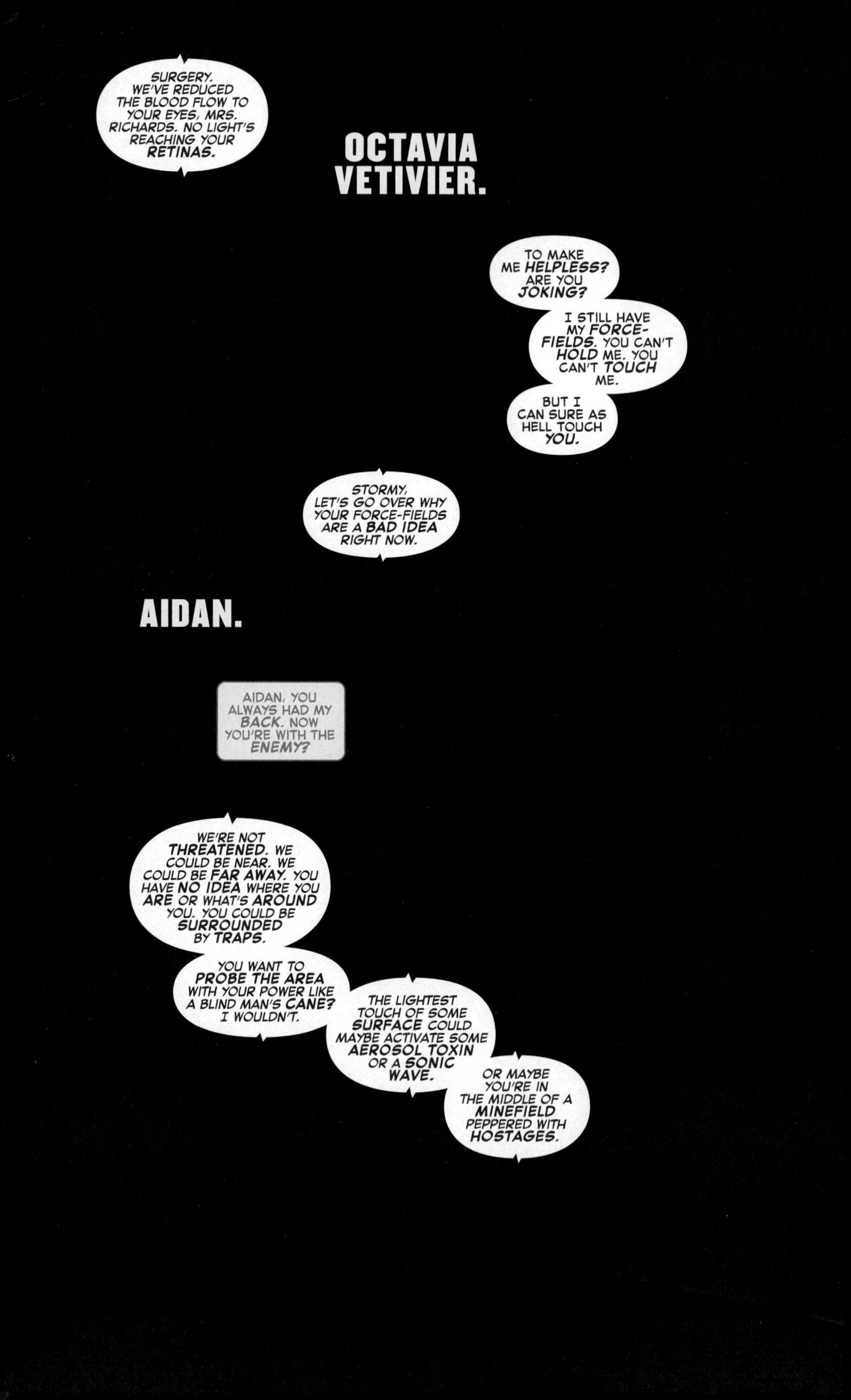
SURGERY. WE'VE REDUCED THE BLOOD FLOW TO YOUR EYES, MRS. RICHARDS. NO LIGHT'S REACHING YOUR RETINAS.
OCTAVIA VETIVIER.
TO MAKE ME HELPLESS? ARE YOU JOKING?
I STILL HAVE MY FORCE-FIELDS. YOU CAN'T HOLD ME. YOU CAN'T TOUCH ME.
BUT I CAN SURE AS HELL TOUCH YOU.
STORMY, LET'S GO OVER WHY YOUR FORCE-FIELDS ARE A BAD IDEA RIGHT NOW.
AIDAN.
AIDAN, YOU ALWAYS HAD MY BACK. NOW YOU'RE WITH THE ENEMY?
WE'RE NOT THREATENED. WE COULD BE NEAR. WE COULD BE FAR AWAY. YOU HAVE NO IDEA WHERE YOU ARE OR WHAT'S AROUND YOU. YOU COULD BE SURROUNDED BY TRAPS.
YOU WANT TO PROBE THE AREA WITH YOUR POWER LIKE A BLIND MAN'S CANE? I WOULDN'T.
THE LIGHTEST TOUCH OF SOME SURFACE COULD MAYBE ACTIVATE SOME AEROSOL TOXIN OR A SONIC WAVE.
OR MAYBE YOU'RE IN THE MIDDLE OF A MINEFIELD PEPPERED WITH HOSTAGES.

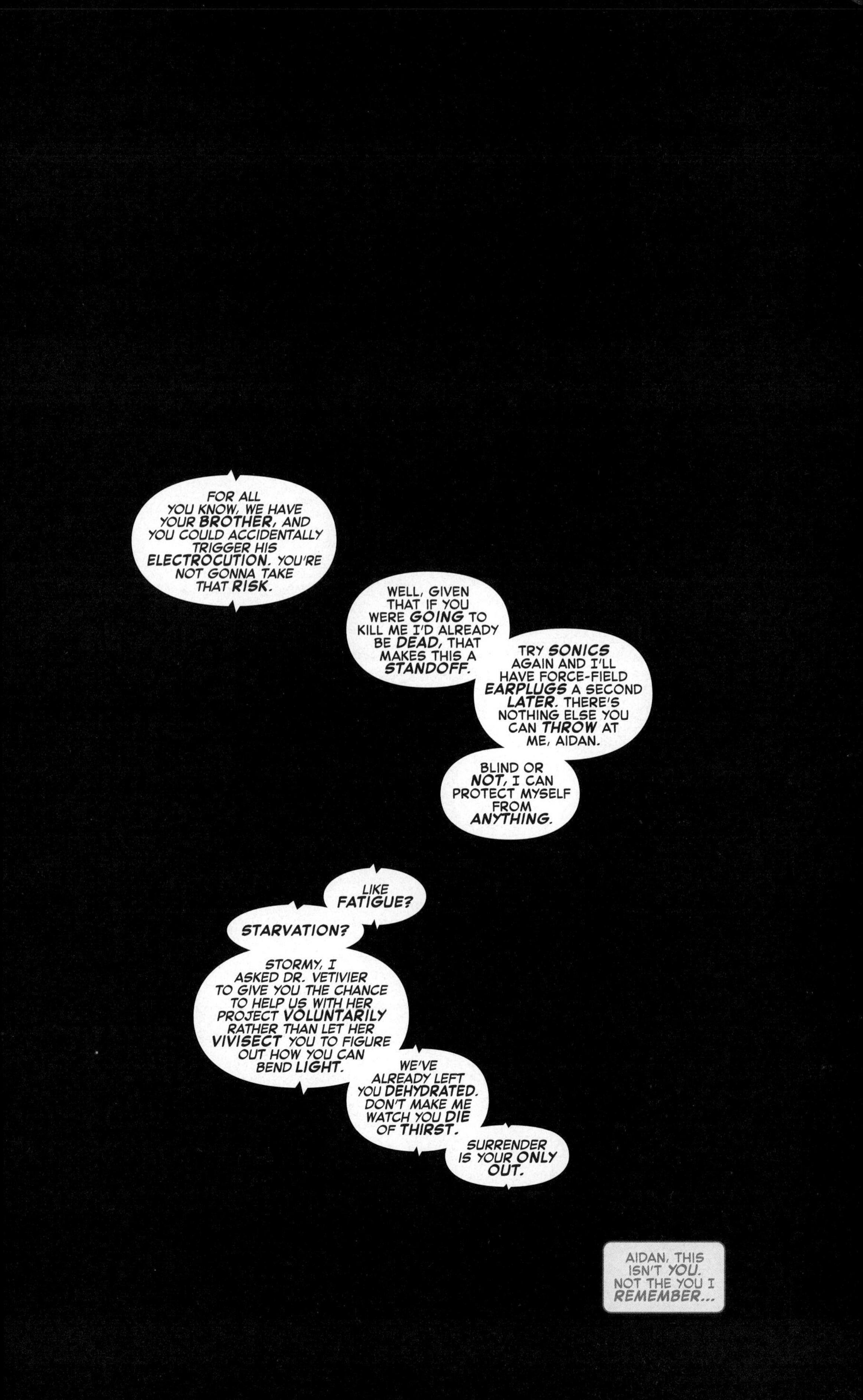
FOR ALL YOU KNOW, WE HAVE YOUR BROTHER, AND YOU COULD ACCIDENTALLY TRIGGER HIS ELECTROCUTION. YOU'RE NOT GONNA TAKE THAT RISK.
WELL, GIVEN THAT IF YOU WERE GOING TO KILL ME I'D ALREADY BE DEAD, THAT MAKES THIS A STANDOFF.
TRY SONICS AGAIN AND I'LL HAVE FORCE-FIELD EARPLUGS A SECOND LATER. THERE'S NOTHING ELSE YOU CAN THROW AT ME, AIDAN.
BLIND OR NOT, I CAN PROTECT MYSELF FROM ANYTHING.
LIKE FATIGUE?
STARVATION?
STORMY, I ASKED DR. VETIVIER TO GIVE YOU THE CHANCE TO HELP US WITH HER PROJECT VOLUNTARILY RATHER THAN LET HER VIVISECT YOU TO FIGURE OUT HOW YOU CAN BEND LIGHT.
WE'VE ALREADY LEFT YOU DEHYDRATED. DON'T MAKE ME WATCH YOU DIE OF THIRST.
SURRENDER IS YOUR ONLY OUT.
AIDAN, THIS ISN'T YOU. NOT THE YOU I REMEMBER...

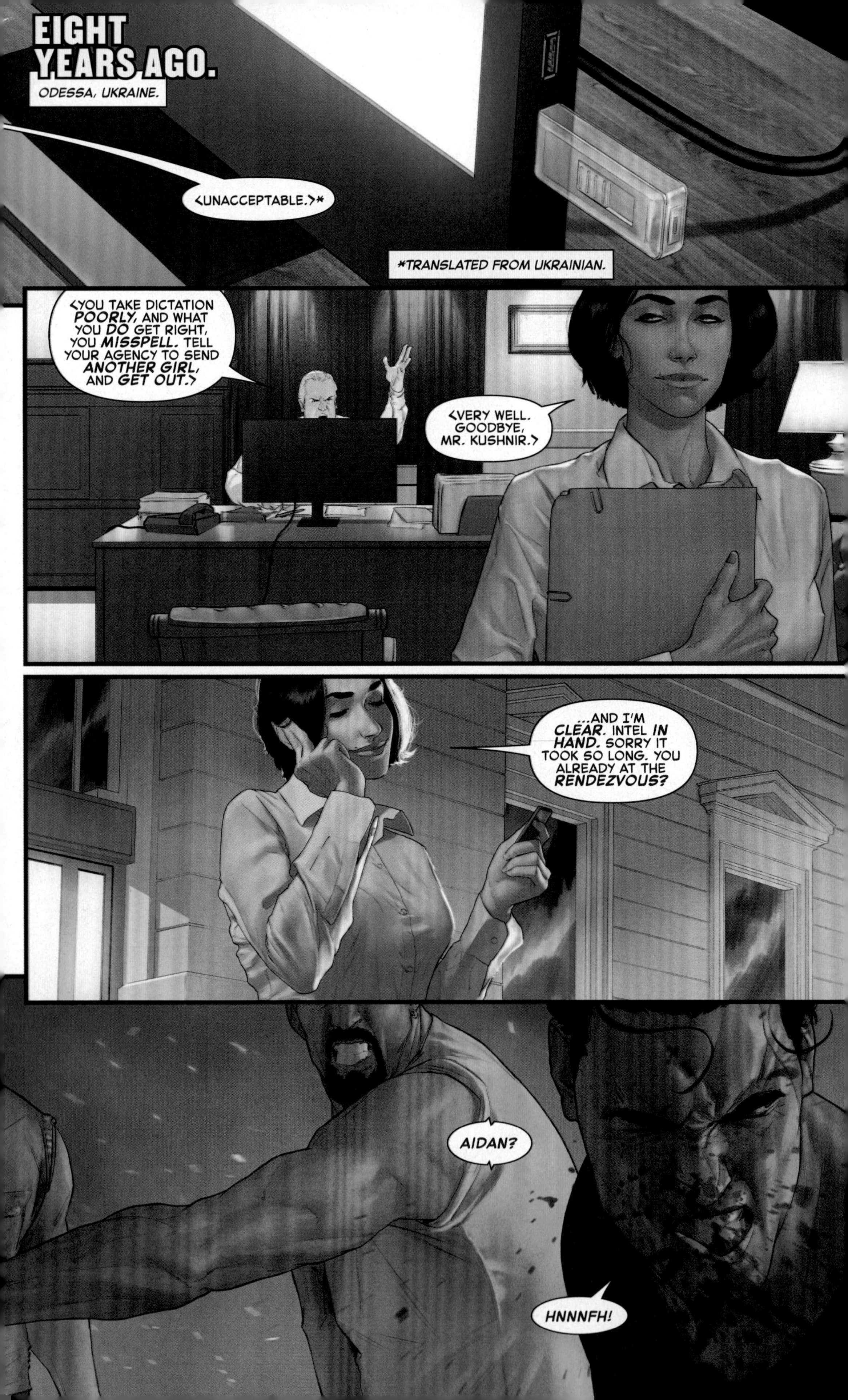
EIGHT YEARS AGO.
ODESSA, UKRAINE.
<UNACCEPTABLE.>*
*TRANSLATED FROM UKRAINIAN.
<YOU TAKE DICTATION POORLY, AND WHAT YOU DO GET RIGHT, YOU MISSPELL. TELL YOUR AGENCY TO SEND ANOTHER GIRL, AND GET OUT.>
<VERY WELL. GOODBYE, MR. KUSHNIR.>
...AND I'M CLEAR. INTEL IN HAND. SORRY IT TOOK SO LONG. YOU ALREADY AT THE RENDEZVOUS?
AIDAN?
HNNNFH!

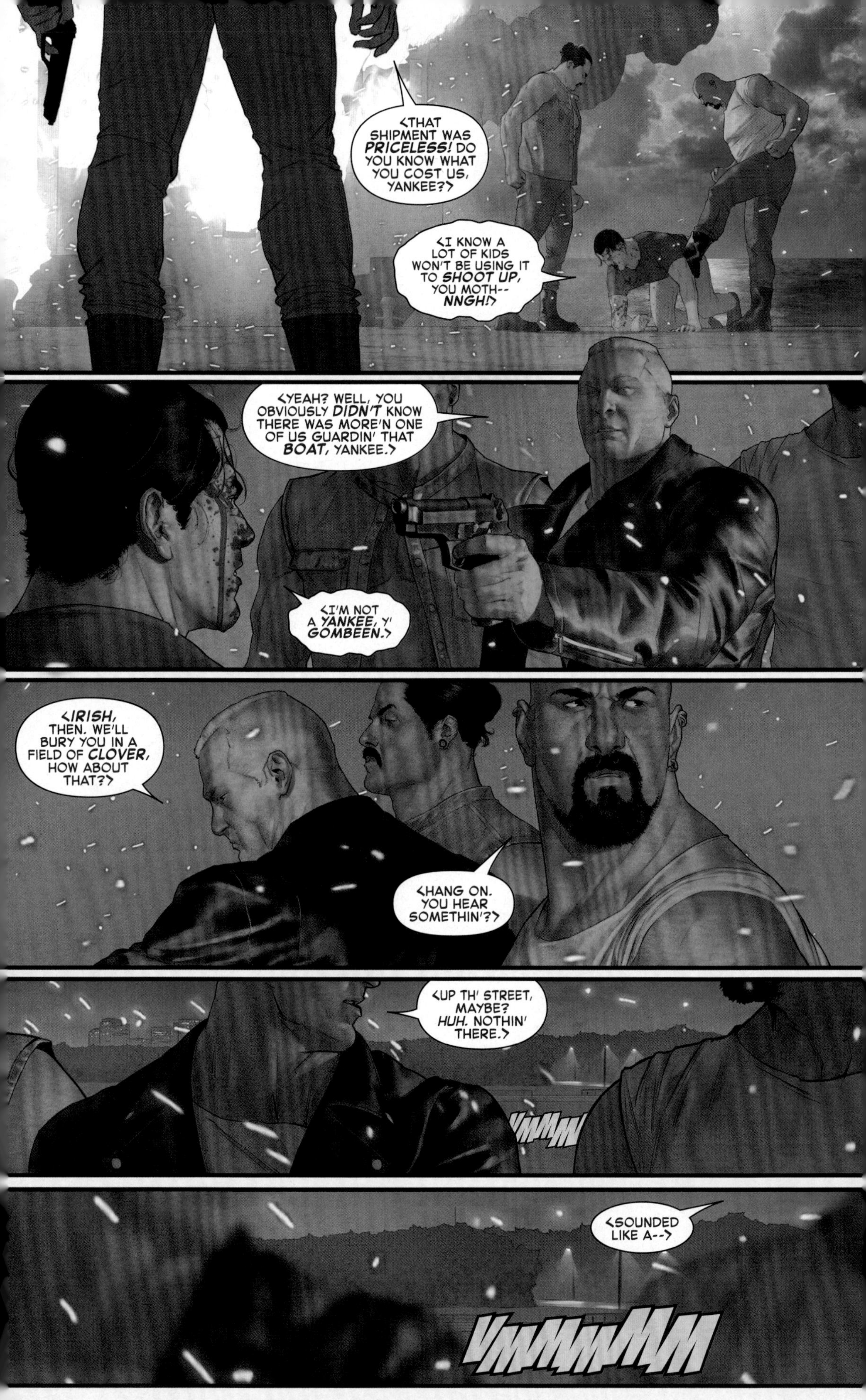
<THAT SHIPMENT WAS PRICELESS! DO YOU KNOW WHAT YOU COST US, YANKEE?>
<I KNOW A LOT OF KIDS WON'T BE USING IT TO SHOOT UP, YOU MOTH-- NNGH!>
<YEAH? WELL, YOU OBVIOUSLY DIDN'T KNOW THERE WAS MORE'N ONE OF US GUARDIN' THAT BOAT, YANKEE.>
<I'M NOT A YANKEE, Y' GOMBEEN.>
<IRISH, THEN. WE'LL BURY YOU IN A FIELD OF CLOVER, HOW ABOUT THAT?>
<HANG ON. YOU HEAR SOMETHIN'?>
<UP TH' STREET, MAYBE? HUH. NOTHIN' THERE.>
<SOUNDED LIKE A-->

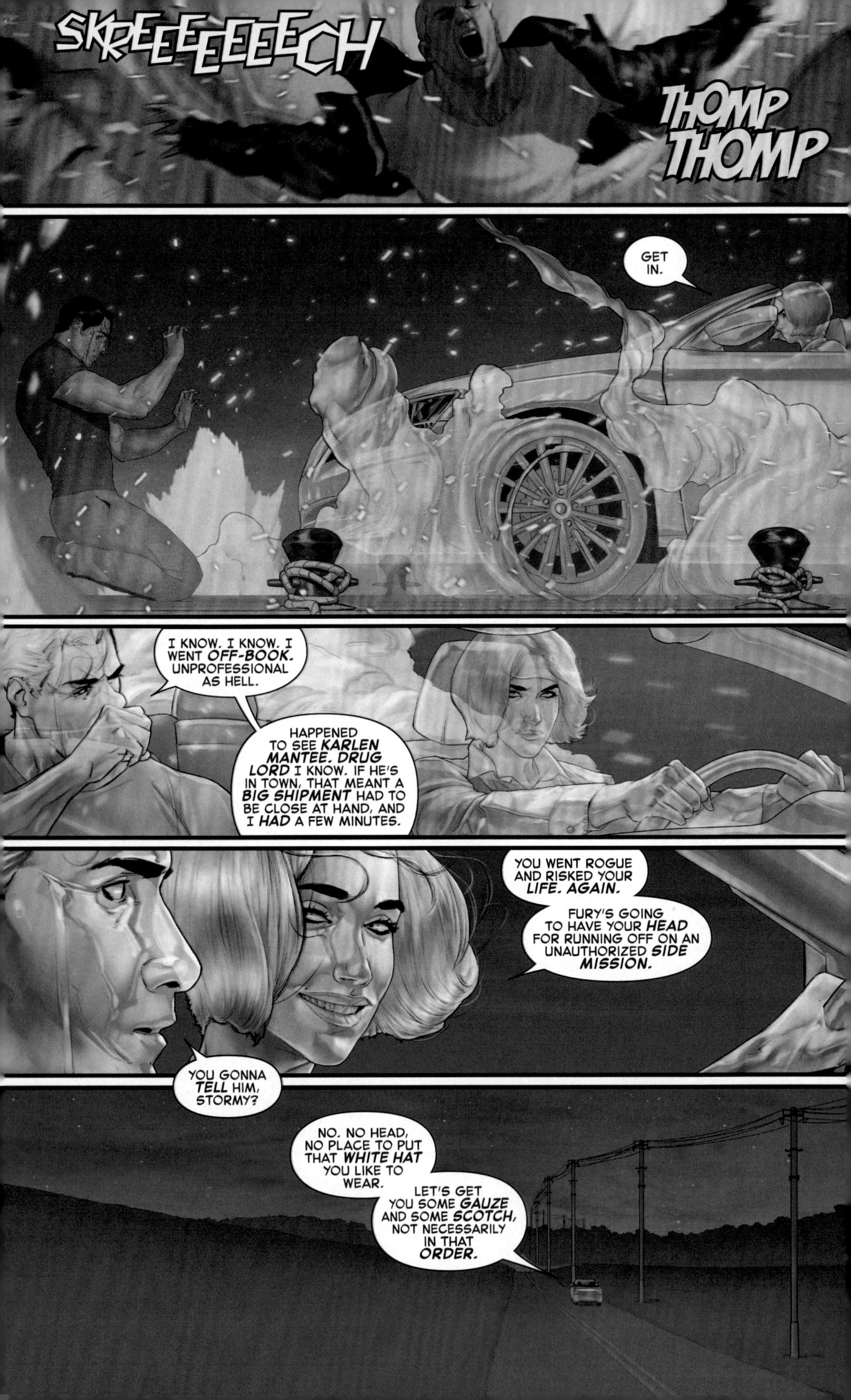

SKREEEEEEEEECH
THOMP THOMP
GET IN.
I KNOW. I KNOW. I WENT OFF-BOOK. UNPROFESSIONAL AS HELL.
HAPPENED TO SEE KARLEN MANTEE. DRUG LORD I KNOW. IF HE'S IN TOWN, THAT MEANT A BIG SHIPMENT HAD TO BE CLOSE AT HAND, AND I HAD A FEW MINUTES.
YOU WENT ROGUE AND RISKED YOUR LIFE. AGAIN.
FURY'S GOING TO HAVE YOUR HEAD FOR RUNNING OFF ON AN UNAUTHORIZED SIDE MISSION.
YOU GONNA TELL HIM, STORMY?
NO. NO HEAD, NO PLACE TO PUT THAT WHITE HAT YOU LIKE TO WEAR.
LET'S GET YOU SOME GAUZE AND SOME SCOTCH, NOT NECESSARILY IN THAT ORDER.

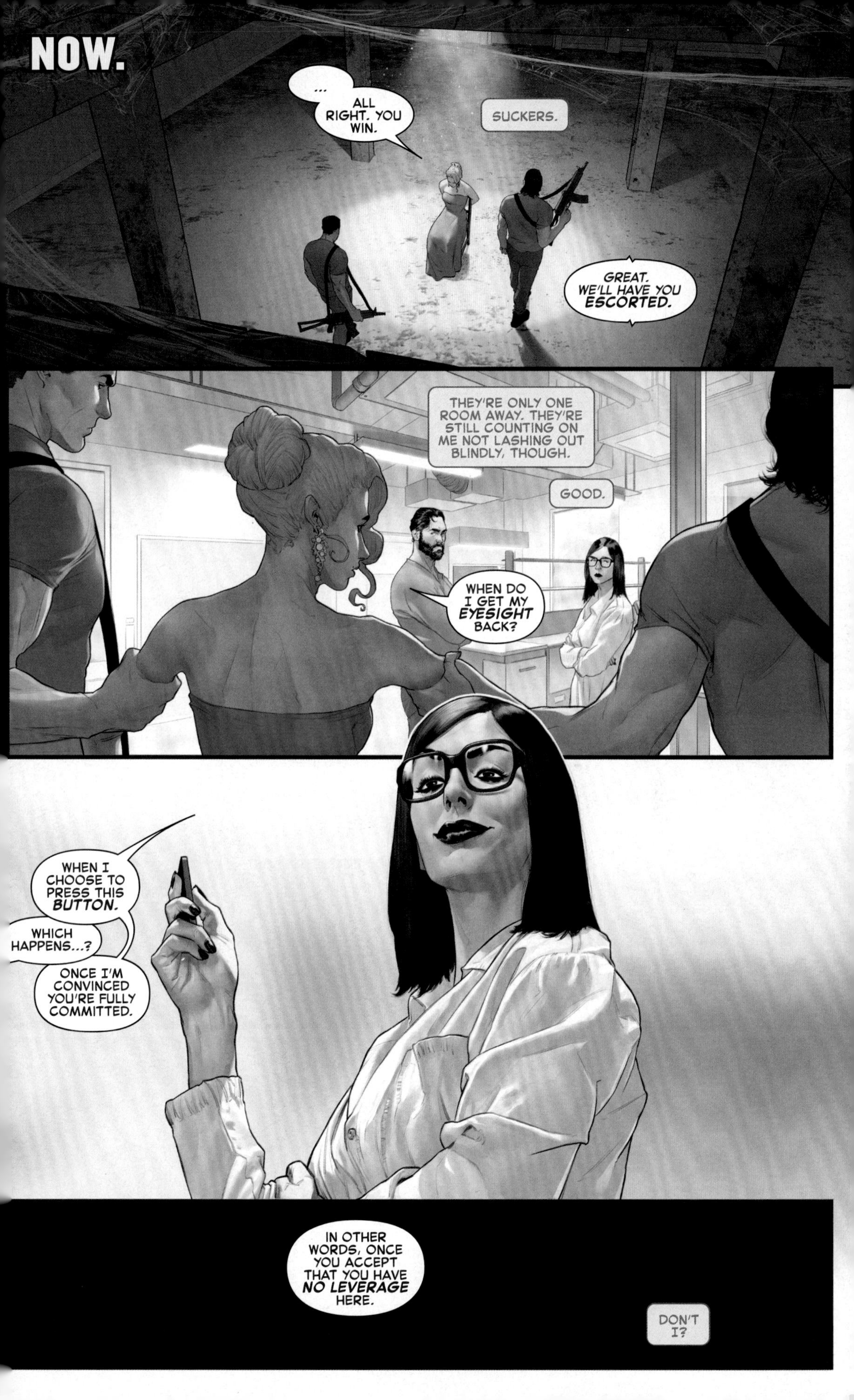
NOW.
...ALL RIGHT. YOU WIN.
SUCKERS.
GREAT. WE'LL HAVE YOU ESCORTED.
THEY'RE ONLY ONE ROOM AWAY. THEY'RE STILL COUNTING ON ME NOT LASHING OUT BLINDLY, THOUGH.
GOOD.
WHEN DO I GET MY EYESIGHT BACK?
WHEN I CHOOSE TO PRESS THIS BUTTON.
WHICH HAPPENS...?
ONCE I'M CONVINCED YOU'RE FULLY COMMITTED.
IN OTHER WORDS, ONCE YOU ACCEPT THAT YOU HAVE NO LEVERAGE HERE.
DON'T I?

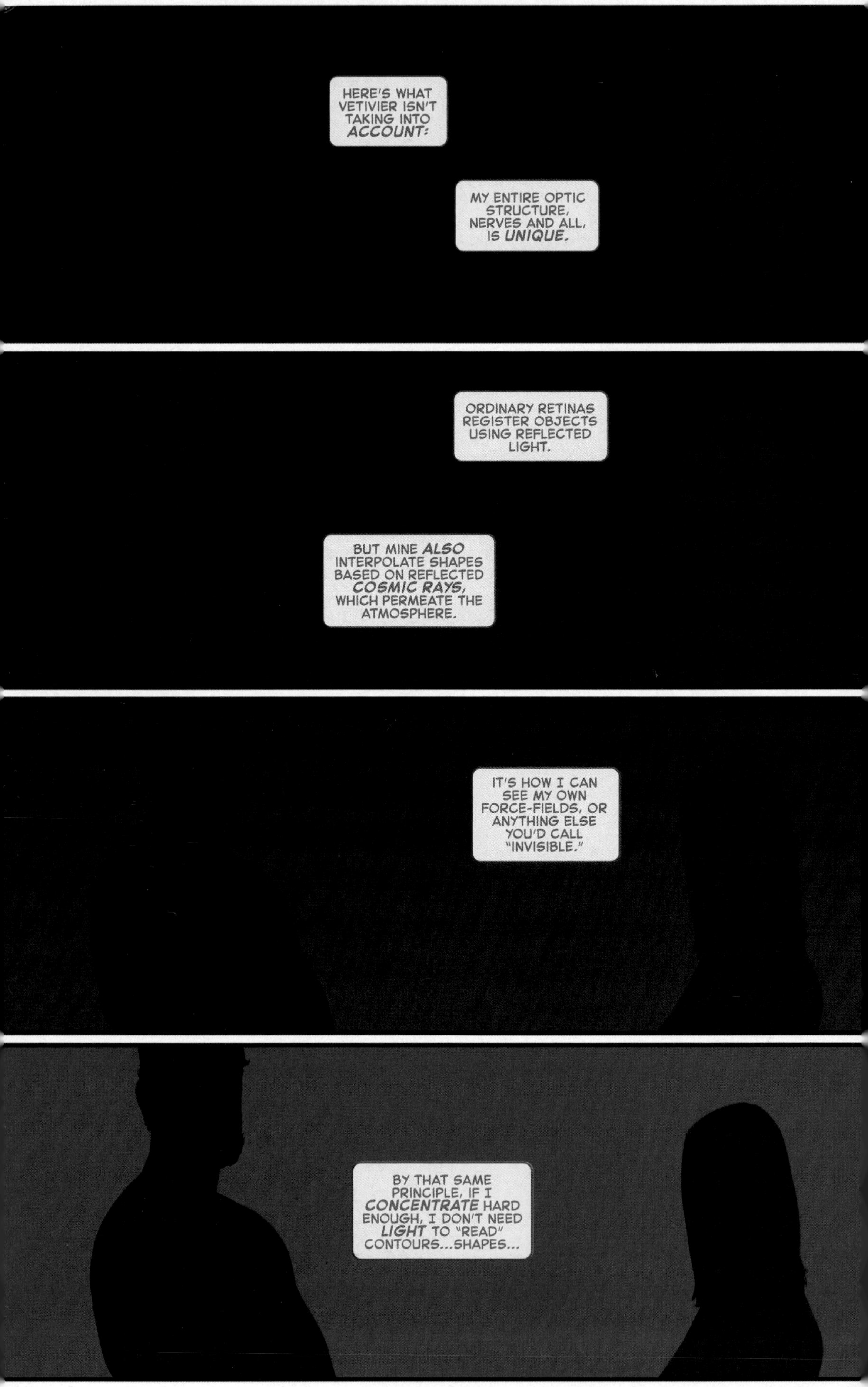
HERE'S WHAT VETIVIER ISN'T TAKING INTO ACCOUNT:
MY ENTIRE OPTIC STRUCTURE, NERVES AND ALL, IS UNIQUE.
ORDINARY RETINAS REGISTER OBJECTS USING REFLECTED LIGHT.
BUT MINE ALSO INTERPOLATE SHAPES BASED ON REFLECTED COSMIC RAYS, WHICH PERMEATE THE ATMOSPHERE.
IT'S HOW I CAN SEE MY OWN FORCE-FIELDS, OR ANYTHING ELSE YOU'D CALL "INVISIBLE."
BY THAT SAME PRINCIPLE, IF I CONCENTRATE HARD ENOUGH, I DON'T NEED LIGHT TO "READ" CONTOURS...SHAPES...

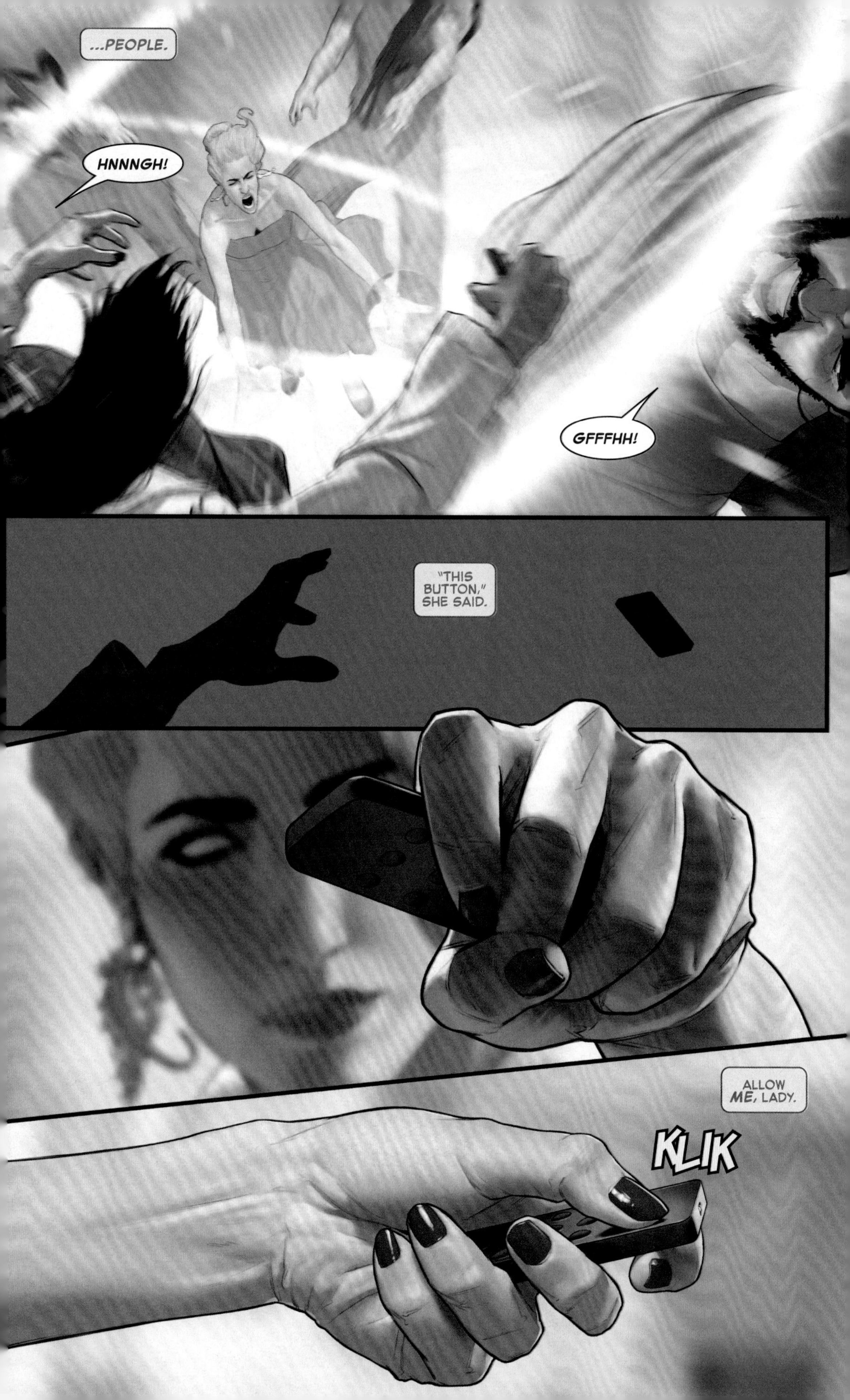
...PEOPLE.
HNNNGH!
GFFFHH!
"THIS BUTTON," SHE SAID.
ALLOW ME, LADY.
KLIK

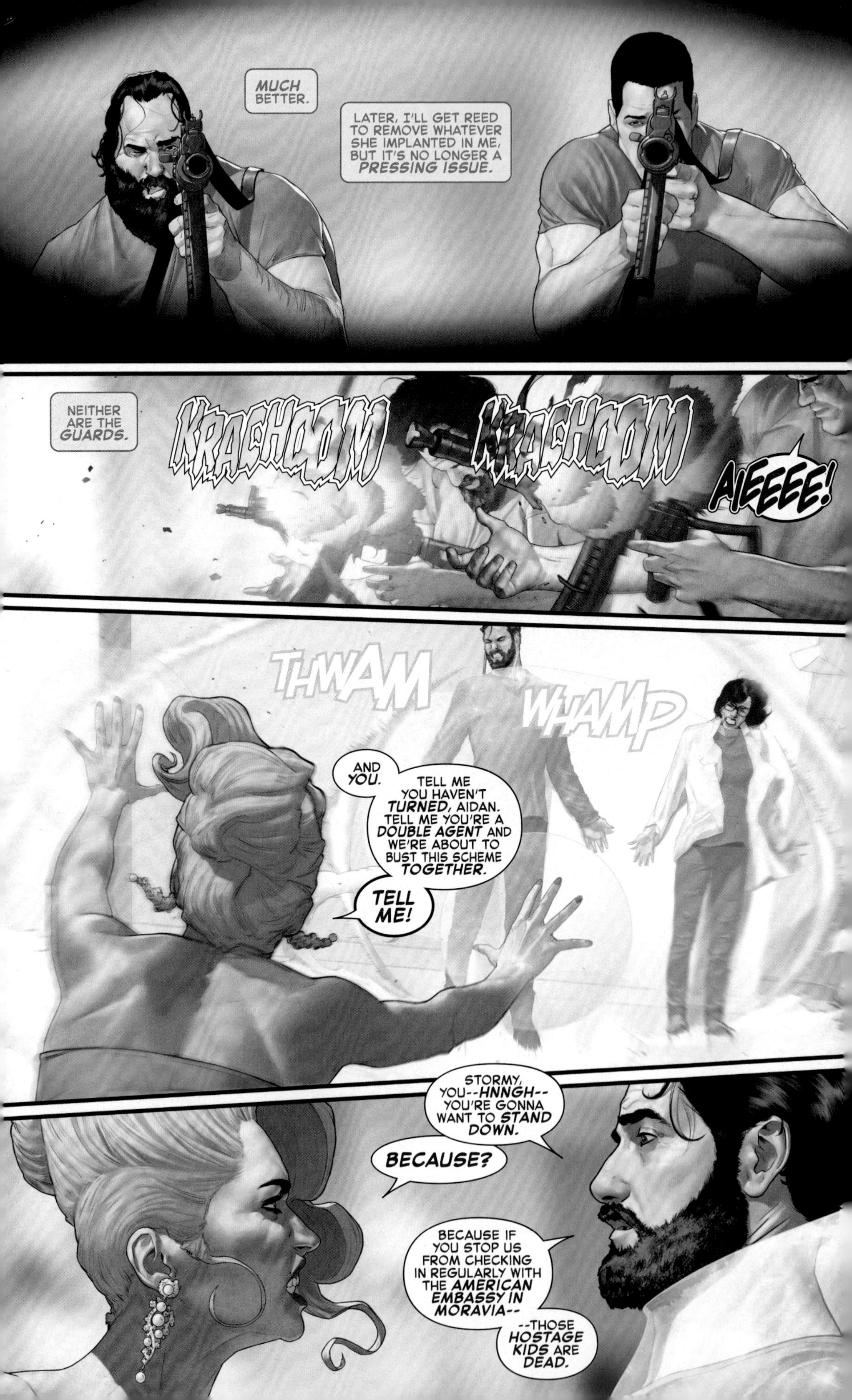

MUCH BETTER.
LATER, I'LL GET REED TO REMOVE WHATEVER SHE IMPLANTED IN ME, BUT IT'S NO LONGER A PRESSING ISSUE.
NEITHER ARE THE GUARDS.
KRACHOOM
KRACHOOM
AIEEEE!
THWAM
WHAMP
AND YOU.
TELL ME YOU HAVEN'T TURNED, AIDAN. TELL ME YOU'RE A DOUBLE AGENT AND WE'RE ABOUT TO BUST THIS SCHEME TOGETHER.
TELL ME!
STORMY, YOU--HNNGH-- YOU'RE GONNA WANT TO STAND DOWN.
BECAUSE?
BECAUSE IF YOU STOP US FROM CHECKING IN REGULARLY WITH THE AMERICAN EMBASSY IN MORAVIA--
--THOSE HOSTAGE KIDS ARE DEAD.

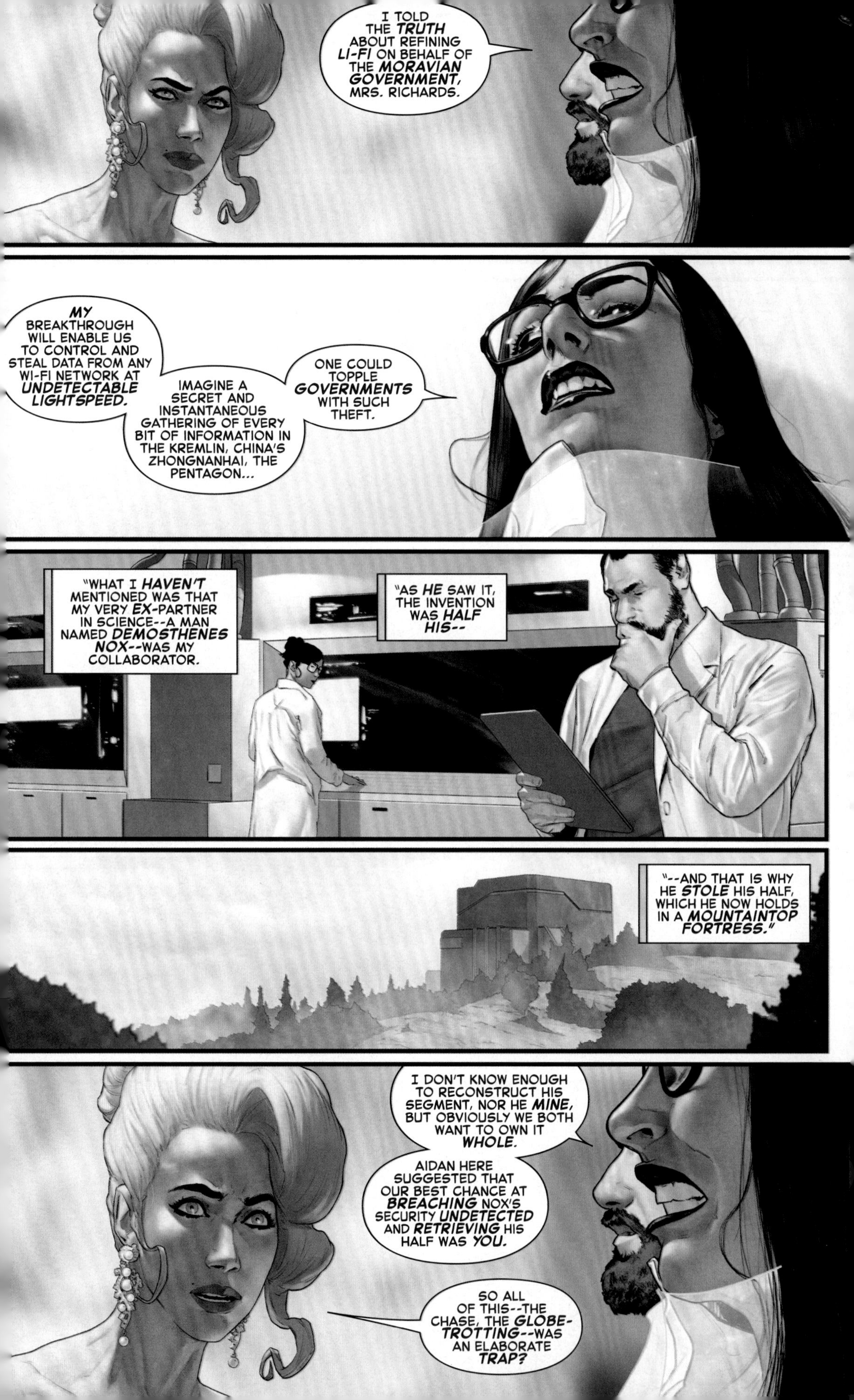

I TOLD THE TRUTH ABOUT REFINING LI-FI ON BEHALF OF THE MORAVIAN GOVERNMENT, MRS. RICHARDS.
MY BREAKTHROUGH WILL ENABLE US TO CONTROL AND STEAL DATA FROM ANY WI-FI NETWORK AT UNDETECTABLE LIGHTSPEED.
IMAGINE A SECRET AND INSTANTANEOUS GATHERING OF EVERY BIT OF INFORMATION IN THE KREMLIN, CHINA'S ZHONGNANHAI, THE PENTAGON...
ONE COULD TOPPLE GOVERNMENTS WITH SUCH THEFT.
"WHAT I HAVEN'T MENTIONED WAS THAT MY VERY EX-PARTNER IN SCIENCE--A MAN NAMED DEMOSTHENES NOX--WAS MY COLLABORATOR.
"AS HE SAW IT, THE INVENTION WAS HALF HIS--
"--AND THAT IS WHY HE STOLE HIS HALF, WHICH HE NOW HOLDS IN A MOUNTAINTOP FORTRESS."
I DON'T KNOW ENOUGH TO RECONSTRUCT HIS SEGMENT, NOR HE MINE, BUT OBVIOUSLY WE BOTH WANT TO OWN IT WHOLE.
AIDAN HERE SUGGESTED THAT OUR BEST CHANCE AT BREACHING NOX'S SECURITY UNDETECTED AND RETRIEVING HIS HALF WAS YOU.
SO ALL OF THIS--THE CHASE, THE GLOBE-TROTTING--WAS AN ELABORATE TRAP?

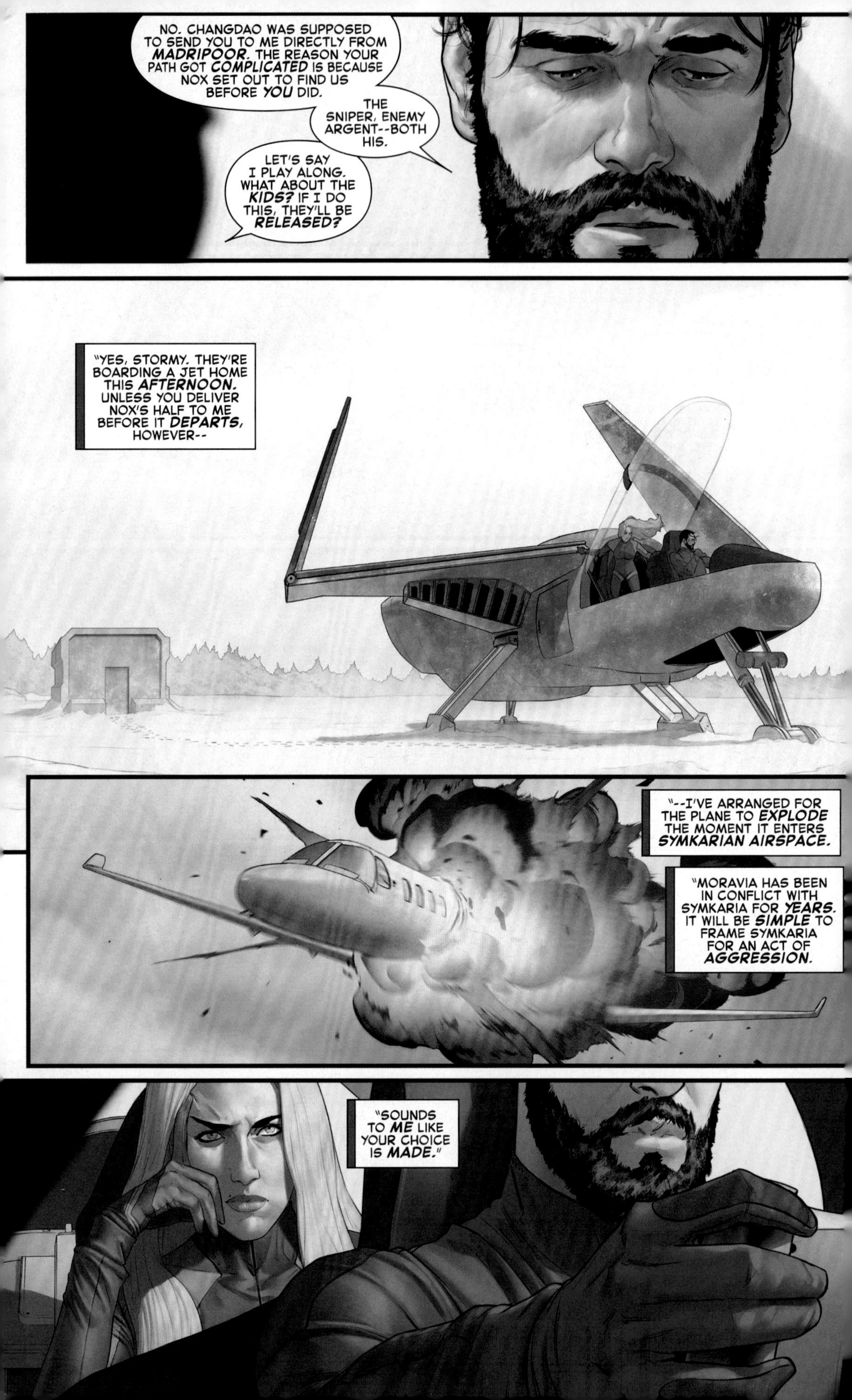
NO. CHANGDAO WAS SUPPOSED TO SEND YOU TO ME DIRECTLY FROM MADRIPOOR. THE REASON YOUR PATH GOT COMPLICATED IS BECAUSE NOX SET OUT TO FIND US BEFORE YOU DID.
THE SNIPER, ENEMY ARGENT--BOTH HIS.
LET'S SAY I PLAY ALONG. WHAT ABOUT THE KIDS? IF I DO THIS, THEY'LL BE RELEASED?
"YES, STORMY. THEY'RE BOARDING A JET HOME THIS AFTERNOON. UNLESS YOU DELIVER NOX'S HALF TO ME BEFORE IT DEPARTS, HOWEVER--
"--I'VE ARRANGED FOR THE PLANE TO EXPLODE THE MOMENT IT ENTERS SYMKARIAN AIRSPACE.
"MORAVIA HAS BEEN IN CONFLICT WITH SYMKARIA FOR YEARS. IT WILL BE SIMPLE TO FRAME SYMKARIA FOR AN ACT OF AGGRESSION.
"SOUNDS TO ME LIKE YOUR CHOICE IS MADE."

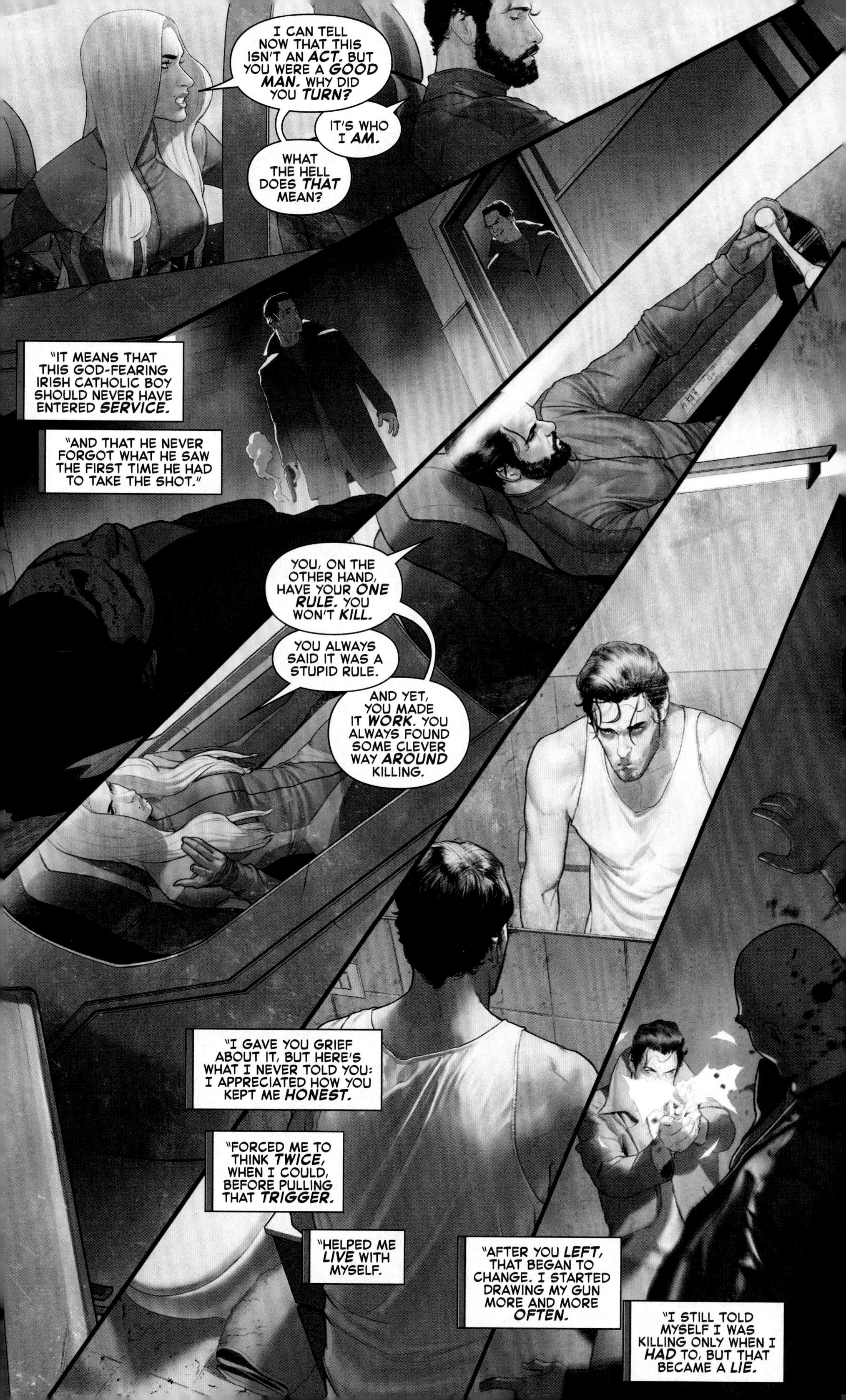
I CAN TELL NOW THAT THIS ISN'T AN ACT. BUT YOU WERE A GOOD MAN. WHY DID YOU TURN?
IT'S WHO I AM.
WHAT THE HELL DOES THAT MEAN?
"IT MEANS THAT THIS GOD-FEARING IRISH CATHOLIC BOY SHOULD NEVER HAVE ENTERED SERVICE.
"AND THAT HE NEVER FORGOT WHAT HE SAW THE FIRST TIME HE HAD TO TAKE THE SHOT."
YOU, ON THE OTHER HAND, HAVE YOUR ONE RULE. YOU WON'T KILL.
YOU ALWAYS SAID IT WAS A STUPID RULE.
AND YET, YOU MADE IT WORK. YOU ALWAYS FOUND SOME CLEVER WAY AROUND KILLING.
"I GAVE YOU GRIEF ABOUT IT, BUT HERE'S WHAT I NEVER TOLD YOU: I APPRECIATED HOW YOU KEPT ME HONEST.
"FORCED ME TO THINK TWICE, WHEN I COULD, BEFORE PULLING THAT TRIGGER.
"HELPED ME LIVE WITH MYSELF.
"AFTER YOU LEFT, THAT BEGAN TO CHANGE. I STARTED DRAWING MY GUN MORE AND MORE OFTEN.
"I STILL TOLD MYSELF I WAS KILLING ONLY WHEN I HAD TO, BUT THAT BECAME A LIE.

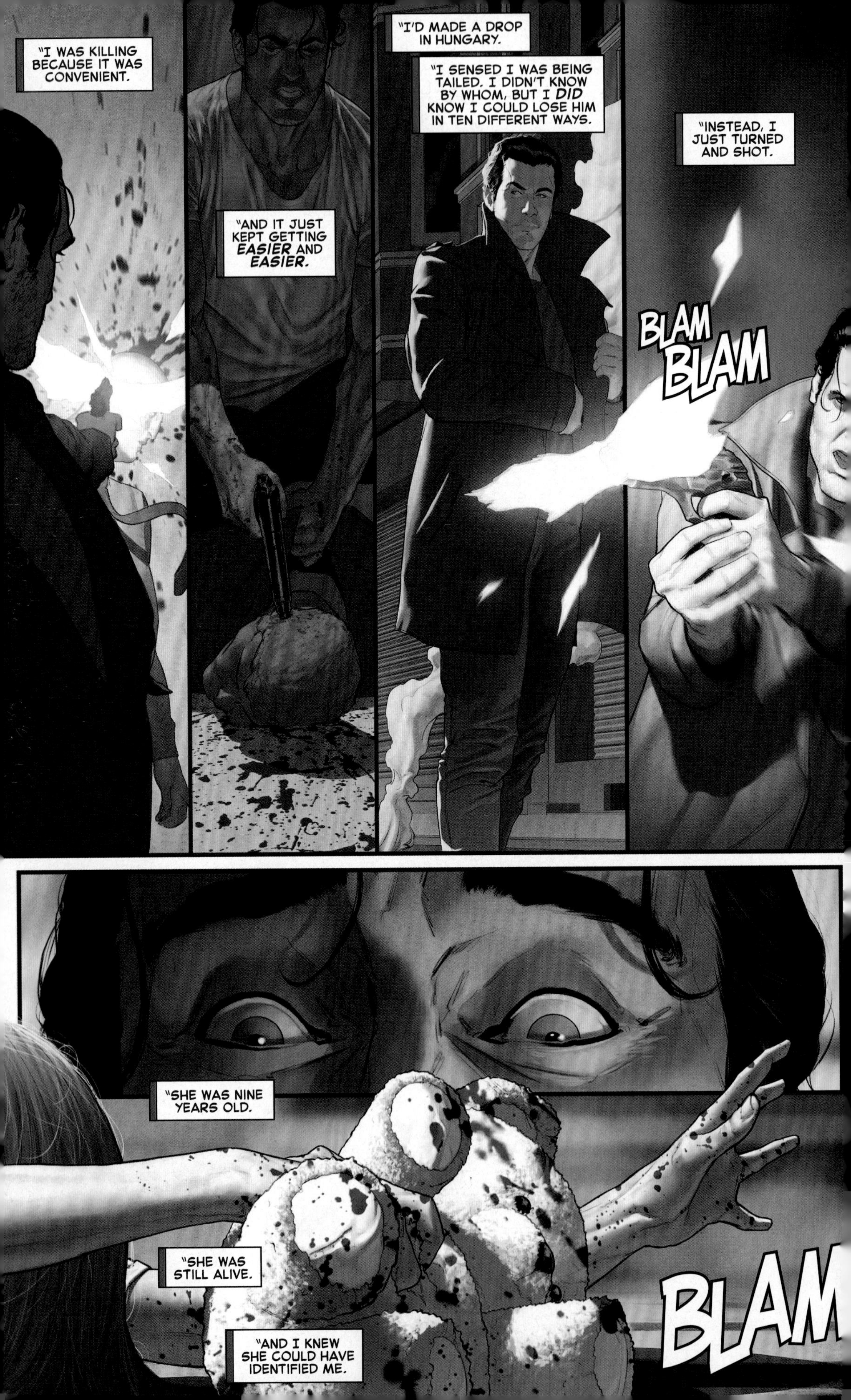
"I WAS KILLING BECAUSE IT WAS CONVENIENT.
"AND IT JUST KEPT GETTING *EASIER* AND *EASIER.*
"I'D MADE A DROP IN HUNGARY.
"I SENSED I WAS BEING TAILED. I DIDN'T KNOW BY WHOM, BUT I *DID* KNOW I COULD LOSE HIM IN TEN DIFFERENT WAYS.
"INSTEAD, I JUST TURNED AND SHOT.
BLAM
BLAM
"SHE WAS NINE YEARS OLD.
"SHE WAS STILL ALIVE.
"AND I KNEW SHE COULD HAVE IDENTIFIED ME.
BLAM

"YOU'RE ASKING ME WHY DID I 'TURN'? I *DIDN'T*.

"TURNS OUT I WAS ALWAYS THIS WAY."

MY GOD.

THE NEXT TIME MORAVIA MADE AN OFFER, I WENT FULL *DOUBLE AGENT*. I MEAN, WHY NOT? *DESTINY* CALLED.

I KNEW WHERE I BELONGED.

I'M LEFT WITH NOTHING TO SAY. THE AIDAN I KNEW IS LONG GONE.

THIS MAN'S A *PSYCHOPATH*.

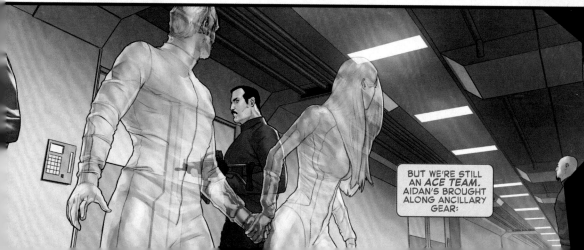

BUT WE'RE STILL AN *ACE TEAM*. AIDAN'S BROUGHT ALONG ANCILLARY GEAR:

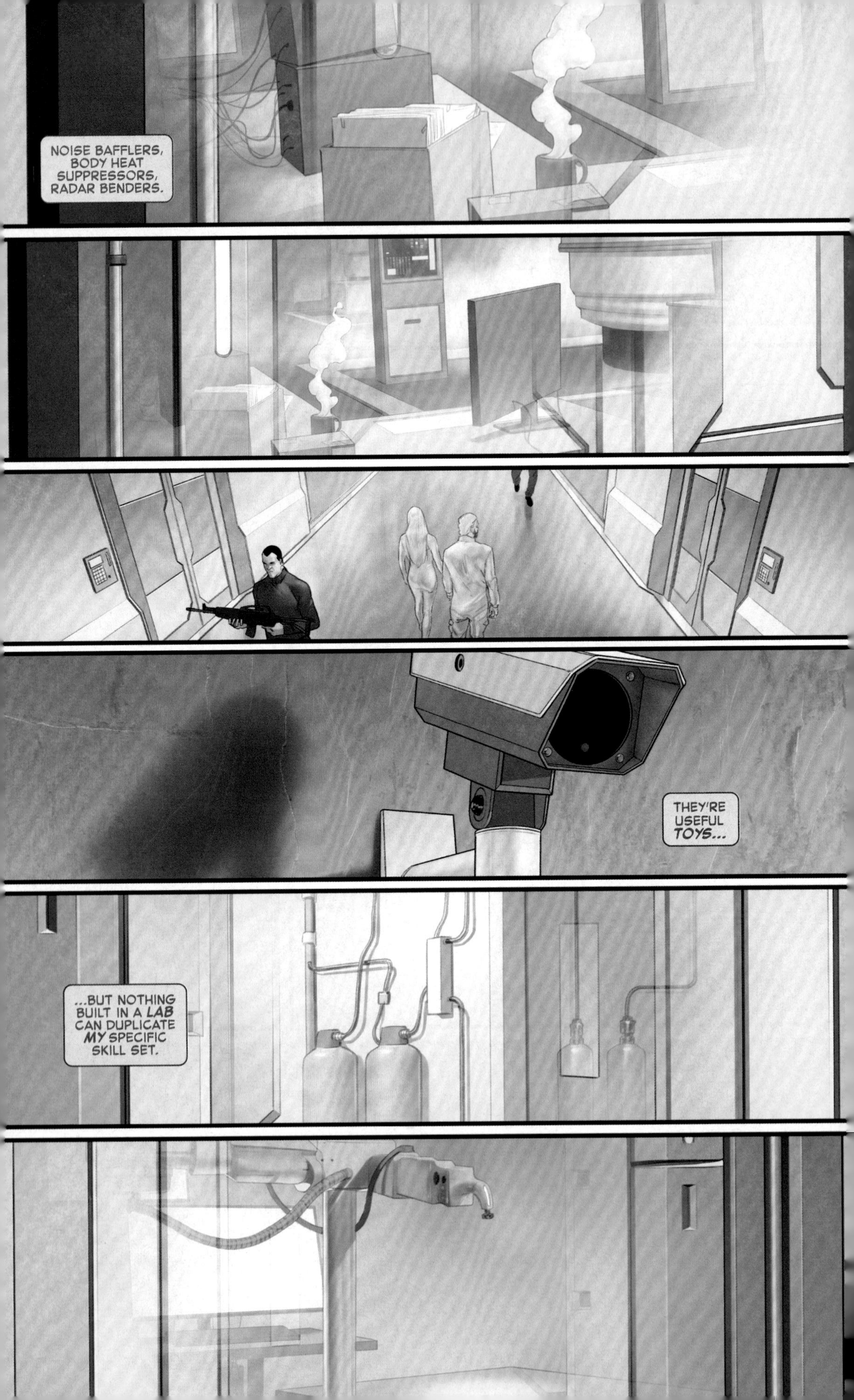
NOISE BAFFLERS, BODY HEAT SUPPRESSORS, RADAR BENDERS.
THEY'RE USEFUL *TOYS*...
...BUT NOTHING BUILT IN A *LAB* CAN DUPLICATE *MY* SPECIFIC SKILL SET.

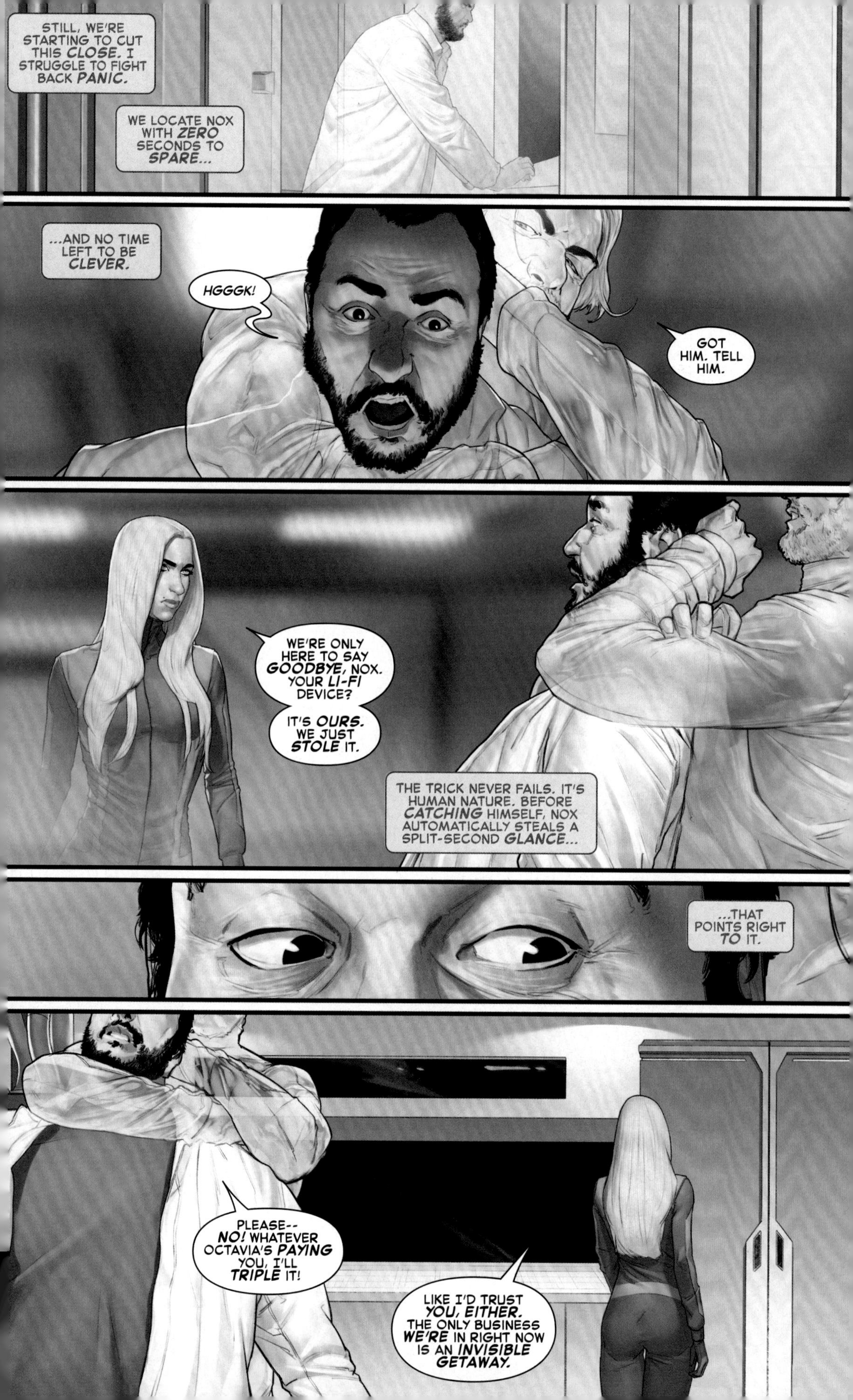
STILL, WE'RE STARTING TO CUT THIS CLOSE. I STRUGGLE TO FIGHT BACK PANIC.
WE LOCATE NOX WITH ZERO SECONDS TO SPARE...
...AND NO TIME LEFT TO BE CLEVER.
HGGGK!
GOT HIM. TELL HIM.
WE'RE ONLY HERE TO SAY GOODBYE, NOX. YOUR LI-FI DEVICE?
IT'S OURS. WE JUST STOLE IT.
THE TRICK NEVER FAILS. IT'S HUMAN NATURE. BEFORE CATCHING HIMSELF, NOX AUTOMATICALLY STEALS A SPLIT-SECOND GLANCE...
...THAT POINTS RIGHT TO IT.
PLEASE-- NO! WHATEVER OCTAVIA'S PAYING YOU, I'LL TRIPLE IT!
LIKE I'D TRUST YOU, EITHER. THE ONLY BUSINESS WE'RE IN RIGHT NOW IS AN INVISIBLE GETAWAY.

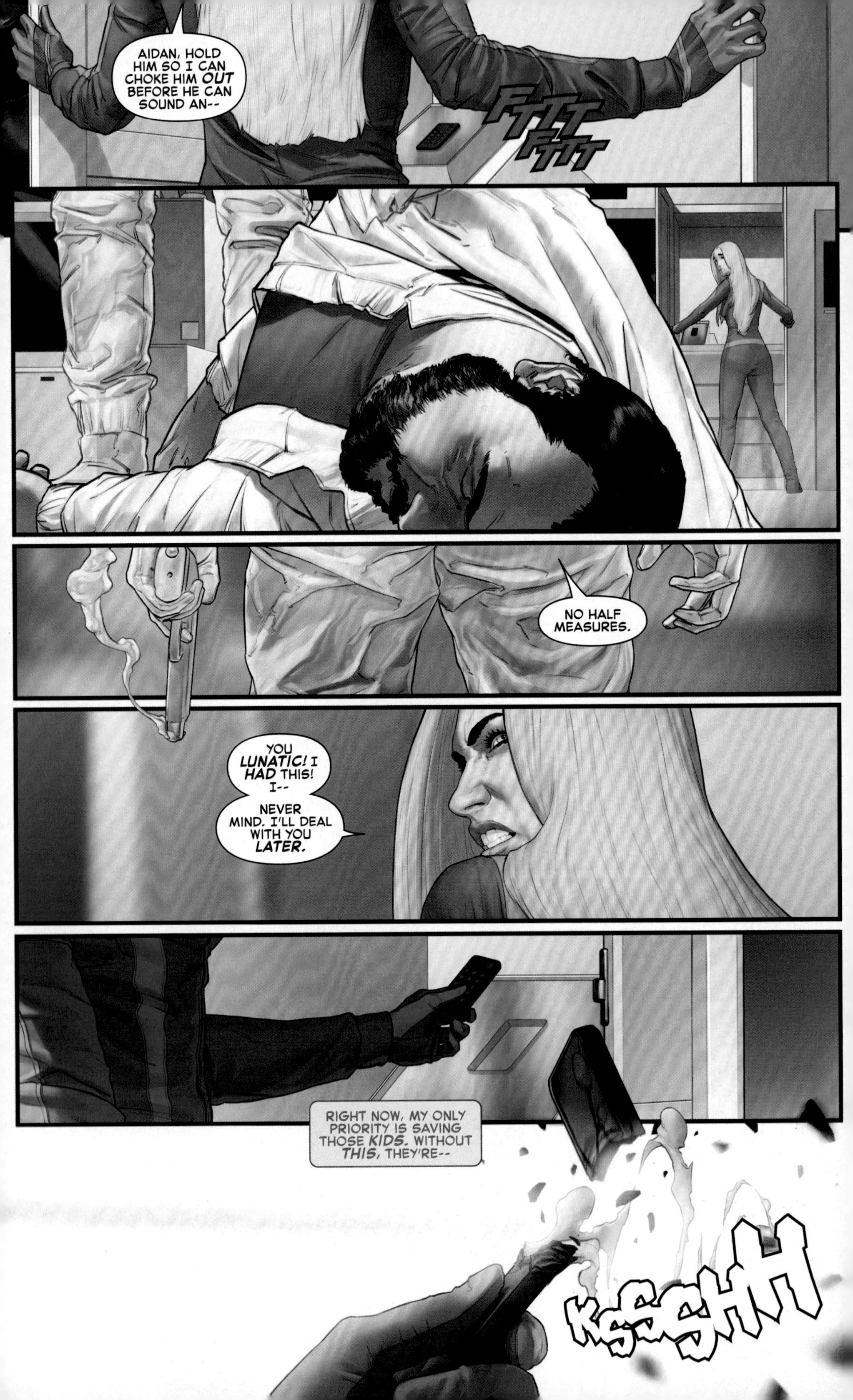
AIDAN, HOLD HIM SO I CAN CHOKE HIM OUT BEFORE HE CAN SOUND AN--
FTTT FTTT
NO HALF MEASURES.
YOU LUNATIC! I HAD THIS! I--
NEVER MIND. I'LL DEAL WITH YOU LATER.
RIGHT NOW, MY ONLY PRIORITY IS SAVING THOSE KIDS. WITHOUT THIS, THEY'RE--
KSSSHH

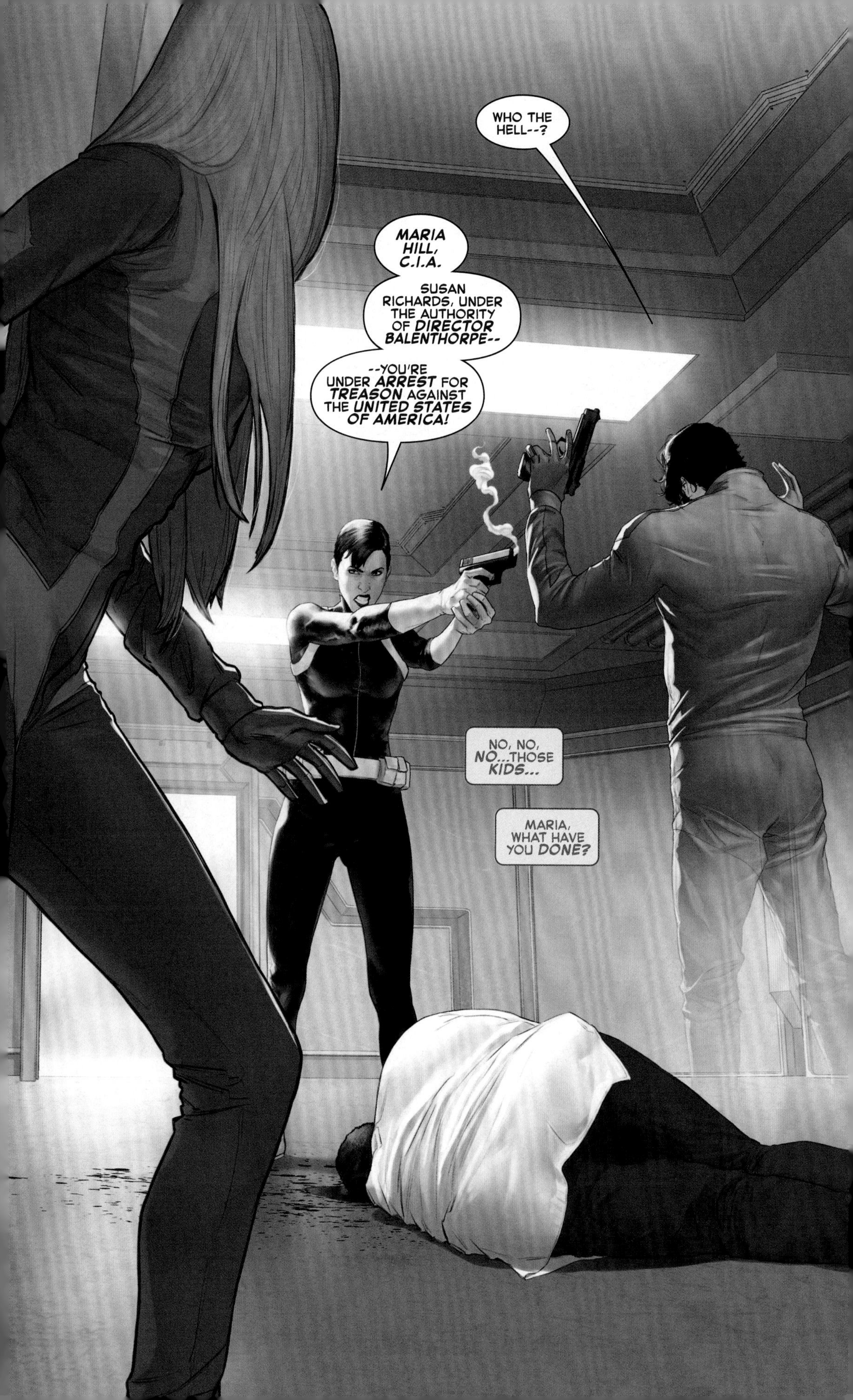
WHO THE HELL--?
MARIA HILL, C.I.A.
SUSAN RICHARDS, UNDER THE AUTHORITY OF DIRECTOR BALENTHORPE--
--YOU'RE UNDER ARREST FOR TREASON AGAINST THE UNITED STATES OF AMERICA!
NO, NO, NO...THOSE KIDS...
MARIA, WHAT HAVE YOU DONE?

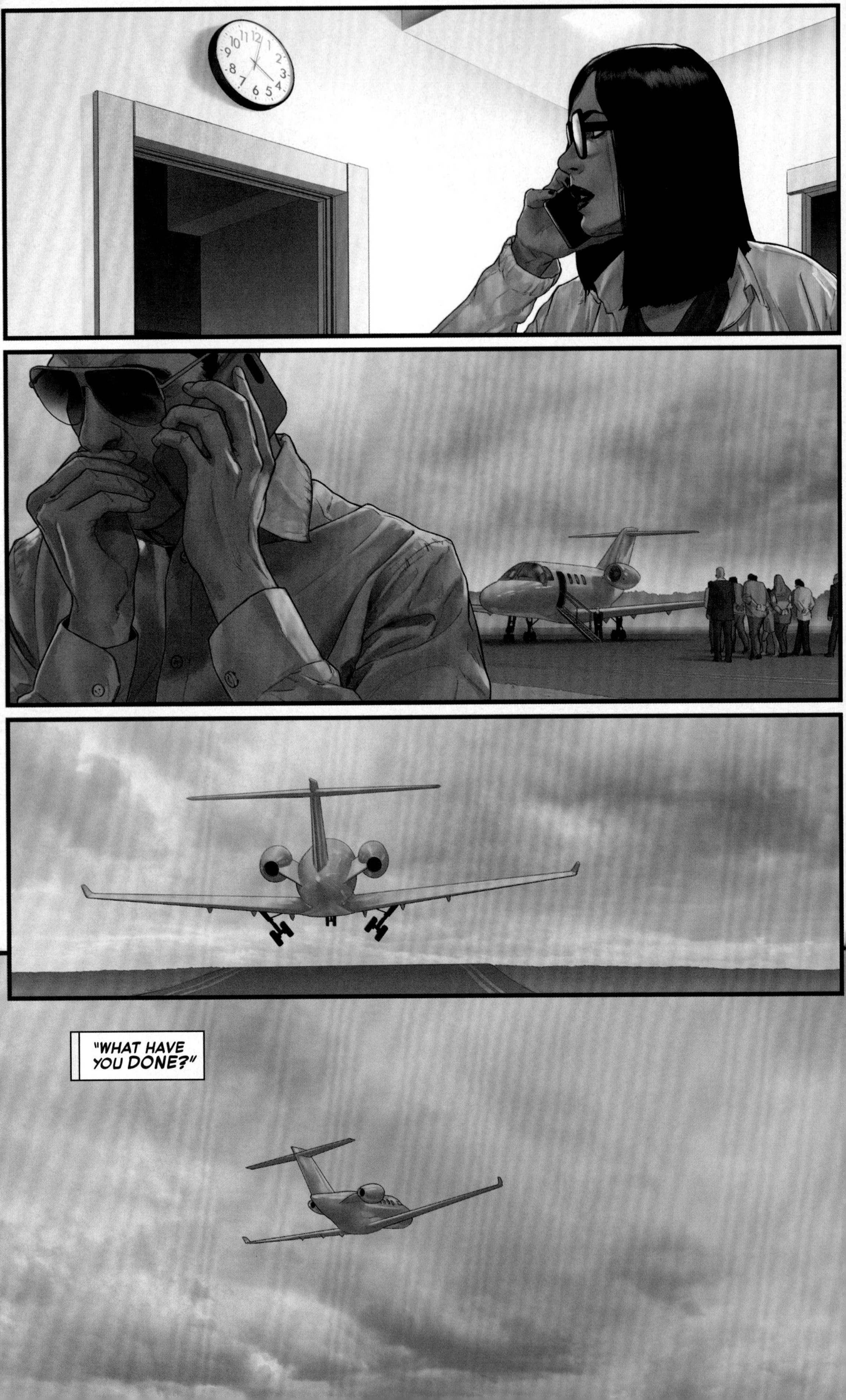
"WHAT HAVE YOU DONE?"

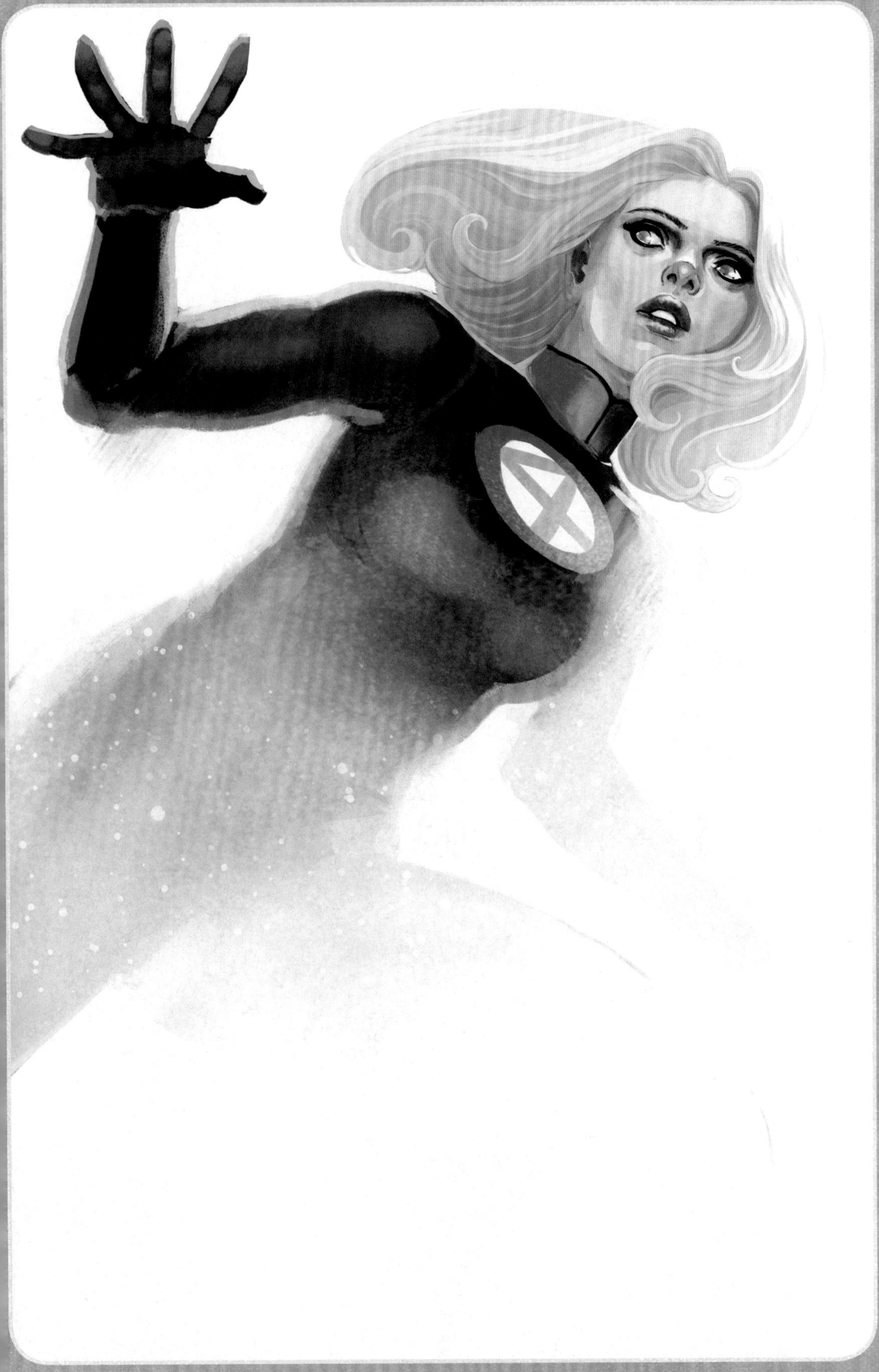

STEPHANIE HANS
1 VARIANT

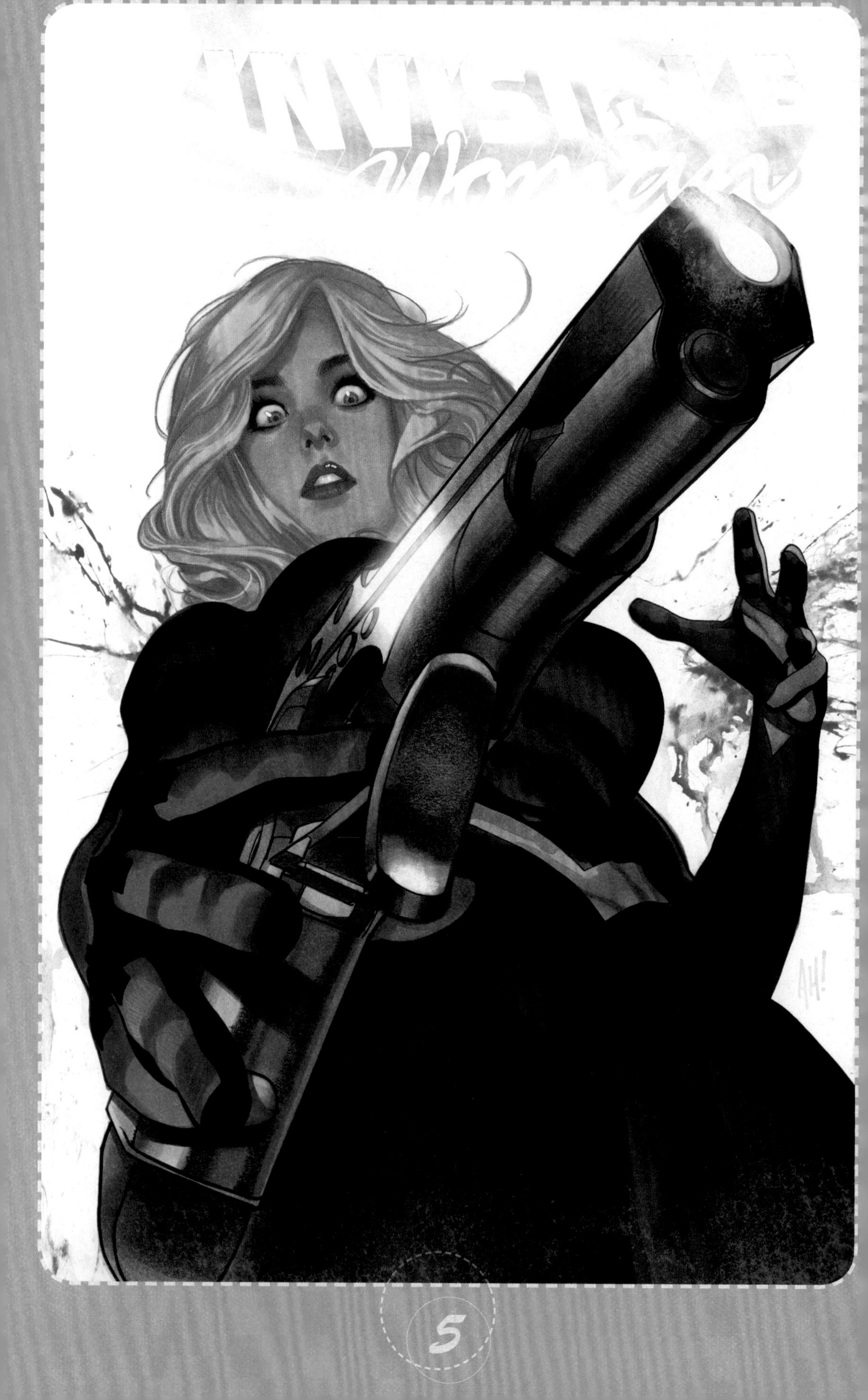
AH!

5

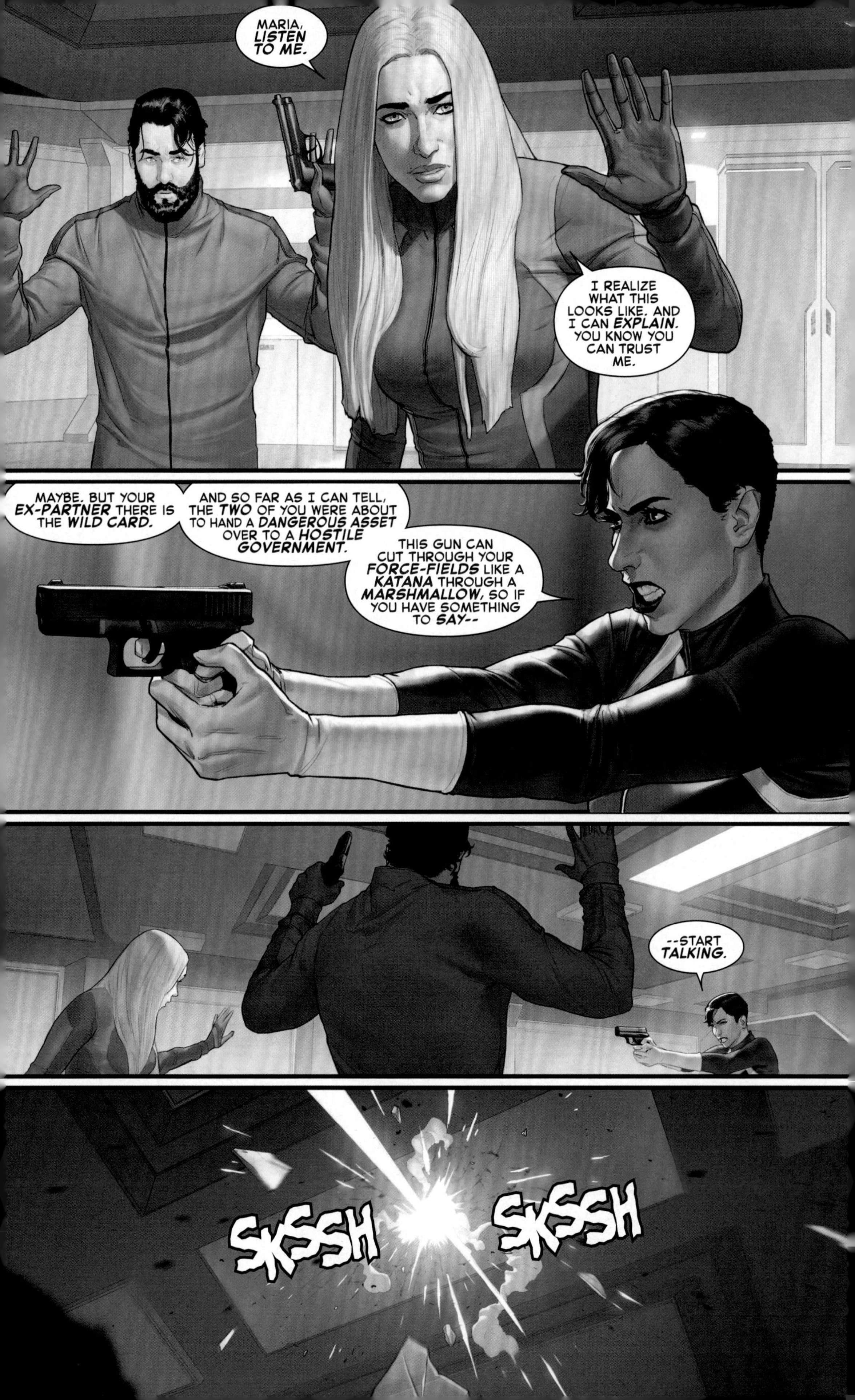
MARIA, LISTEN TO ME.
I REALIZE WHAT THIS LOOKS LIKE. AND I CAN EXPLAIN. YOU KNOW YOU CAN TRUST ME.
MAYBE. BUT YOUR EX-PARTNER THERE IS THE WILD CARD.
AND SO FAR AS I CAN TELL, THE TWO OF YOU WERE ABOUT TO HAND A DANGEROUS ASSET OVER TO A HOSTILE GOVERNMENT.
THIS GUN CAN CUT THROUGH YOUR FORCE-FIELDS LIKE A KATANA THROUGH A MARSHMALLOW, SO IF YOU HAVE SOMETHING TO SAY--
--START TALKING.
SKSSH
SKSSH

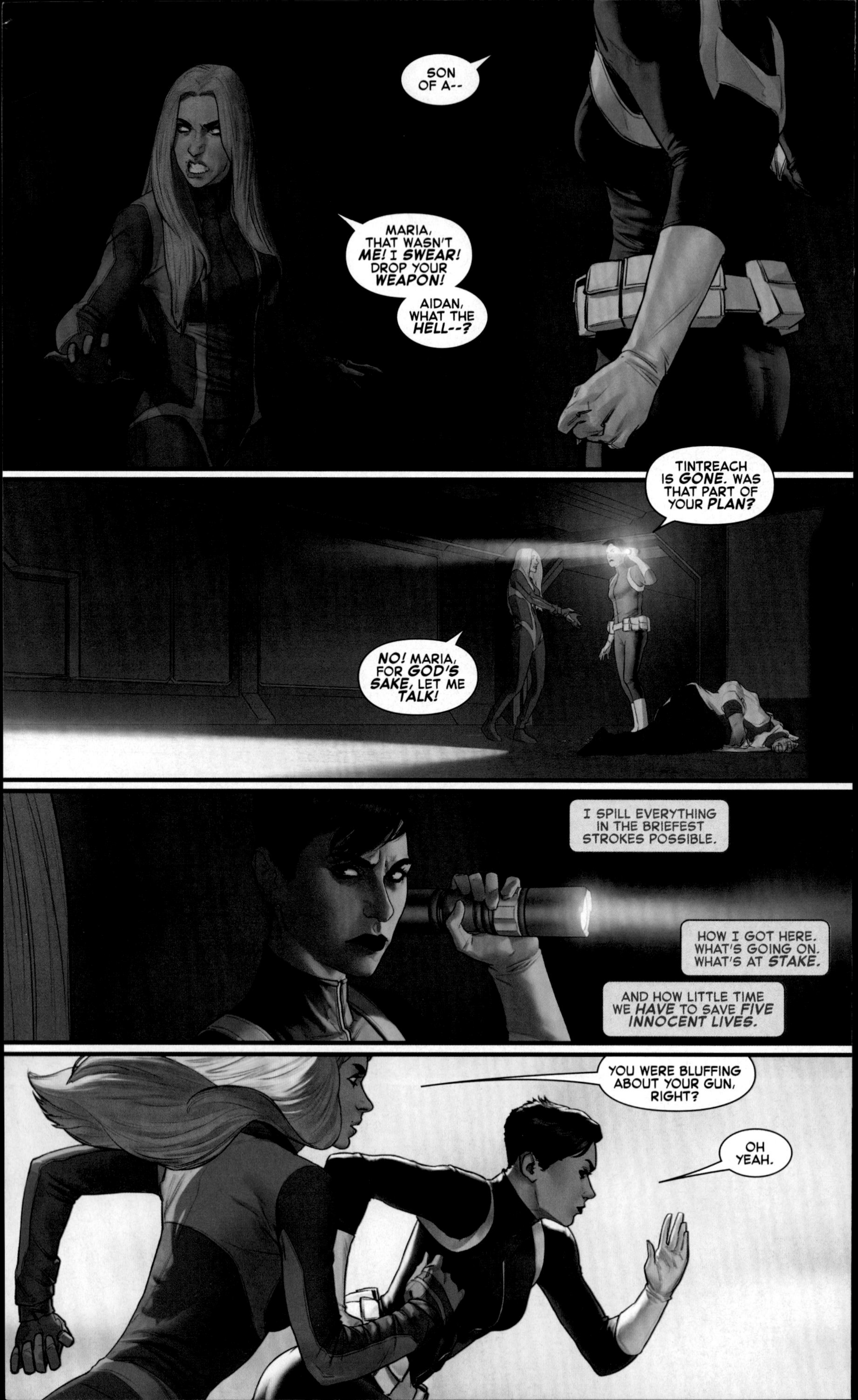
SON OF A--
MARIA, THAT WASN'T ME! I SWEAR! DROP YOUR WEAPON!
AIDAN, WHAT THE HELL--?
TINTREACH IS GONE. WAS THAT PART OF YOUR PLAN?
NO! MARIA, FOR GOD'S SAKE, LET ME TALK!
I SPILL EVERYTHING IN THE BRIEFEST STROKES POSSIBLE.
HOW I GOT HERE. WHAT'S GOING ON. WHAT'S AT STAKE.
AND HOW LITTLE TIME WE HAVE TO SAVE FIVE INNOCENT LIVES.
YOU WERE BLUFFING ABOUT YOUR GUN, RIGHT?
OH YEAH.

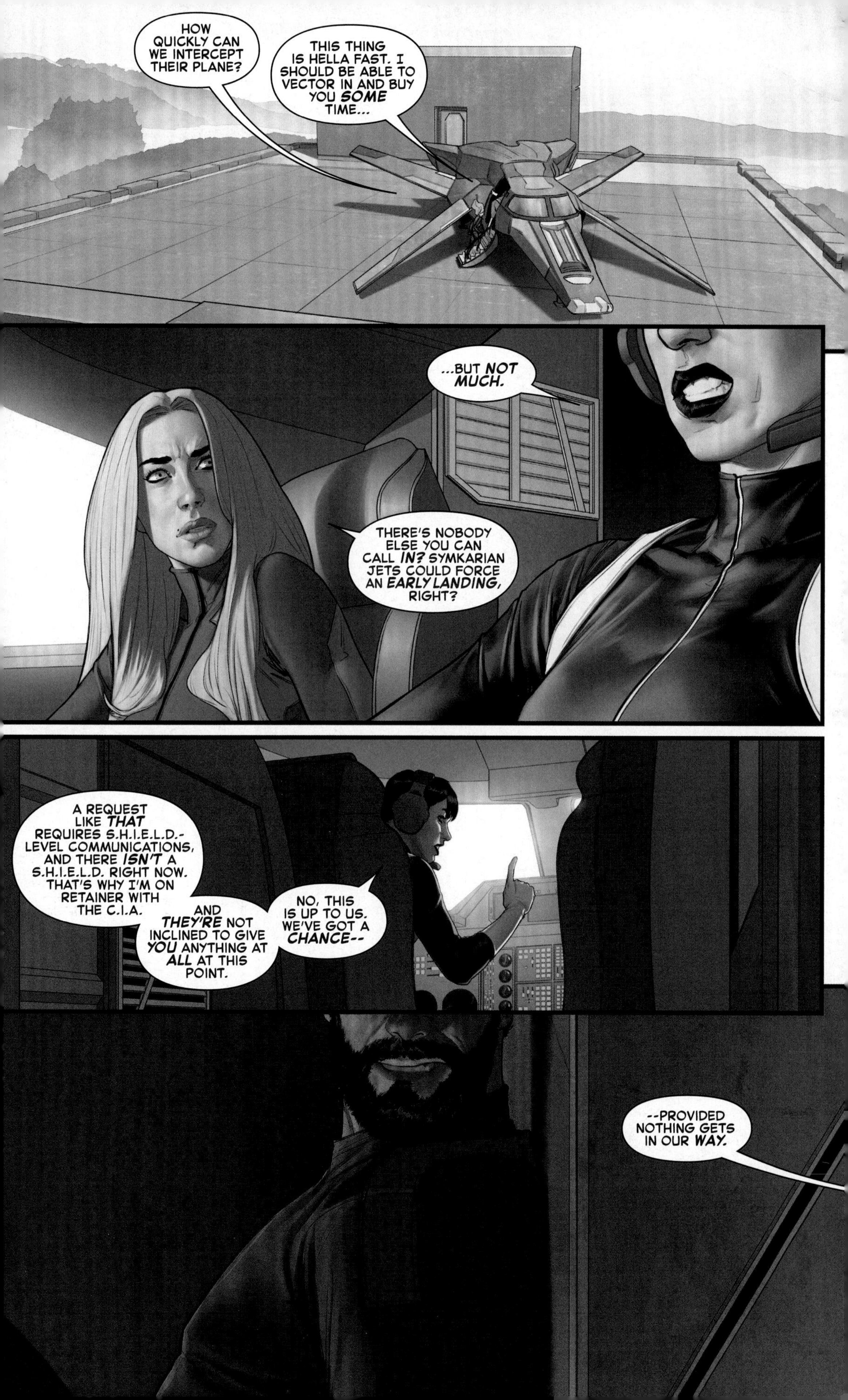
HOW QUICKLY CAN WE INTERCEPT THEIR PLANE?
THIS THING IS HELLA FAST. I SHOULD BE ABLE TO VECTOR IN AND BUY YOU SOME TIME...
...BUT NOT MUCH.
THERE'S NOBODY ELSE YOU CAN CALL IN? SYMKARIAN JETS COULD FORCE AN EARLY LANDING, RIGHT?
A REQUEST LIKE THAT REQUIRES S.H.I.E.L.D.-LEVEL COMMUNICATIONS, AND THERE ISN'T A S.H.I.E.L.D. RIGHT NOW. THAT'S WHY I'M ON RETAINER WITH THE C.I.A.
AND THEY'RE NOT INCLINED TO GIVE YOU ANYTHING AT ALL AT THIS POINT.
NO, THIS IS UP TO US. WE'VE GOT A CHANCE--
--PROVIDED NOTHING GETS IN OUR WAY.

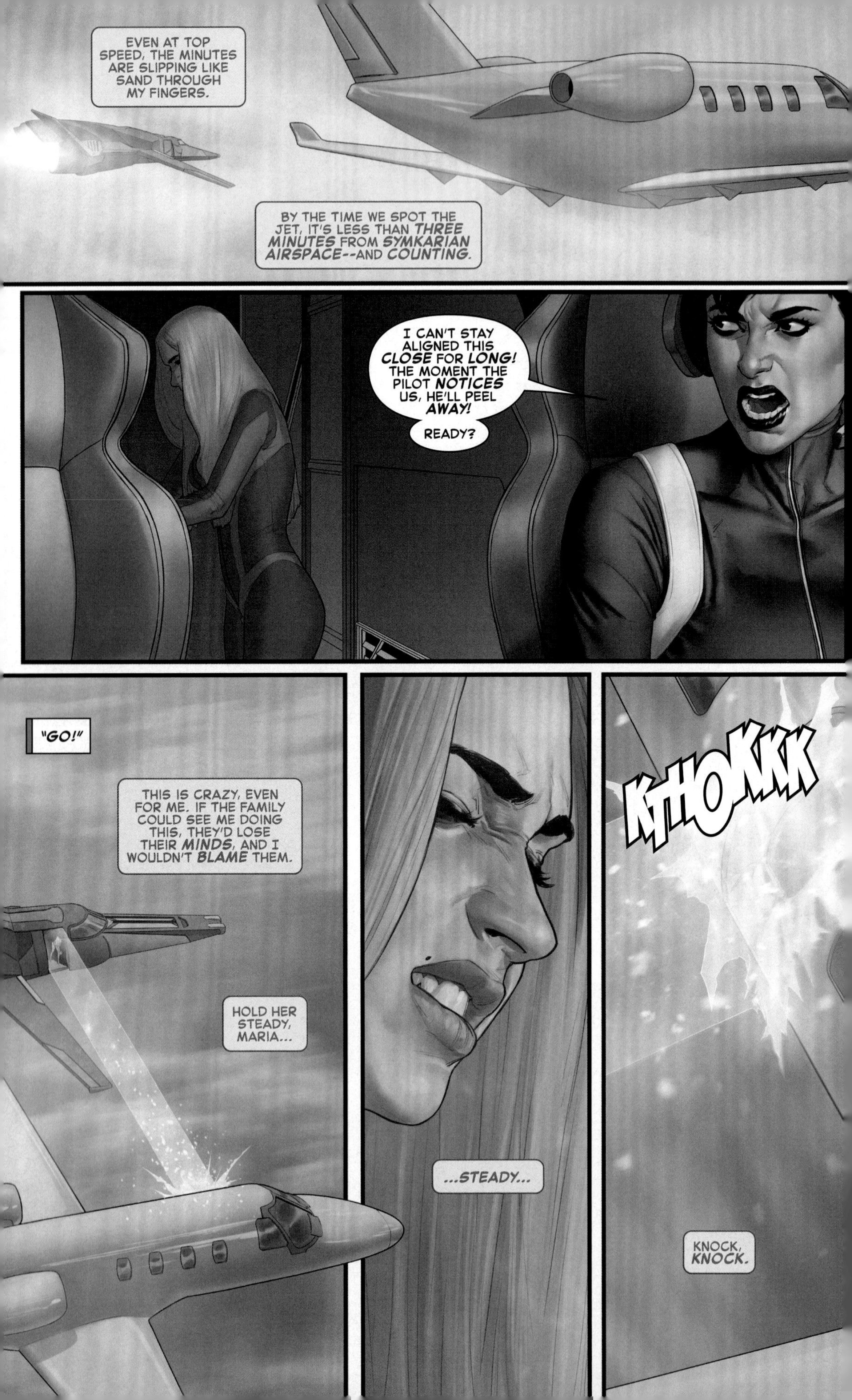
EVEN AT TOP SPEED, THE MINUTES ARE SLIPPING LIKE SAND THROUGH MY FINGERS.
BY THE TIME WE SPOT THE JET, IT'S LESS THAN *THREE MINUTES* FROM *SYMKARIAN AIRSPACE*--AND *COUNTING*.
I CAN'T STAY ALIGNED THIS *CLOSE* FOR *LONG!* THE MOMENT THE PILOT *NOTICES* US, HE'LL PEEL *AWAY!*
READY?
"GO!"
THIS IS CRAZY, EVEN FOR ME. IF THE FAMILY COULD SEE ME DOING THIS, THEY'D LOSE THEIR *MINDS*, AND I WOULDN'T *BLAME* THEM.
HOLD HER STEADY, MARIA...
...STEADY...
KTHOKKK
KNOCK, *KNOCK.*

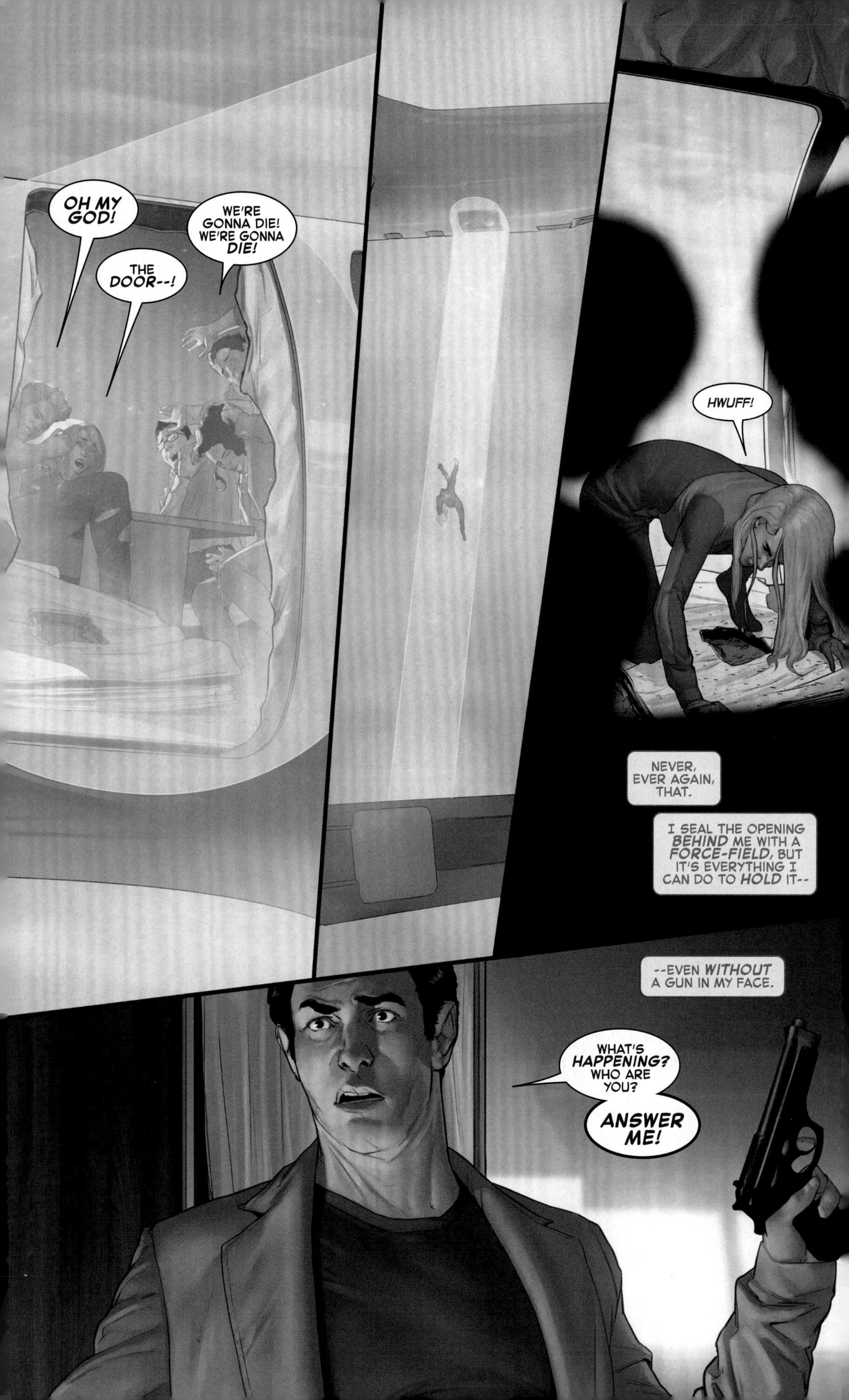
OH MY GOD!
THE DOOR--!
WE'RE GONNA DIE! WE'RE GONNA DIE!
HWUFF!
NEVER, EVER AGAIN, THAT.
I SEAL THE OPENING BEHIND ME WITH A FORCE-FIELD, BUT IT'S EVERYTHING I CAN DO TO HOLD IT--
--EVEN WITHOUT A GUN IN MY FACE.
WHAT'S HAPPENING? WHO ARE YOU?
ANSWER ME!

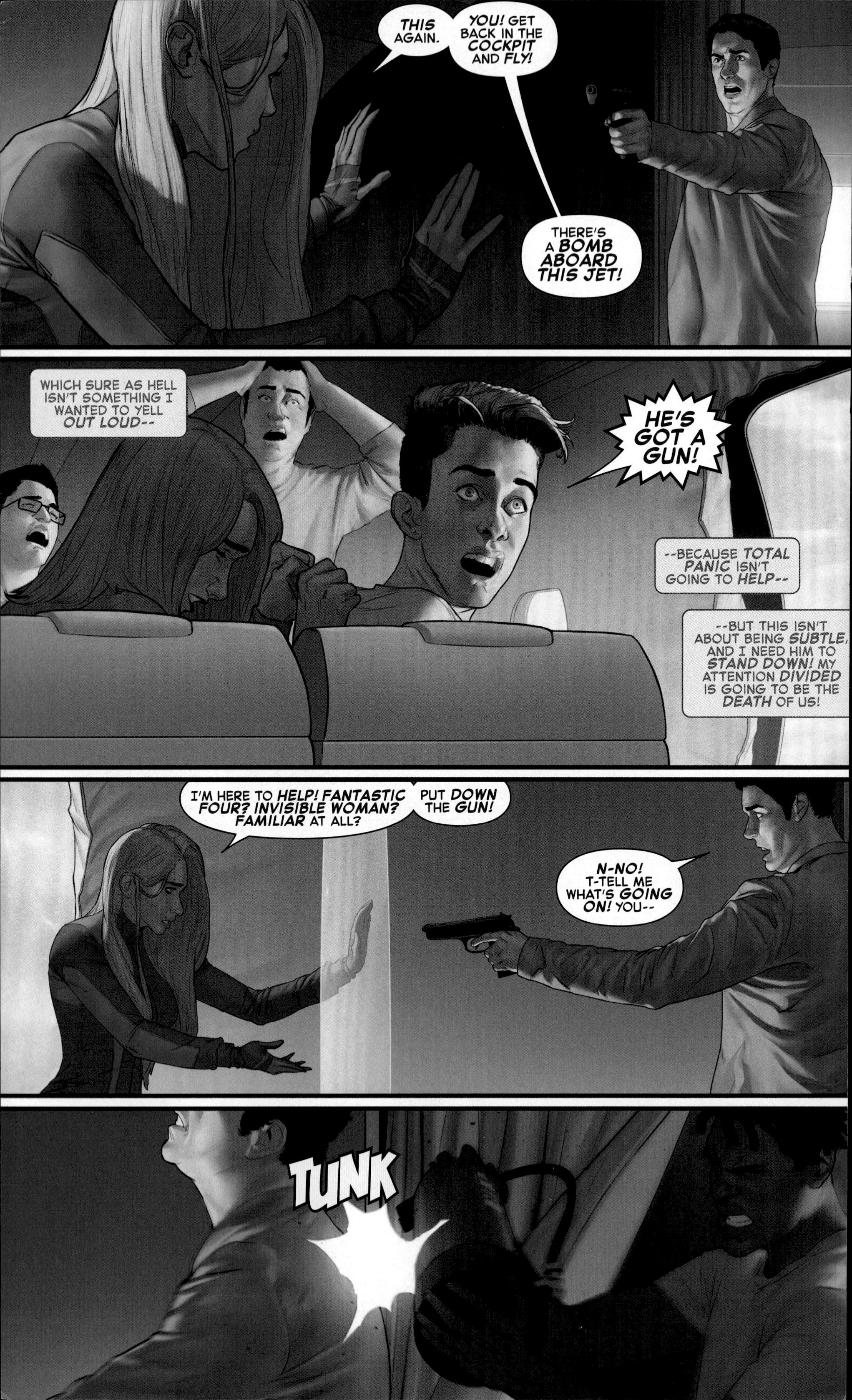
THIS AGAIN.
YOU! GET BACK IN THE COCKPIT AND FLY!
THERE'S A BOMB ABOARD THIS JET!
WHICH SURE AS HELL ISN'T SOMETHING I WANTED TO YELL OUT LOUD--
HE'S GOT A GUN!
--BECAUSE TOTAL PANIC ISN'T GOING TO HELP--
--BUT THIS ISN'T ABOUT BEING SUBTLE, AND I NEED HIM TO STAND DOWN! MY ATTENTION DIVIDED IS GOING TO BE THE DEATH OF US!
I'M HERE TO HELP! FANTASTIC FOUR? INVISIBLE WOMAN? FAMILIAR AT ALL?
PUT DOWN THE GUN!
N-NO! T-TELL ME WHAT'S GOING ON! YOU--
TUNK

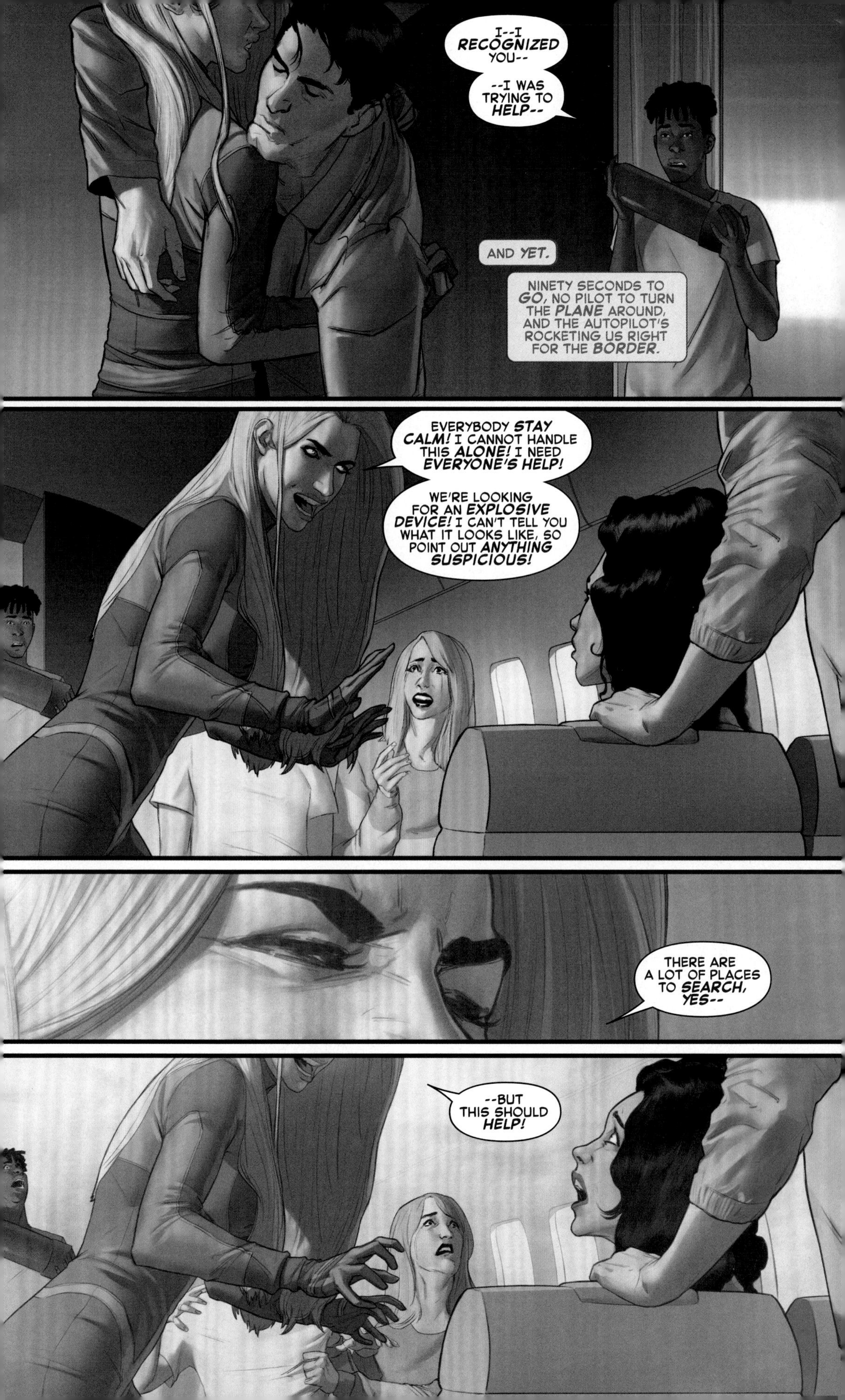
I--I RECOGNIZED YOU--
--I WAS TRYING TO HELP--
AND YET.
NINETY SECONDS TO GO, NO PILOT TO TURN THE PLANE AROUND, AND THE AUTOPILOT'S ROCKETING US RIGHT FOR THE BORDER.
EVERYBODY STAY CALM! I CANNOT HANDLE THIS ALONE! I NEED EVERYONE'S HELP!
WE'RE LOOKING FOR AN EXPLOSIVE DEVICE! I CAN'T TELL YOU WHAT IT LOOKS LIKE, SO POINT OUT ANYTHING SUSPICIOUS!
THERE ARE A LOT OF PLACES TO SEARCH, YES--
--BUT THIS SHOULD HELP!

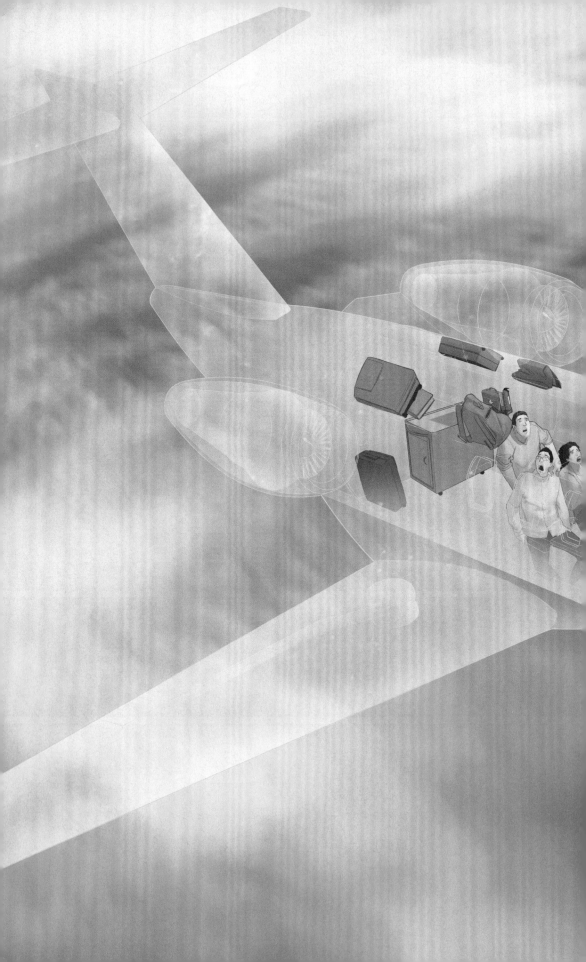

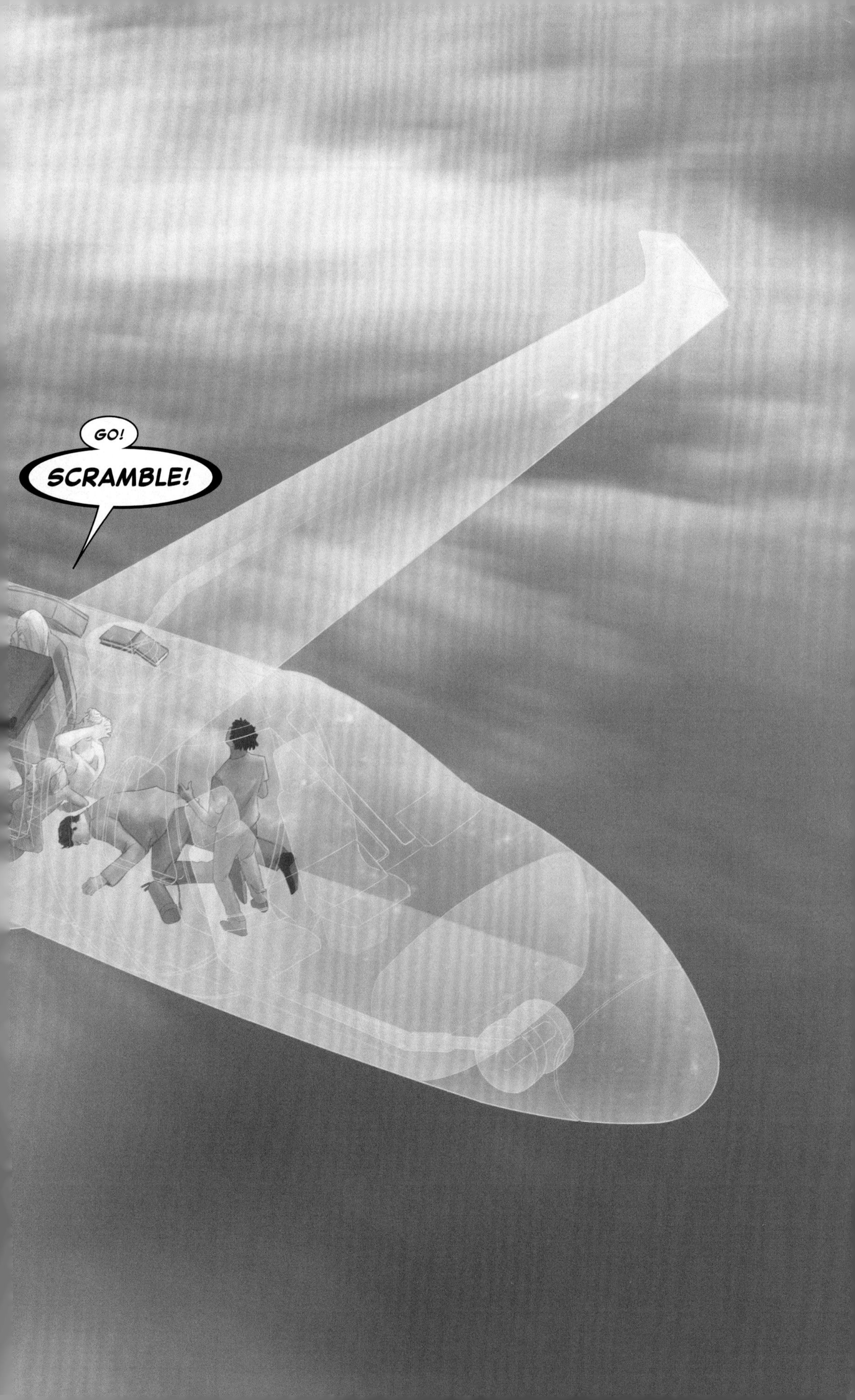
GO!
SCRAMBLE!

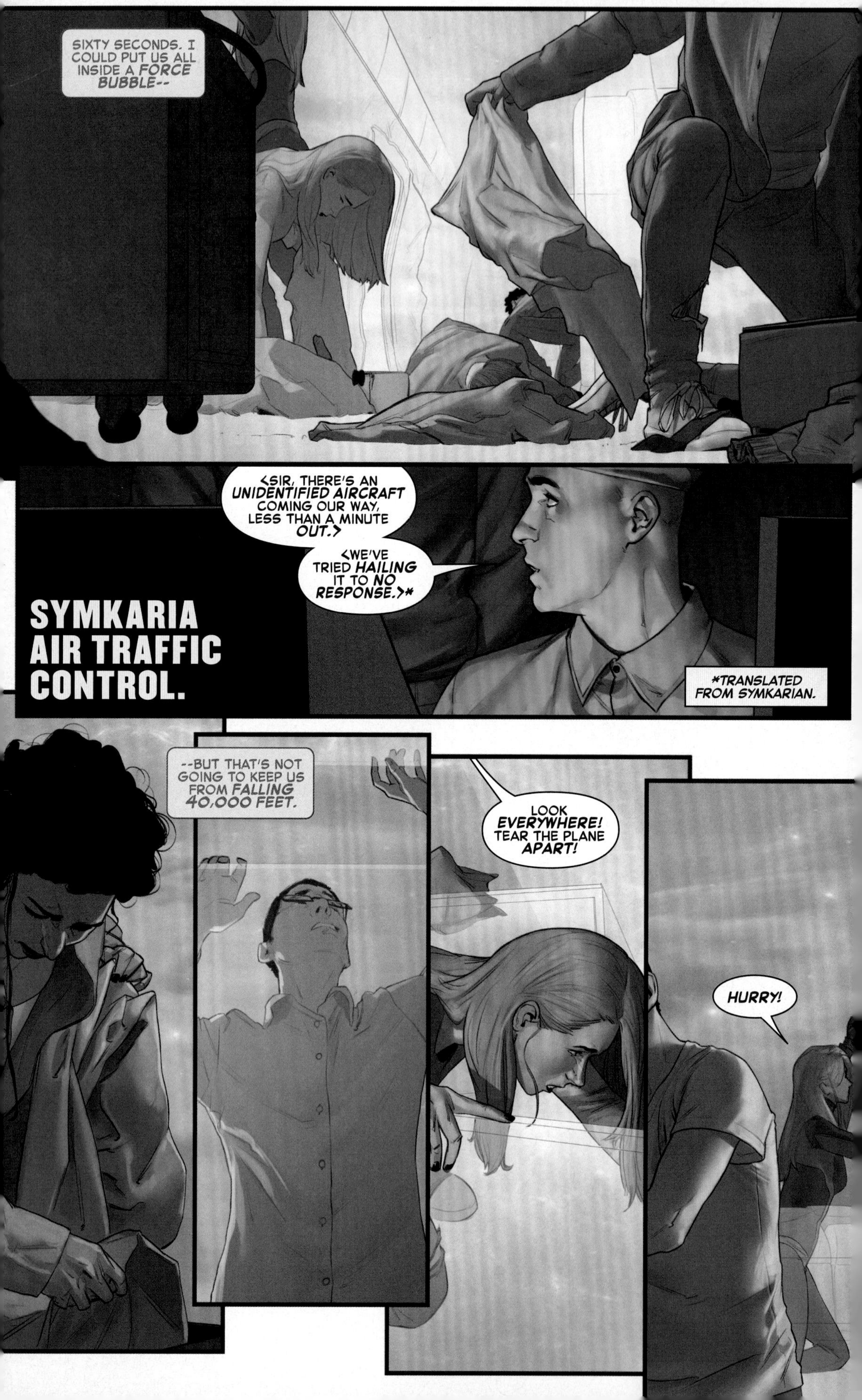
SIXTY SECONDS. I COULD PUT US ALL INSIDE A FORCE BUBBLE--
<SIR, THERE'S AN UNIDENTIFIED AIRCRAFT COMING OUR WAY, LESS THAN A MINUTE OUT.>
<WE'VE TRIED HAILING IT TO NO RESPONSE.>*
SYMKARIA AIR TRAFFIC CONTROL.
*TRANSLATED FROM SYMKARIAN.
--BUT THAT'S NOT GOING TO KEEP US FROM FALLING 40,000 FEET.
LOOK EVERYWHERE! TEAR THE PLANE APART!
HURRY!

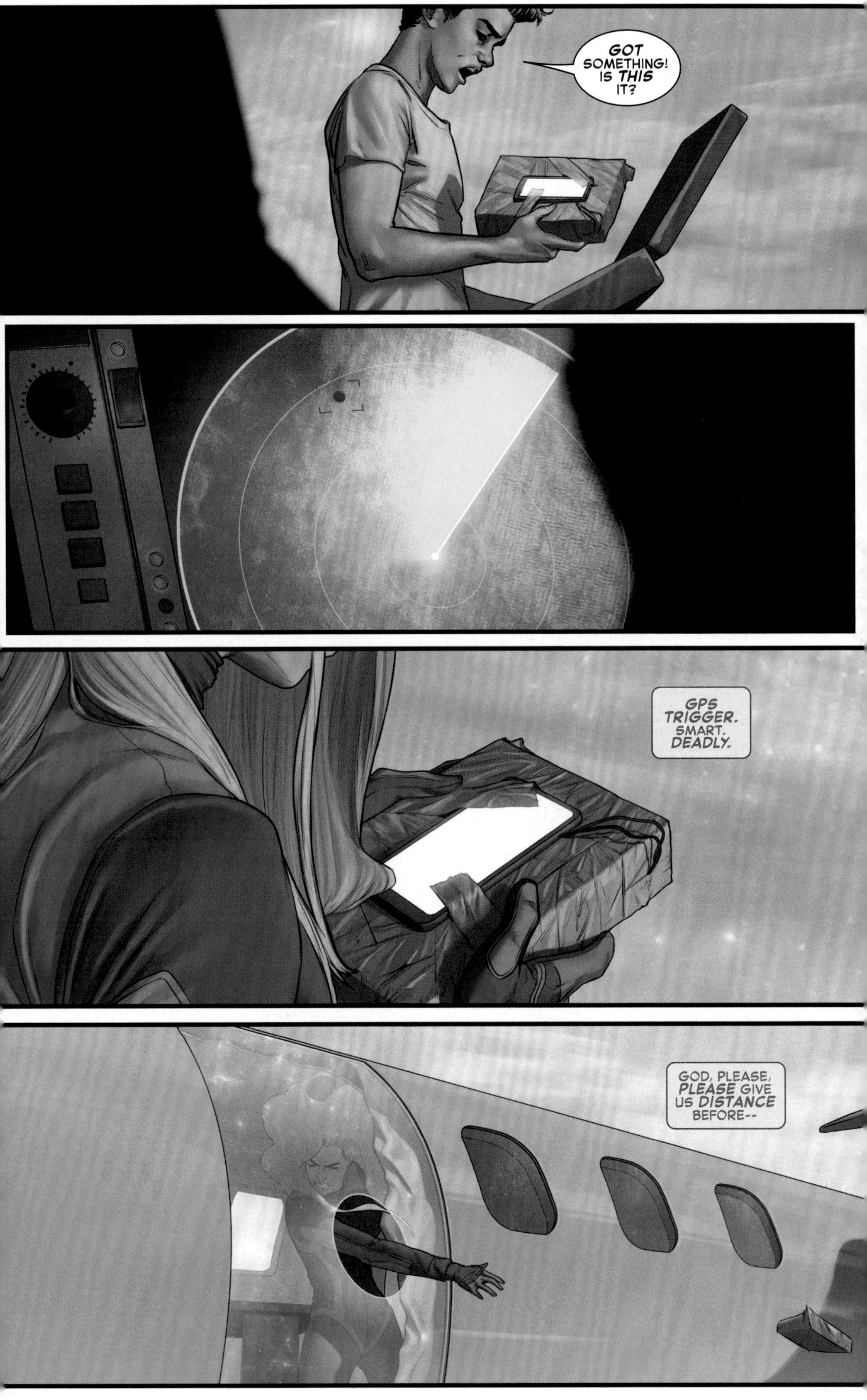
GOT SOMETHING! IS THIS IT?
GPS TRIGGER. SMART. DEADLY.
GOD, PLEASE, PLEASE GIVE US DISTANCE BEFORE--

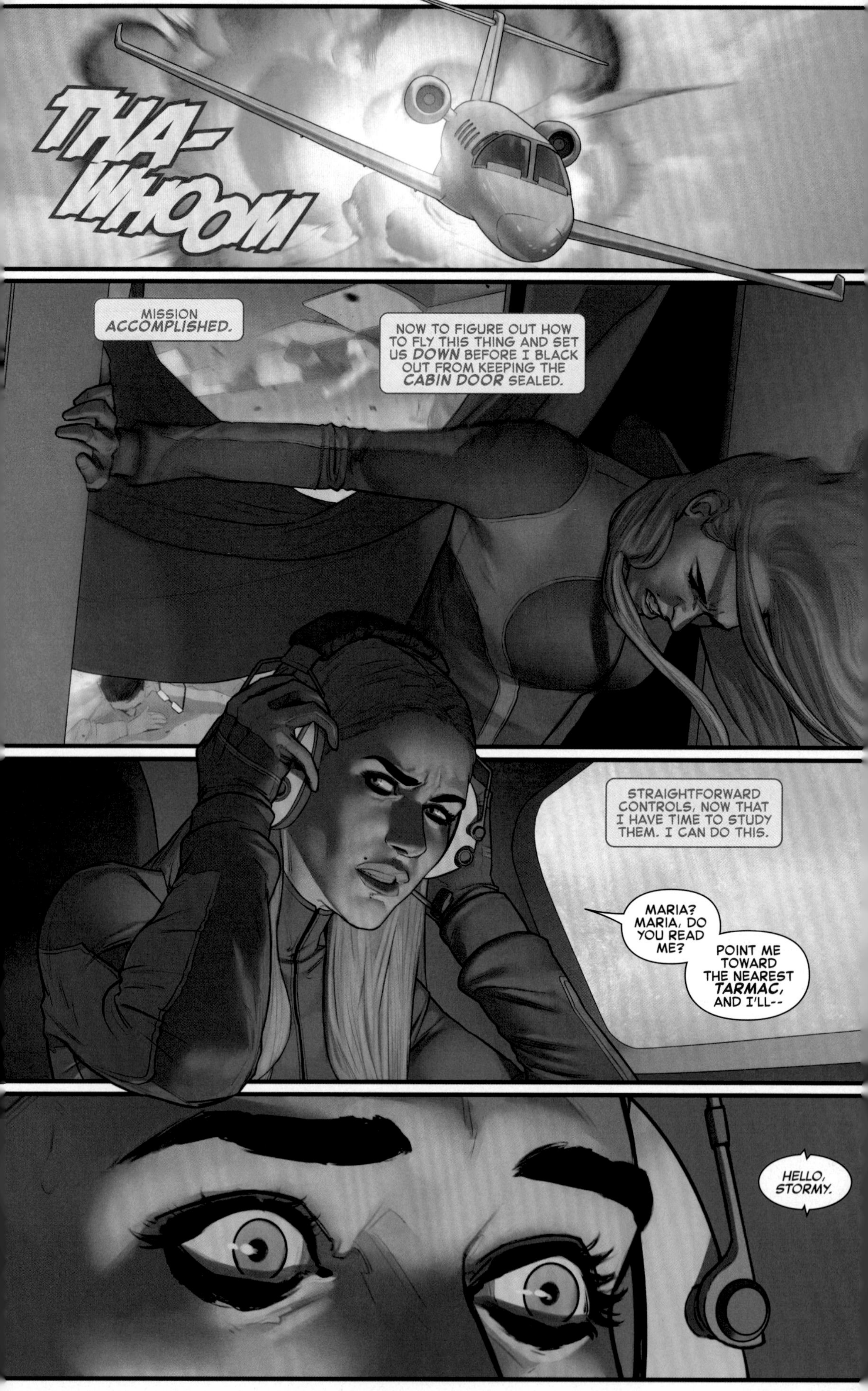
THA-WHOOM
MISSION ACCOMPLISHED.
NOW TO FIGURE OUT HOW TO FLY THIS THING AND SET US DOWN BEFORE I BLACK OUT FROM KEEPING THE CABIN DOOR SEALED.
STRAIGHTFORWARD CONTROLS, NOW THAT I HAVE TIME TO STUDY THEM. I CAN DO THIS.
MARIA? MARIA, DO YOU READ ME?
POINT ME TOWARD THE NEAREST TARMAC, AND I'LL--
HELLO, STORMY.

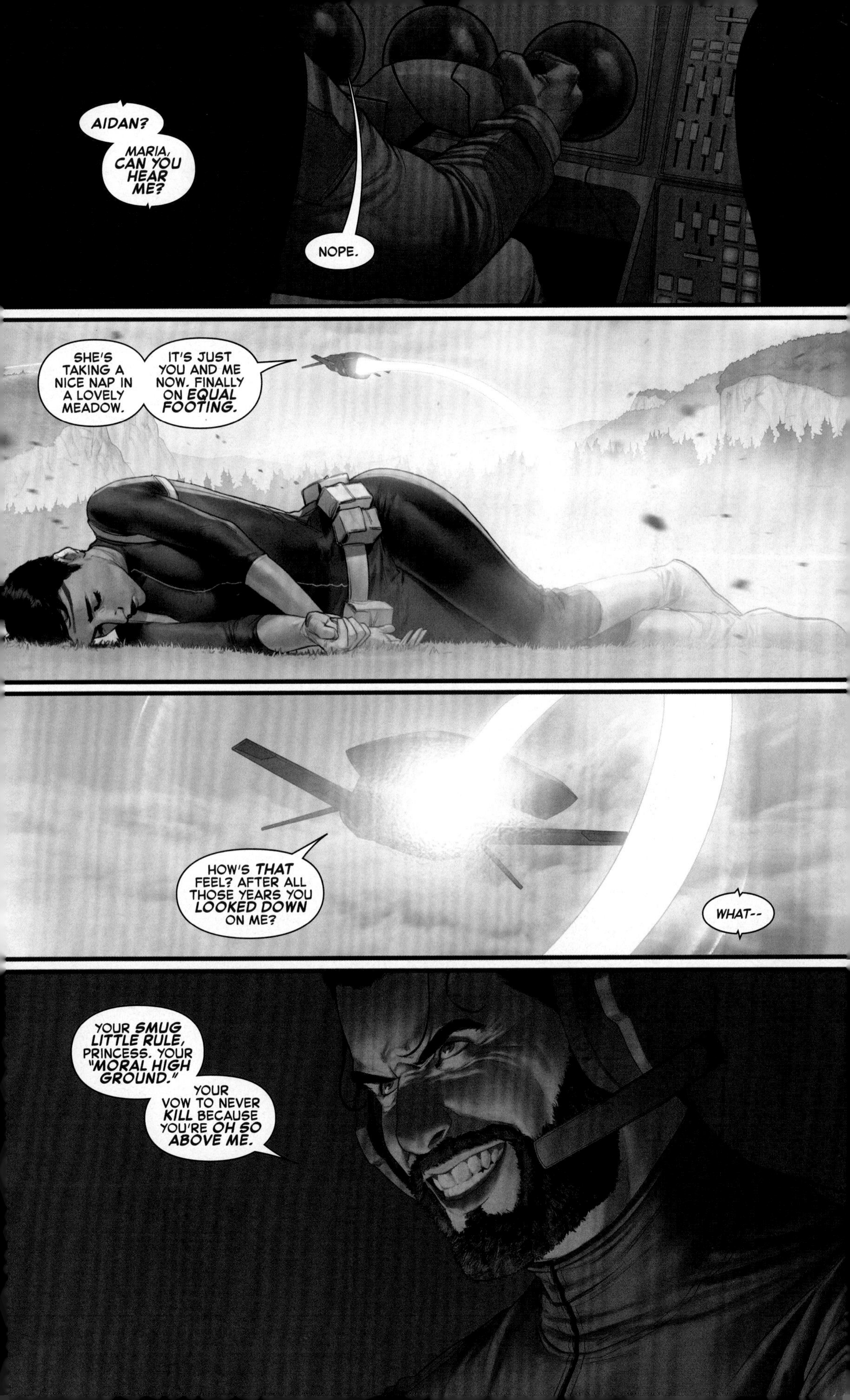
AIDAN?
MARIA, CAN YOU HEAR ME?
NOPE.
SHE'S TAKING A NICE NAP IN A LOVELY MEADOW.
IT'S JUST YOU AND ME NOW. FINALLY ON EQUAL FOOTING.
HOW'S THAT FEEL? AFTER ALL THOSE YEARS YOU LOOKED DOWN ON ME?
WHAT--
YOUR SMUG LITTLE RULE, PRINCESS. YOUR "MORAL HIGH GROUND."
YOUR VOW TO NEVER KILL BECAUSE YOU'RE OH SO ABOVE ME.

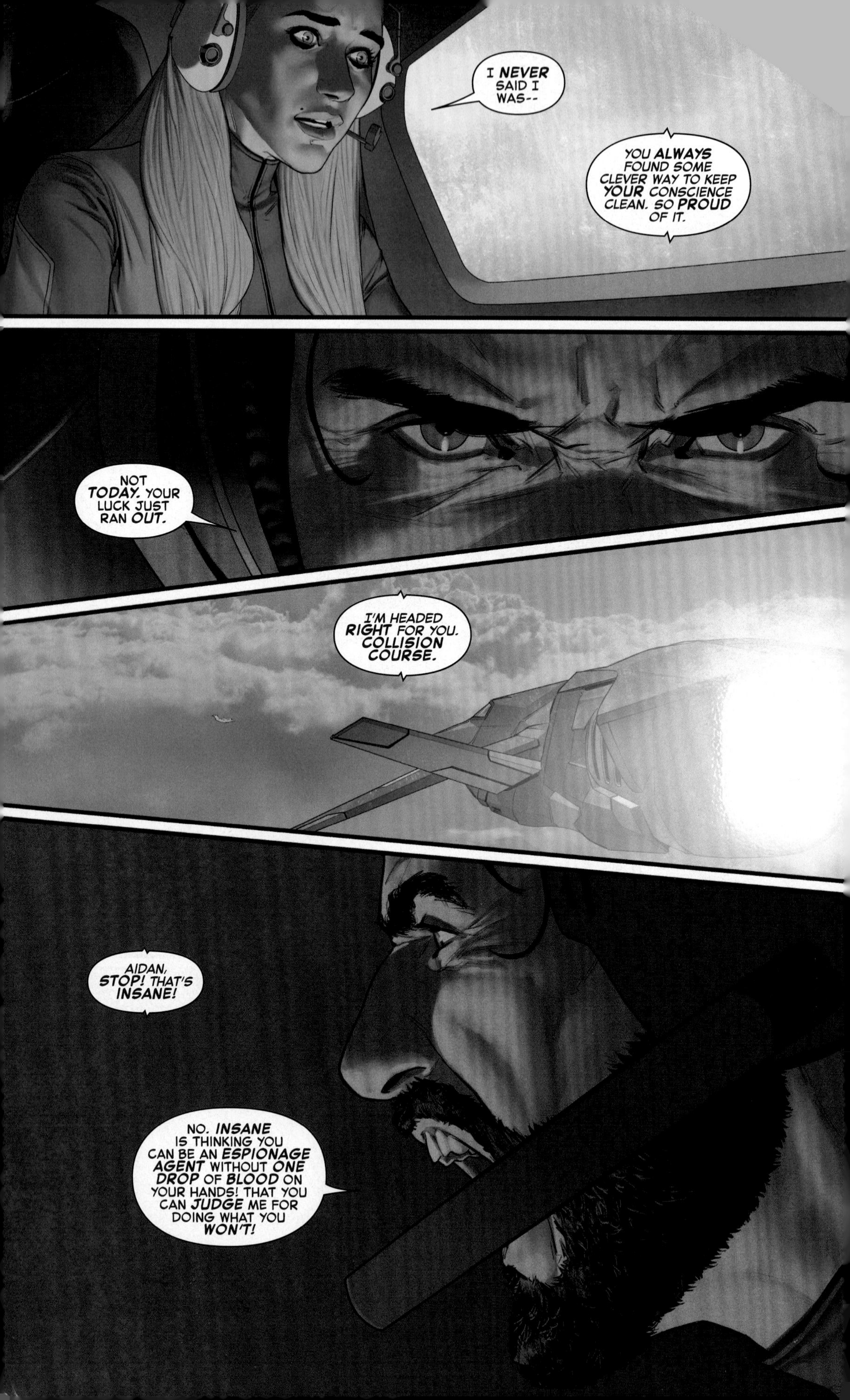
I NEVER SAID I WAS--
YOU ALWAYS FOUND SOME CLEVER WAY TO KEEP YOUR CONSCIENCE CLEAN. SO PROUD OF IT.
NOT TODAY. YOUR LUCK JUST RAN OUT.
I'M HEADED RIGHT FOR YOU. COLLISION COURSE.
AIDAN, STOP! THAT'S INSANE!
NO. INSANE IS THINKING YOU CAN BE AN ESPIONAGE AGENT WITHOUT ONE DROP OF BLOOD ON YOUR HANDS! THAT YOU CAN JUDGE ME FOR DOING WHAT YOU WON'T!

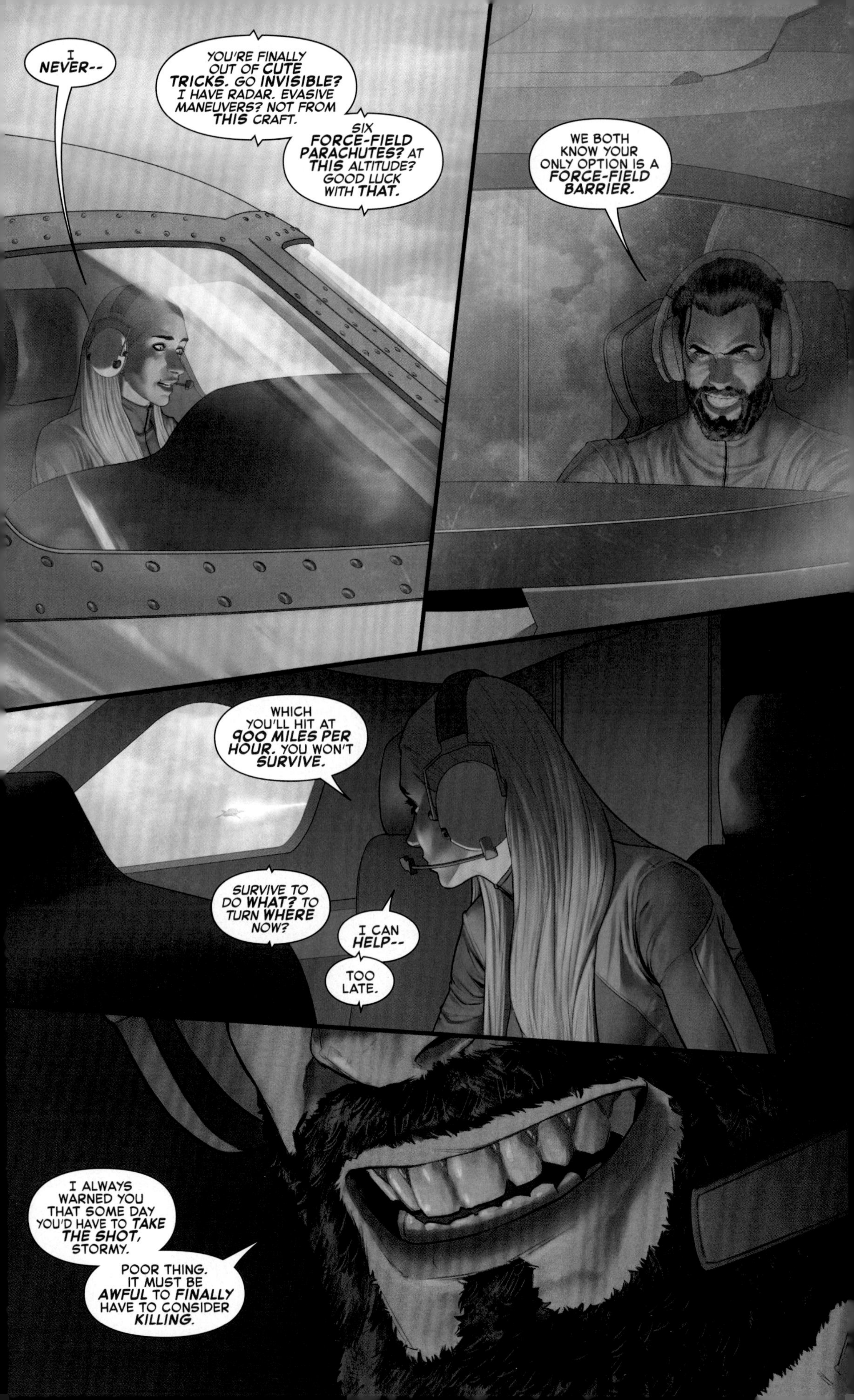
I NEVER--
YOU'RE FINALLY OUT OF CUTE TRICKS. GO INVISIBLE? I HAVE RADAR. EVASIVE MANEUVERS? NOT FROM THIS CRAFT.
SIX FORCE-FIELD PARACHUTES? AT THIS ALTITUDE? GOOD LUCK WITH THAT.
WE BOTH KNOW YOUR ONLY OPTION IS A FORCE-FIELD BARRIER.
WHICH YOU'LL HIT AT 900 MILES PER HOUR. YOU WON'T SURVIVE.
SURVIVE TO DO WHAT? TO TURN WHERE NOW?
I CAN HELP--
TOO LATE.
I ALWAYS WARNED YOU THAT SOME DAY YOU'D HAVE TO TAKE THE SHOT, STORMY.
POOR THING. IT MUST BE AWFUL TO FINALLY HAVE TO CONSIDER KILLING.

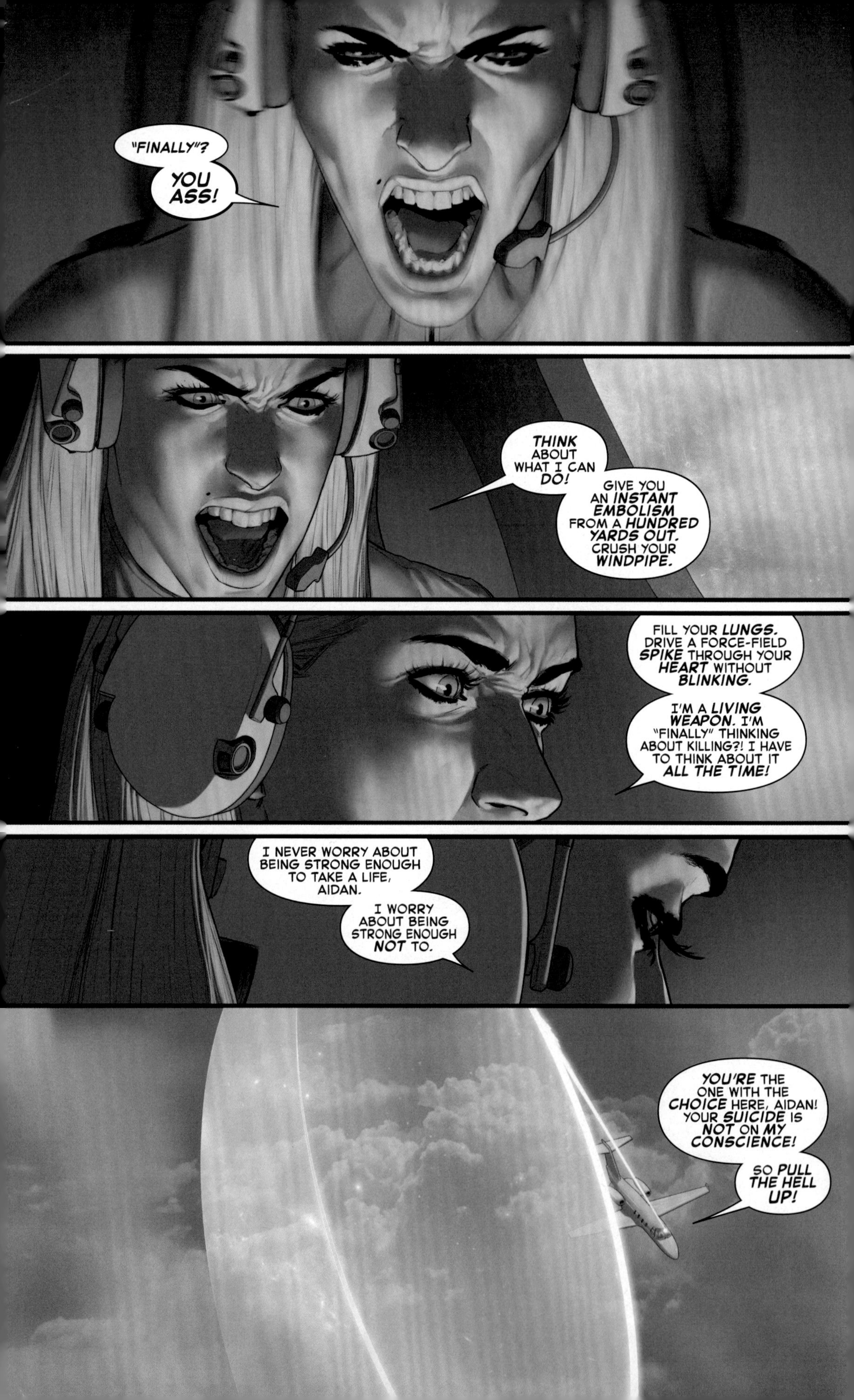
"FINALLY"?
YOU ASS!
THINK ABOUT WHAT I CAN DO!
GIVE YOU AN INSTANT EMBOLISM FROM A HUNDRED YARDS OUT. CRUSH YOUR WINDPIPE.
FILL YOUR LUNGS. DRIVE A FORCE-FIELD SPIKE THROUGH YOUR HEART WITHOUT BLINKING.
I'M A LIVING WEAPON. I'M "FINALLY" THINKING ABOUT KILLING?! I HAVE TO THINK ABOUT IT ALL THE TIME!
I NEVER WORRY ABOUT BEING STRONG ENOUGH TO TAKE A LIFE, AIDAN.
I WORRY ABOUT BEING STRONG ENOUGH NOT TO.
YOU'RE THE ONE WITH THE CHOICE HERE, AIDAN! YOUR SUICIDE IS NOT ON MY CONSCIENCE!
SO PULL THE HELL UP!

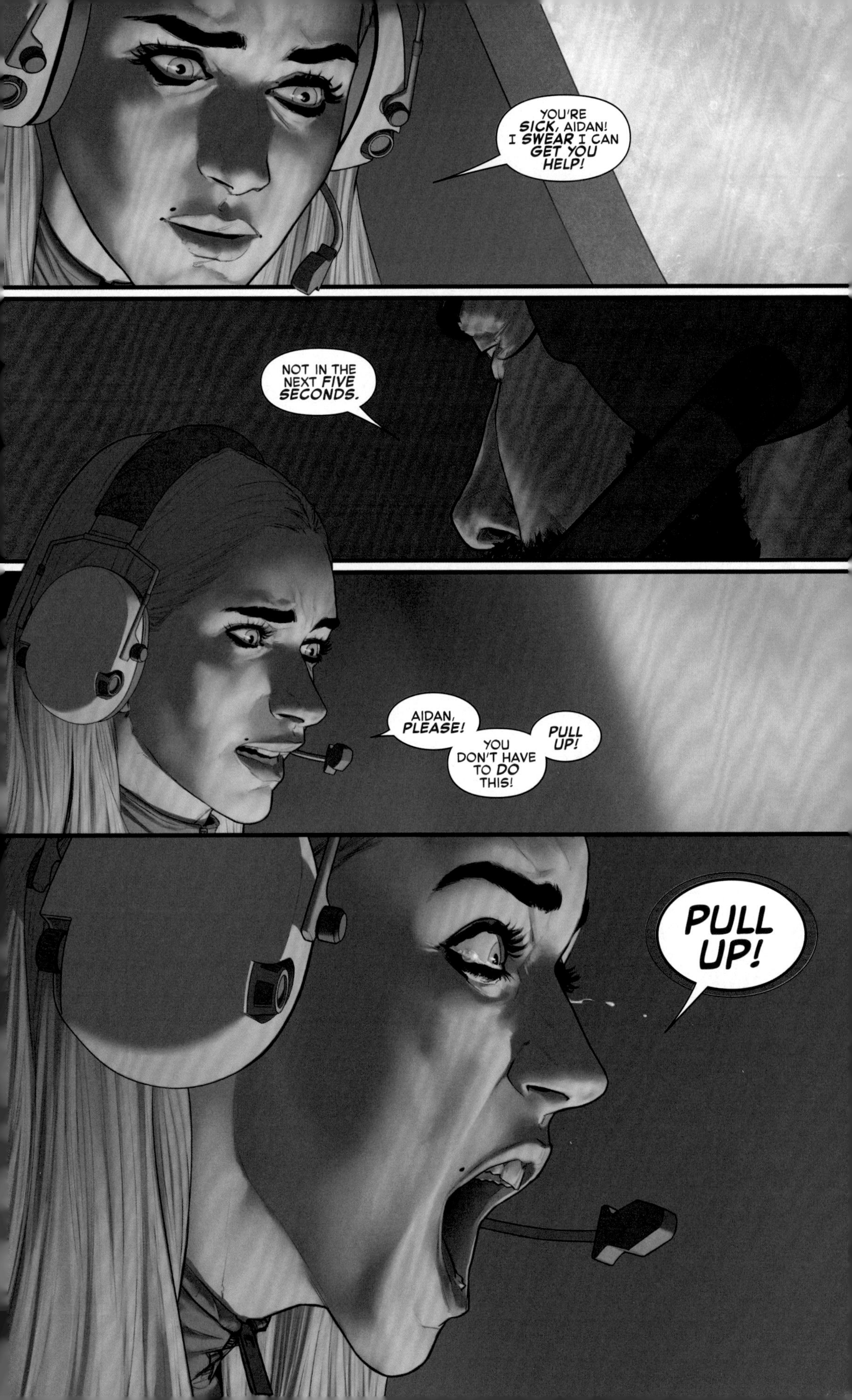
YOU'RE SICK, AIDAN! I SWEAR I CAN GET YOU HELP!
NOT IN THE NEXT FIVE SECONDS.
AIDAN, PLEASE!
YOU DON'T HAVE TO DO THIS!
PULL UP!
PULL UP!

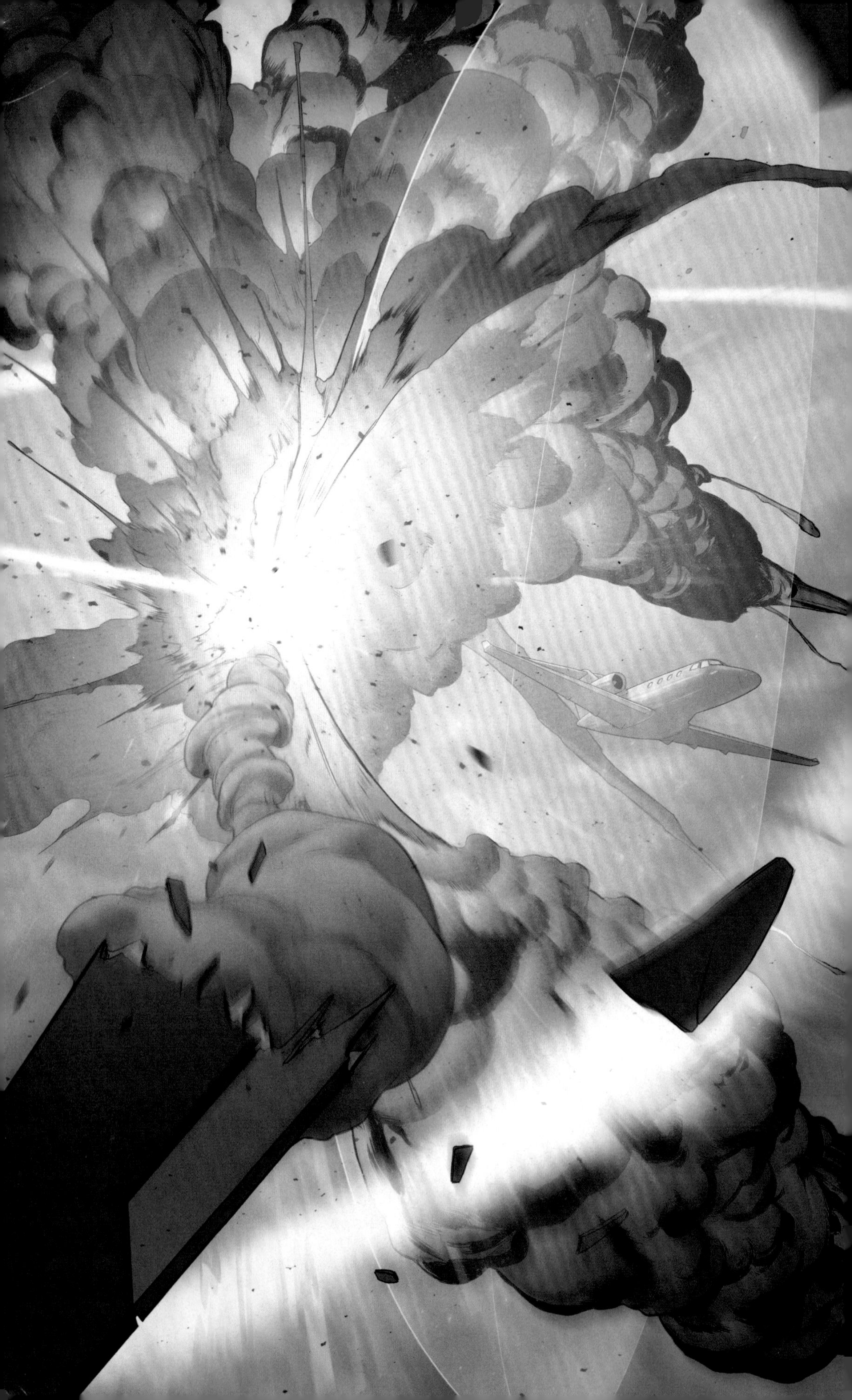

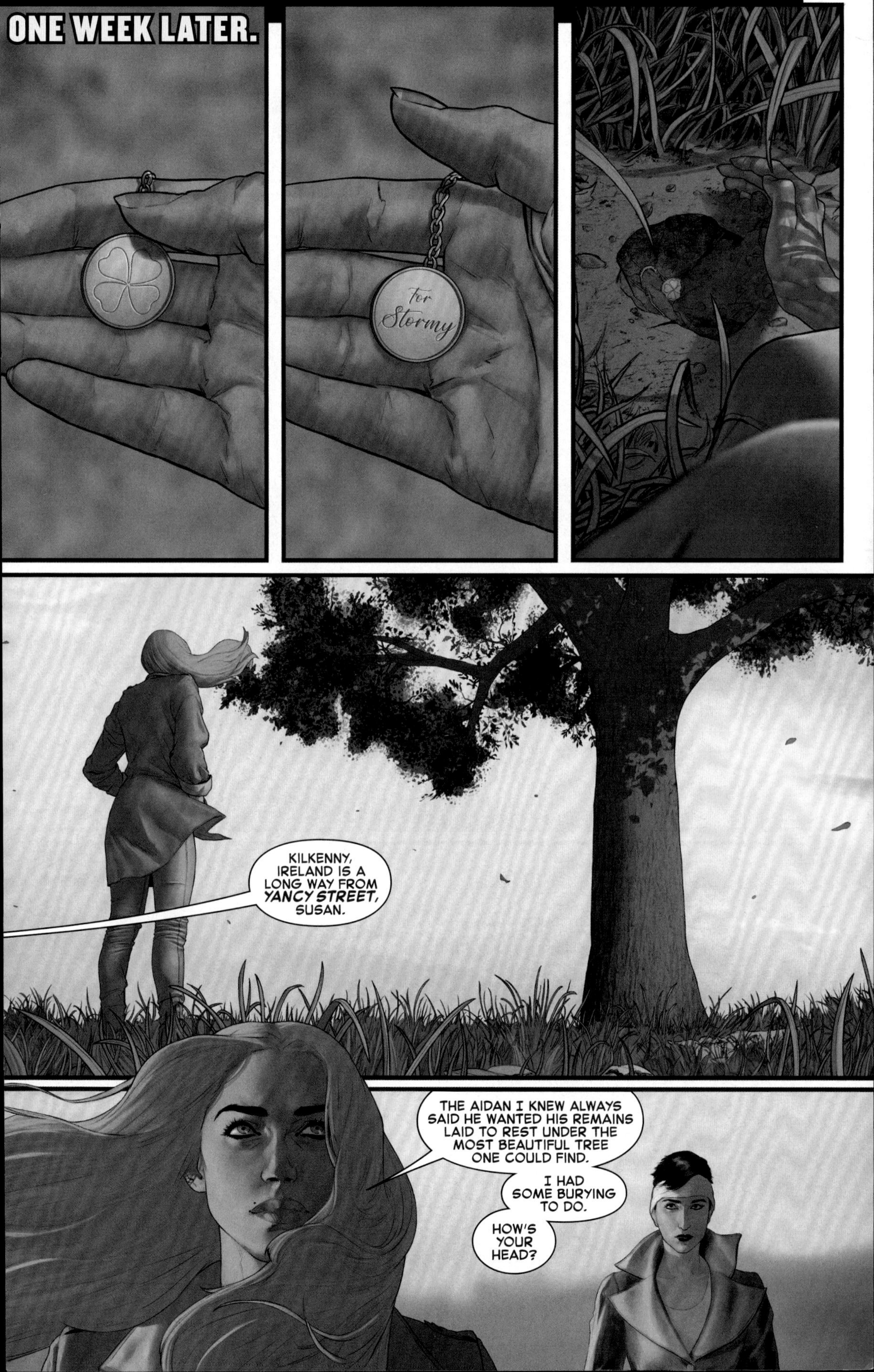
ONE WEEK LATER.
For Stormy
KILKENNY, IRELAND IS A LONG WAY FROM YANCY STREET, SUSAN.
THE AIDAN I KNEW ALWAYS SAID HE WANTED HIS REMAINS LAID TO REST UNDER THE MOST BEAUTIFUL TREE ONE COULD FIND.
I HAD SOME BURYING TO DO.
HOW'S YOUR HEAD?

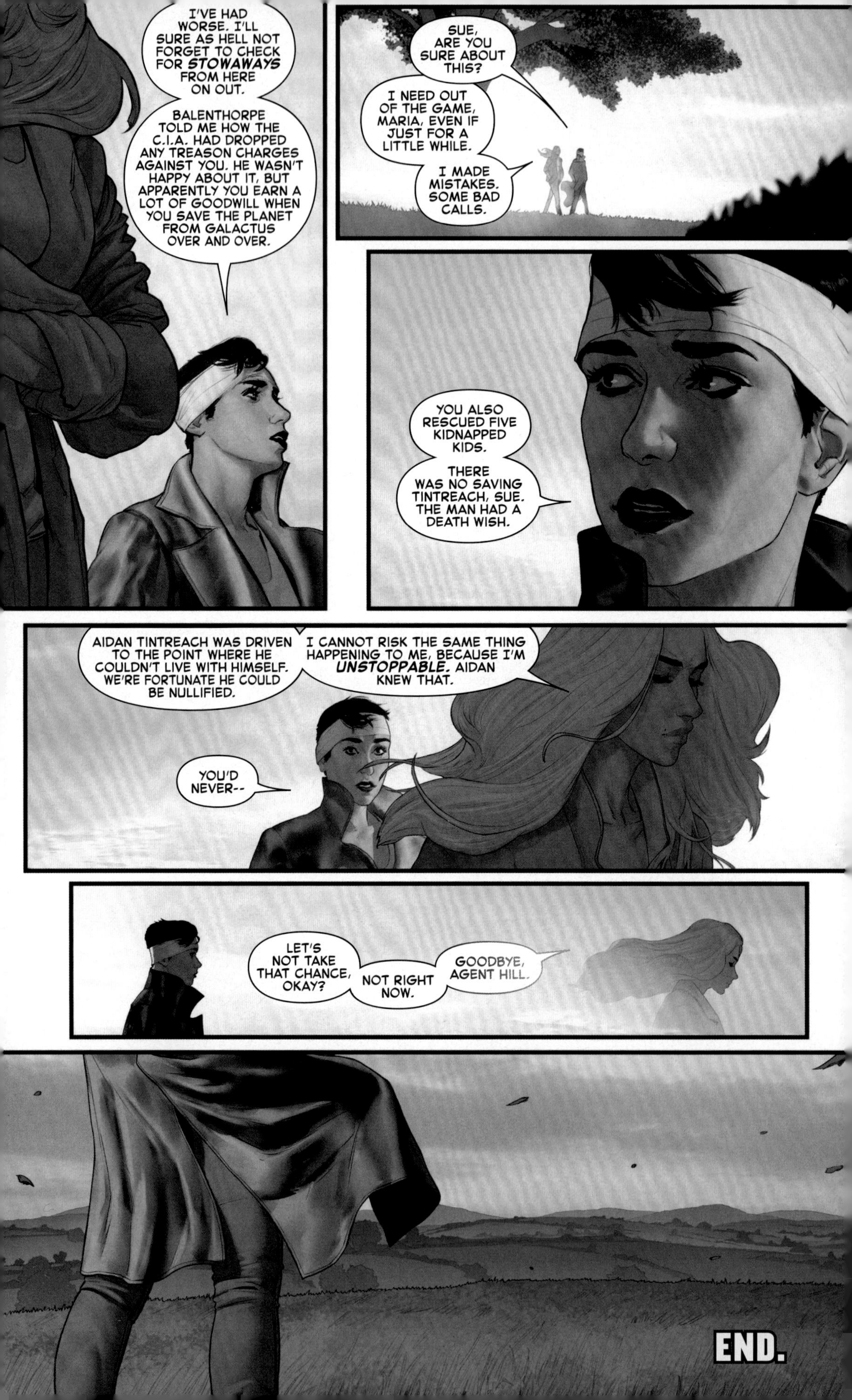
I'VE HAD WORSE. I'LL SURE AS HELL NOT FORGET TO CHECK FOR *STOWAWAYS* FROM HERE ON OUT.
BALENTHORPE TOLD ME HOW THE C.I.A. HAD DROPPED ANY TREASON CHARGES AGAINST YOU. HE WASN'T HAPPY ABOUT IT, BUT APPARENTLY YOU EARN A LOT OF GOODWILL WHEN YOU SAVE THE PLANET FROM GALACTUS OVER AND OVER.
SUE, ARE YOU SURE ABOUT THIS?
I NEED OUT OF THE GAME, MARIA, EVEN IF JUST FOR A LITTLE WHILE.
I MADE MISTAKES. SOME BAD CALLS.
YOU ALSO RESCUED FIVE KIDNAPPED KIDS.
THERE WAS NO SAVING TINTREACH, SUE. THE MAN HAD A DEATH WISH.
AIDAN TINTREACH WAS DRIVEN TO THE POINT WHERE HE COULDN'T LIVE WITH HIMSELF. WE'RE FORTUNATE HE COULD BE NULLIFIED.
I CANNOT RISK THE SAME THING HAPPENING TO ME, BECAUSE I'M *UNSTOPPABLE.* AIDAN KNEW THAT.
YOU'D NEVER--
LET'S NOT TAKE THAT CHANCE, OKAY?
NOT RIGHT NOW.
GOODBYE, AGENT HILL.
END.

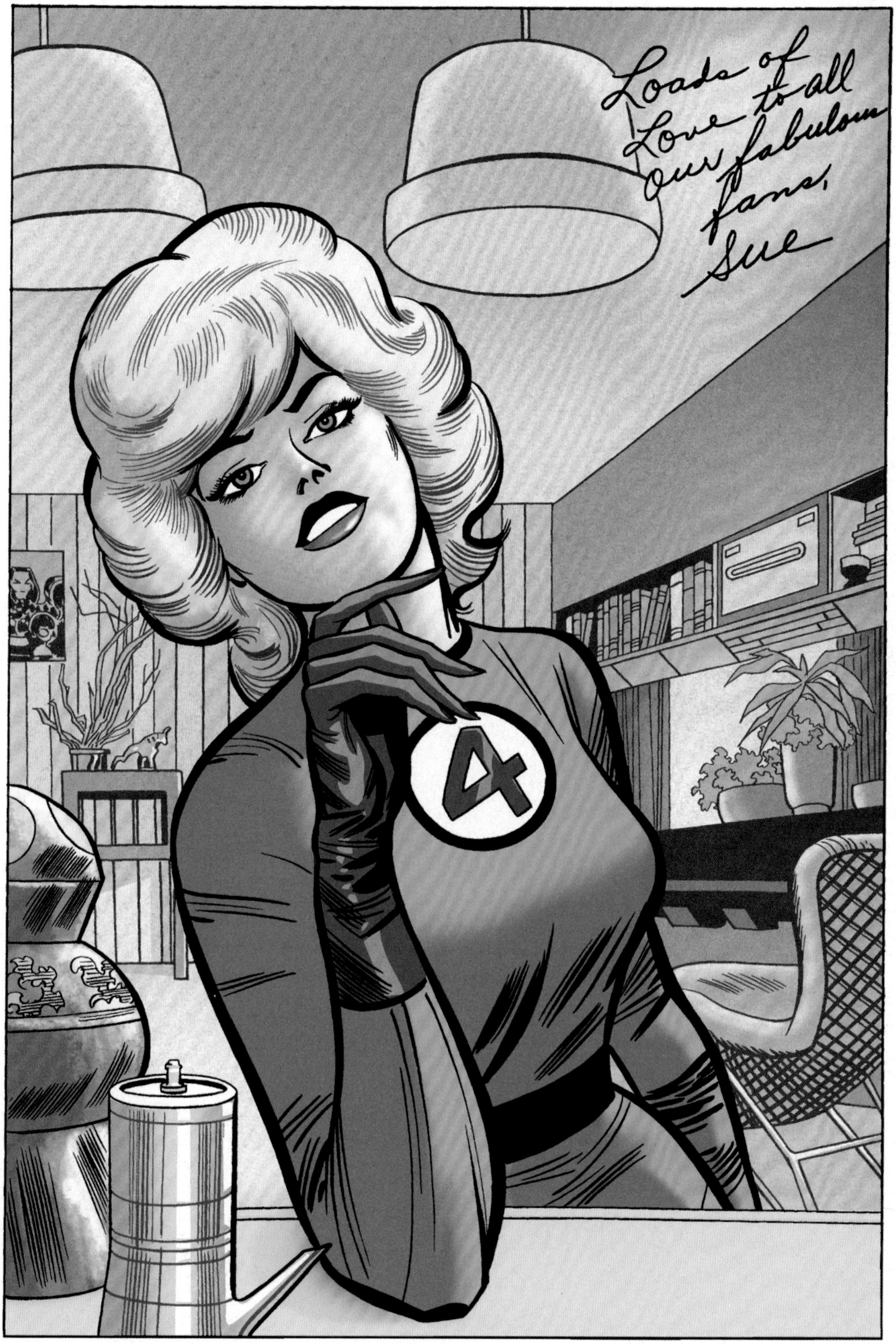
Loads of
Love to all
our fabulous
fans,
Sue

JACK KIRBY & EDGAR DELGADO
1 HIDDEN GEM VARIANT

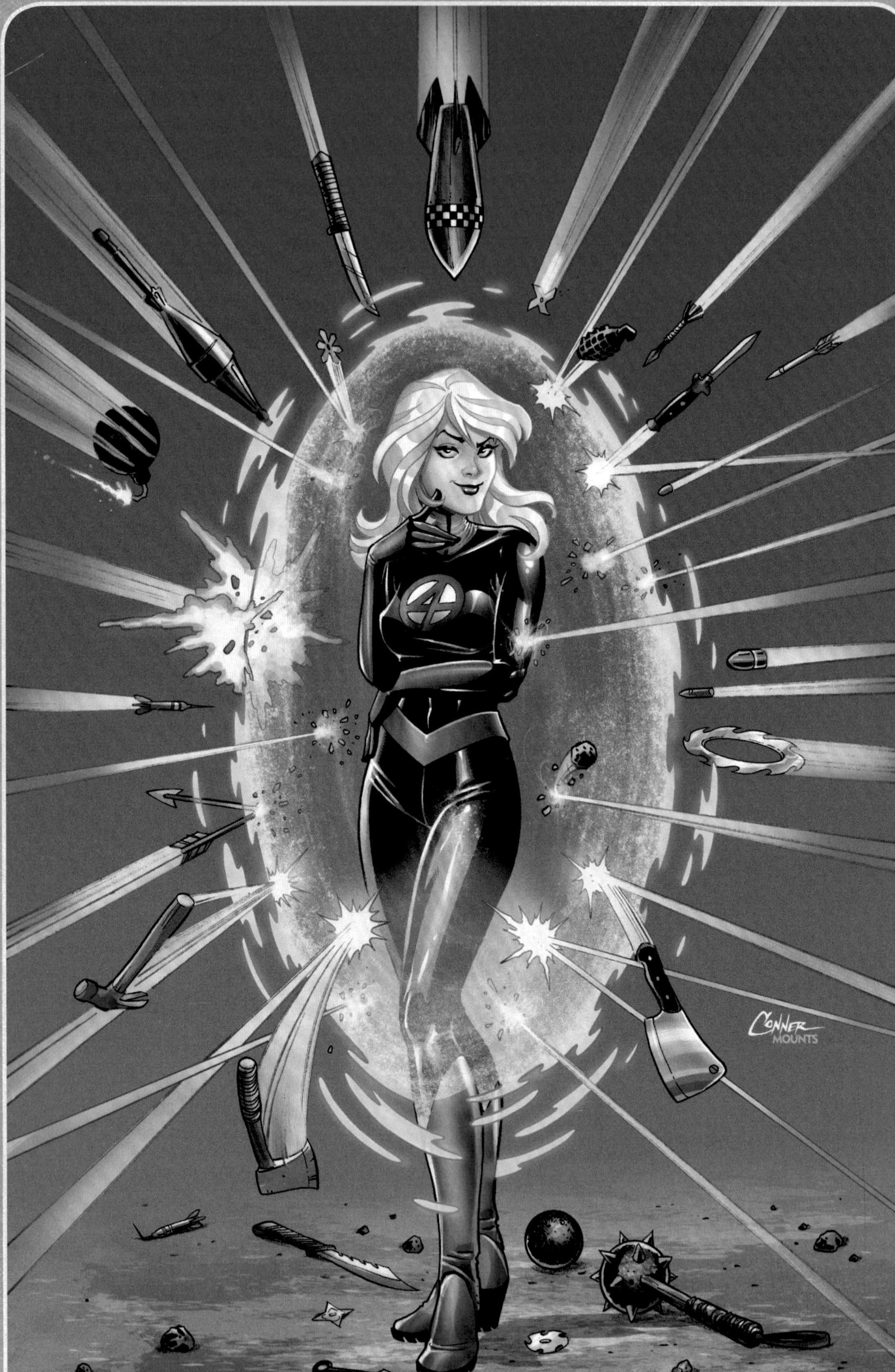
4
CONNER
MOUNTS

AMANDA CONNER & PAUL MOUNTS
2 VARIANT